ALL-NEW
X·FACTOR

01

"We specialize in helping people."

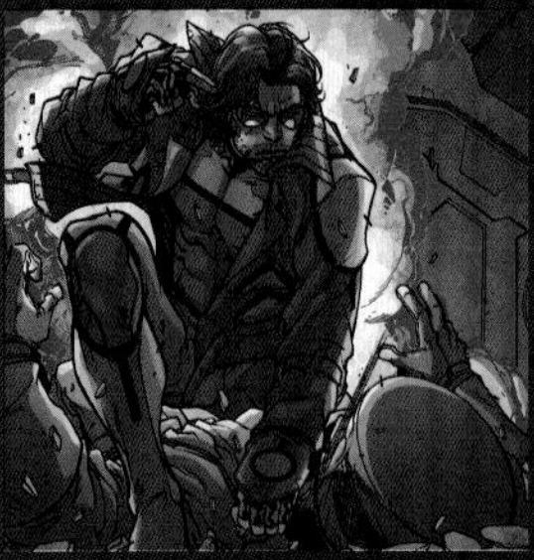

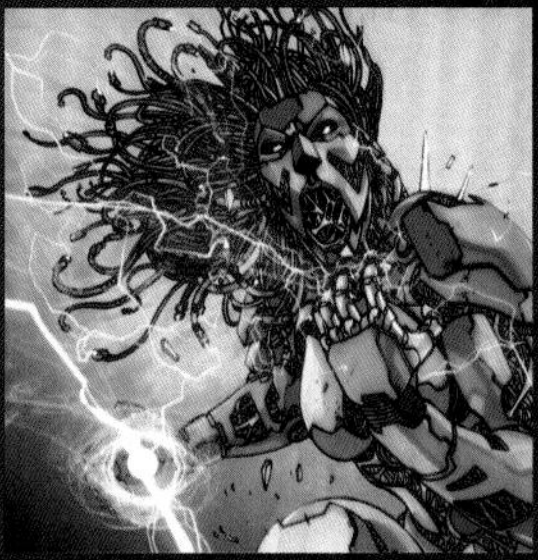

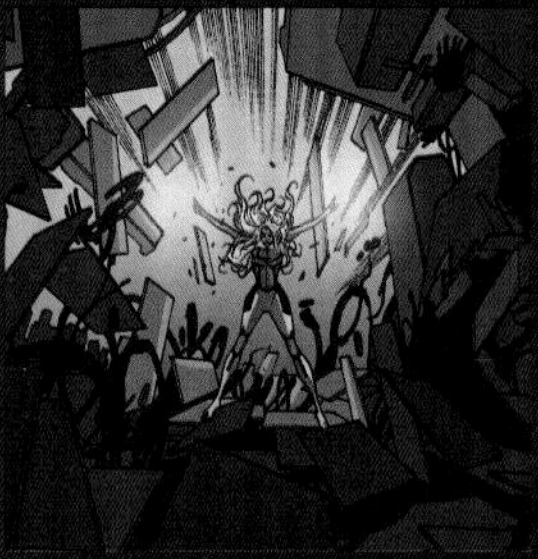

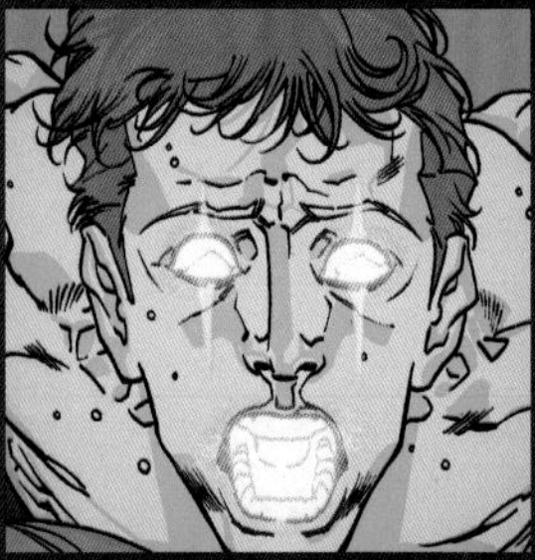

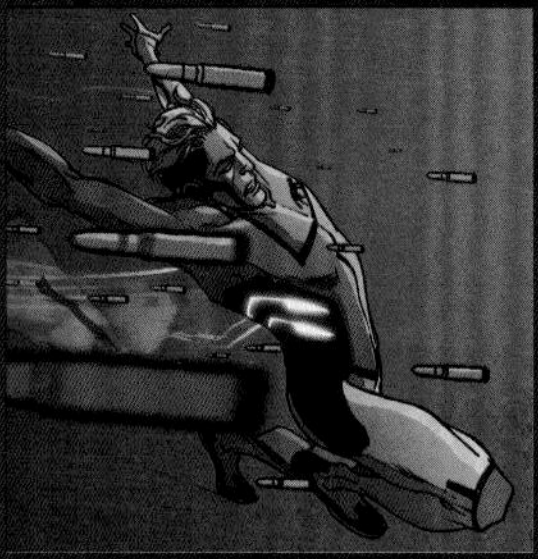

volume 01

NOT BRAND X

PETER DAVID writer
CARMINE DI GIANDOMENICO artist

LEE LOUGHRIDGE colorist #1-3 + #5-6
RACHELLE ROSENBERG colorist #4
VC's CORY PETIT letterer
KRIS ANKA & JARED K. FLETCHER cover art

XANDER JAROWEY assistant editor
JORDAN D. WHITE editor

JENNIFER GRÜNWALD collection editor
SARAH BRUNSTAD assistant editor
ALEX STARBUCK associate managing editor
MARK D. BEAZLEY editor, special projects
JEFF YOUNGQUIST senior editor, special projects
DAVID GABRIEL svp print, sales + marketing
JARED K. FLETCHER book designer

AXEL ALONSO editor in chief
JOE QUESADA chief creative officer
DAN BUCKLEY publisher
ALAN FINE executive producer

ALL-NEW X-FACTOR sponsored by

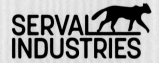

SERVAL INDUSTRIES

ALL-NEW X-FACTOR

ALL-NEW X-FACTOR VOL. 1: NOT BRAND X. Contains material originally published in magazine form as ALL-NEW X-FACTOR #1-6. First printing 2014. ISBN# 978-0-7851-8816-2. Published by MARVEL WORLDWIDE, INC., a subsidiary of MARVEL ENTERTAINMENT, LLC. OFFICE OF PUBLICATION: 135 West 50th Street, New York, NY 10020. Copyright © 2014 Marvel Characters, Inc. All rights reserved. All characters featured in this issue and the distinctive names and likenesses thereof, and all related indicia are trademarks of Marvel Characters, Inc. No similarity between any of the names, characters, persons, and/or institutions in this magazine with those of any living or dead person or institution is intended, and any such similarity which may exist is purely coincidental. Printed in Canada. ALAN FINE, EVP - Office of the President, Marvel Worldwide, Inc. and EVP & CMO Marvel Characters B.V.; DAN BUCKLEY, Publisher & President - Print, Animation & Digital Divisions; JOE QUESADA, Chief Creative Officer; TOM BREVOORT, SVP of Publishing; DAVID BOGART, SVP of Operations & Procurement, Publishing; C.B. CEBULSKI, SVP of Creator & Content Development; DAVID GABRIEL, SVP of Print & Digital Publishing Sales; JIM O'KEEFE, VP of Operations & Logistics; DAN CARR, Executive Director of Publishing Technology; SUSAN CRESPI, Editorial Operations Manager; ALEX MORALES, Publishing Operations Manager; STAN LEE, Chairman Emeritus. For information regarding advertising in Marvel Comics or on Marvel.com, please contact Niza Disla, Director of Marvel Partnerships, at ndisla@marvel.com. For Marvel subscription inquiries, please call 800-217-9158. Manufactured between 4/21/2014 and 5/26/2014 by SOLISCO PRINTERS, SCOTT, QC, CANADA.

10 9 8 7 6 5 4 3 2 1

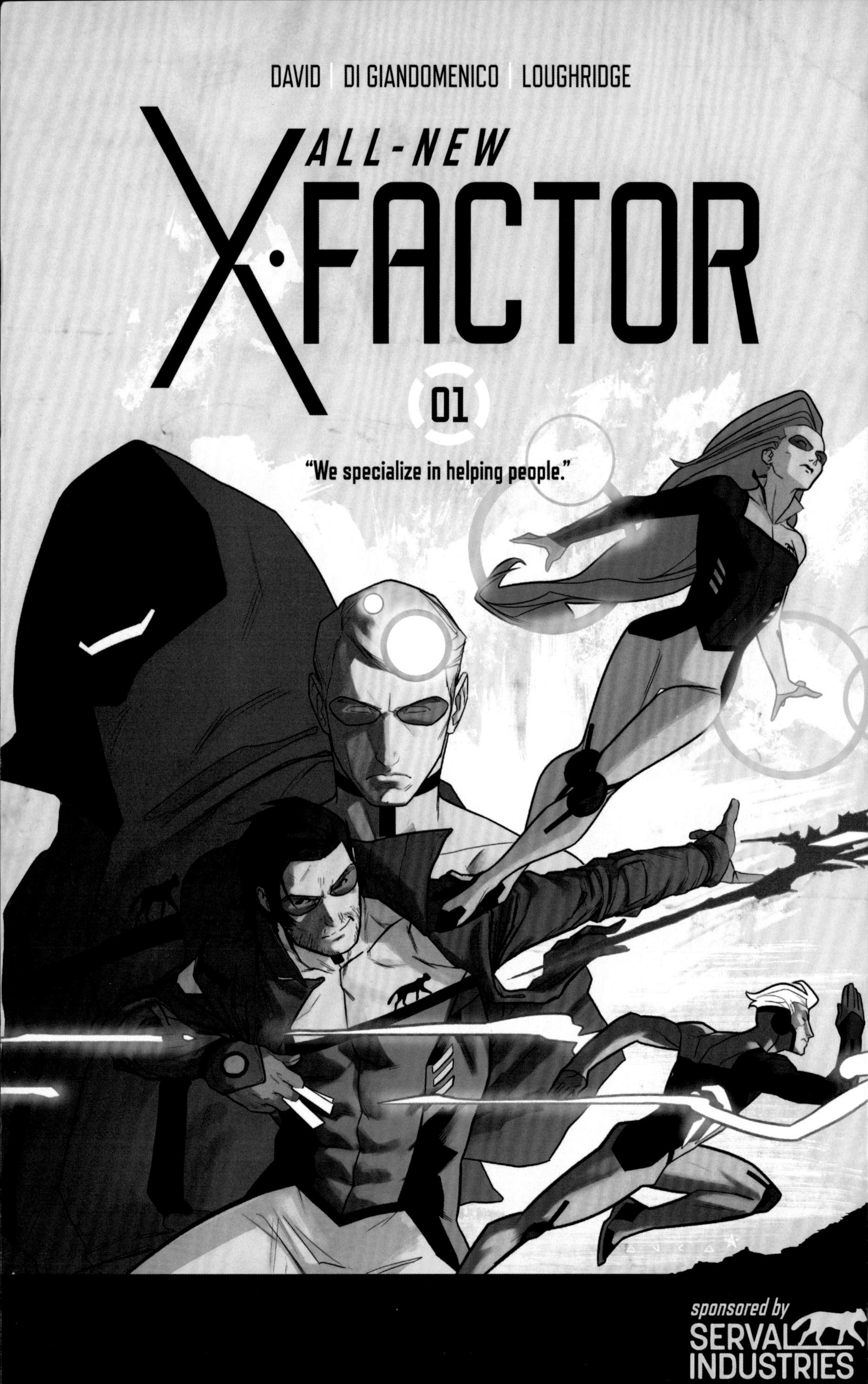
DAVID | DI GIANDOMENICO | LOUGHRIDGE
ALL-NEW
X-FACTOR
01
"We specialize in helping people."
sponsored by
SERVAL INDUSTRIES

THAT'S SUPERB. AN EXCELLENT DAY'S WORK, DON'T YOU THINK?

ABSOLUTELY, SIR.

NOW... TOMORROW IS *ALSO* GOING TO BE A BIG DAY.

YOU MEAN FINALLY...?

I BELIEVE SO. WE'RE FINALLY READY TO BEGIN VIVISECTION.

HOFFMAN...

JUST SO YOU KNOW...WHEN I GET OUT OF THIS... I'LL KILL YOU MYSELF.

I UNDERSTAND HOW YOU FEEL. BUT PLEASE KNOW THAT, ALTHOUGH YOU'RE SUFFERING...

I SWEAR IT'S FOR THE GREATER GOOD.

GOOD NIGHT.

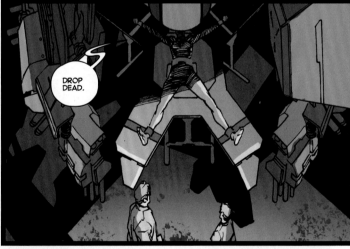

DROP DEAD.

WANT TO GRAB AN ESPRESSO? STARBUCKS IS STILL OPEN.

ABSOLUTELY.

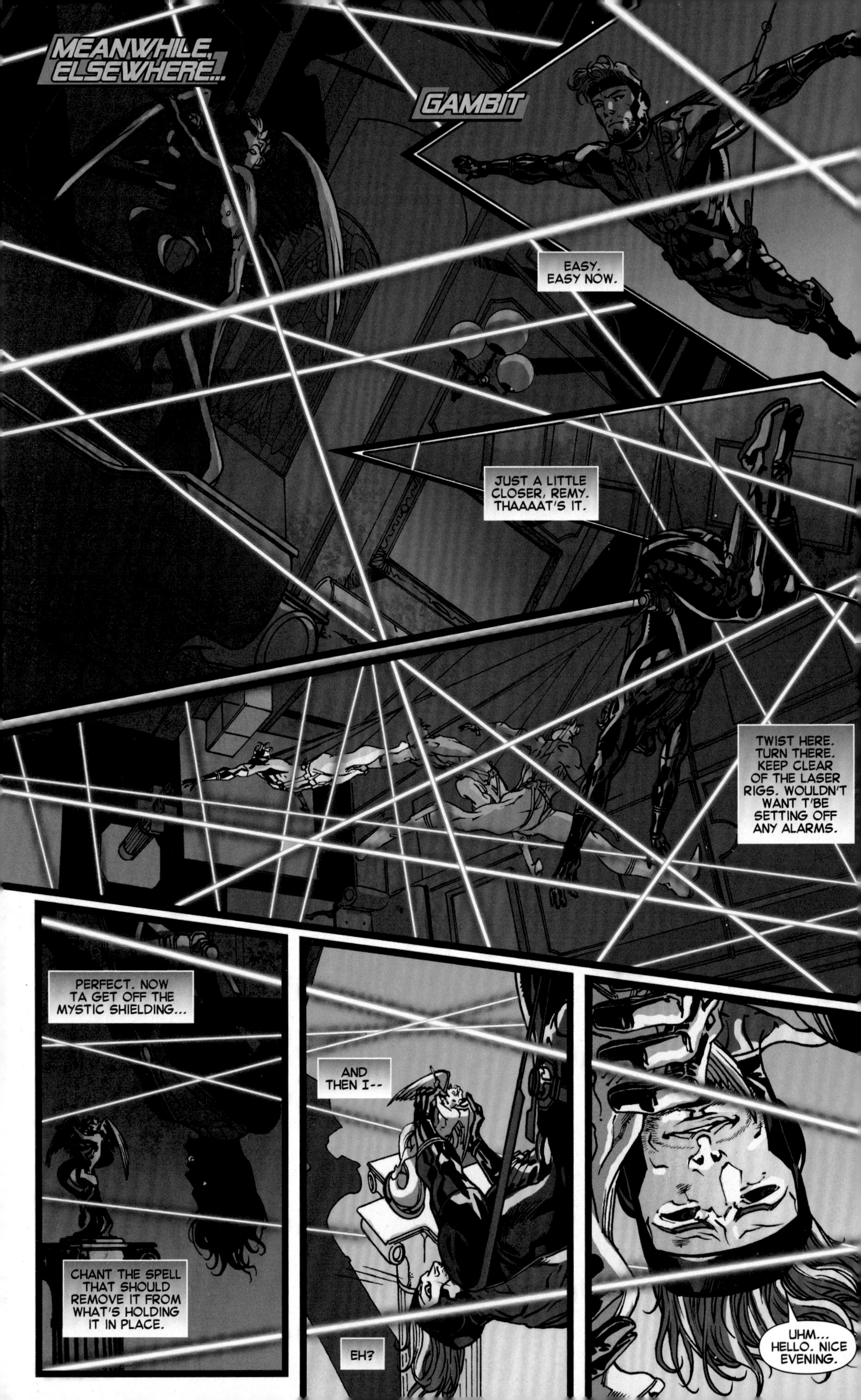
MEANWHILE, ELSEWHERE...
GAMBIT
EASY. EASY NOW.
JUST A LITTLE CLOSER, REMY. THAAAAT'S IT.
TWIST HERE. TURN THERE. KEEP CLEAR OF THE LASER RIGS. WOULDN'T WANT T'BE SETTING OFF ANY ALARMS.
PERFECT. NOW TA GET OFF THE MYSTIC SHIELDING...
CHANT THE SPELL THAT SHOULD REMOVE IT FROM WHAT'S HOLDING IT IN PLACE.
AND THEN I--
EH?
UHM... HELLO. NICE EVENING.

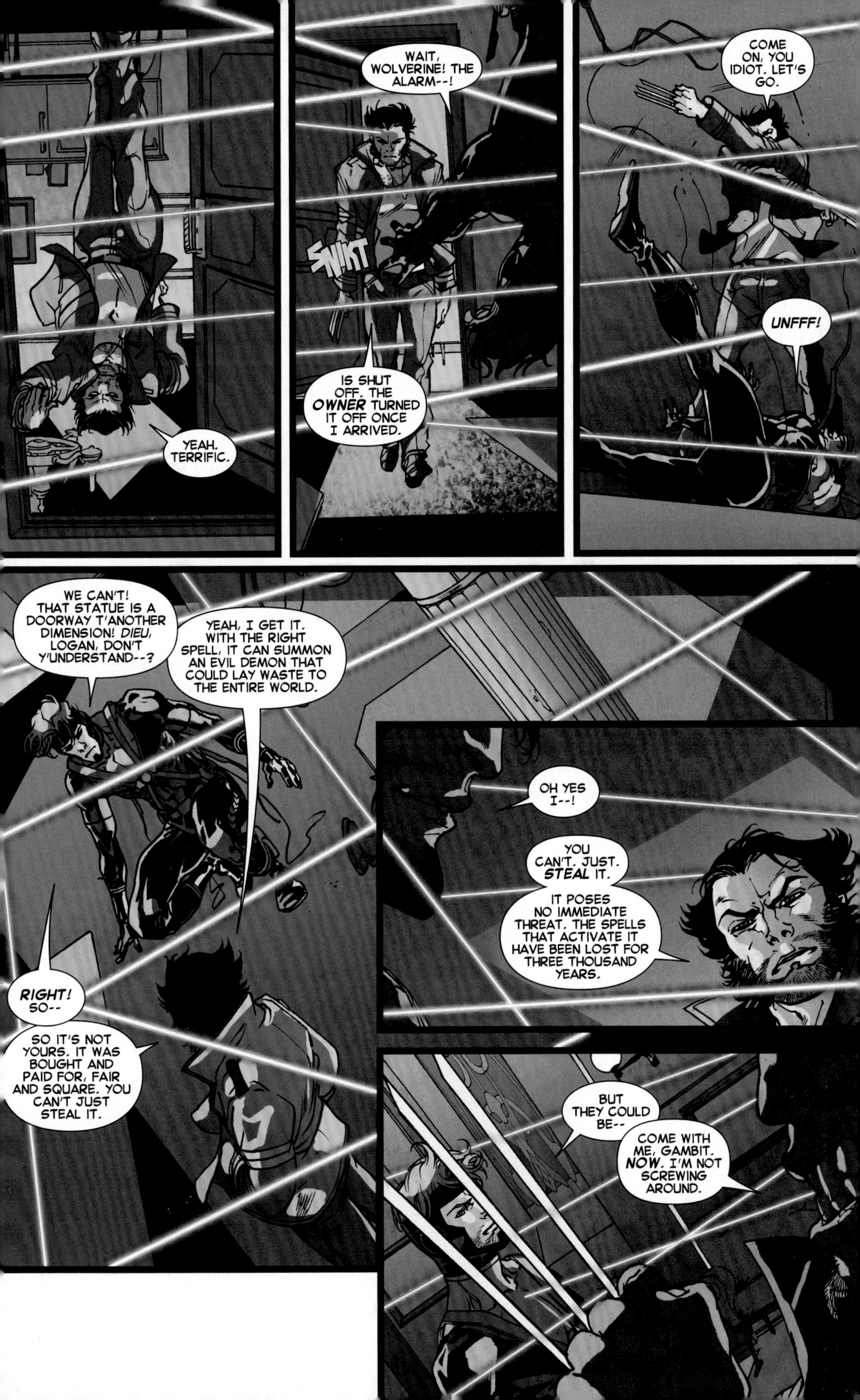

YEAH. TERRIFIC.
WAIT, WOLVERINE! THE ALARM--!
SNIKT
IS SHUT OFF. THE OWNER TURNED IT OFF ONCE I ARRIVED.
COME ON, YOU IDIOT. LET'S GO.
UNFFF!
WE CAN'T! THAT STATUE IS A DOORWAY T'ANOTHER DIMENSION! DIEU, LOGAN, DON'T Y'UNDERSTAND--?
YEAH, I GET IT. WITH THE RIGHT SPELL, IT CAN SUMMON AN EVIL DEMON THAT COULD LAY WASTE TO THE ENTIRE WORLD.
RIGHT! SO--
SO IT'S NOT YOURS. IT WAS BOUGHT AND PAID FOR, FAIR AND SQUARE. YOU CAN'T JUST STEAL IT.
OH YES I--!
YOU CAN'T. JUST. STEAL IT.
IT POSES NO IMMEDIATE THREAT. THE SPELLS THAT ACTIVATE IT HAVE BEEN LOST FOR THREE THOUSAND YEARS.
BUT THEY COULD BE--
COME WITH ME, GAMBIT. NOW. I'M NOT SCREWING AROUND.

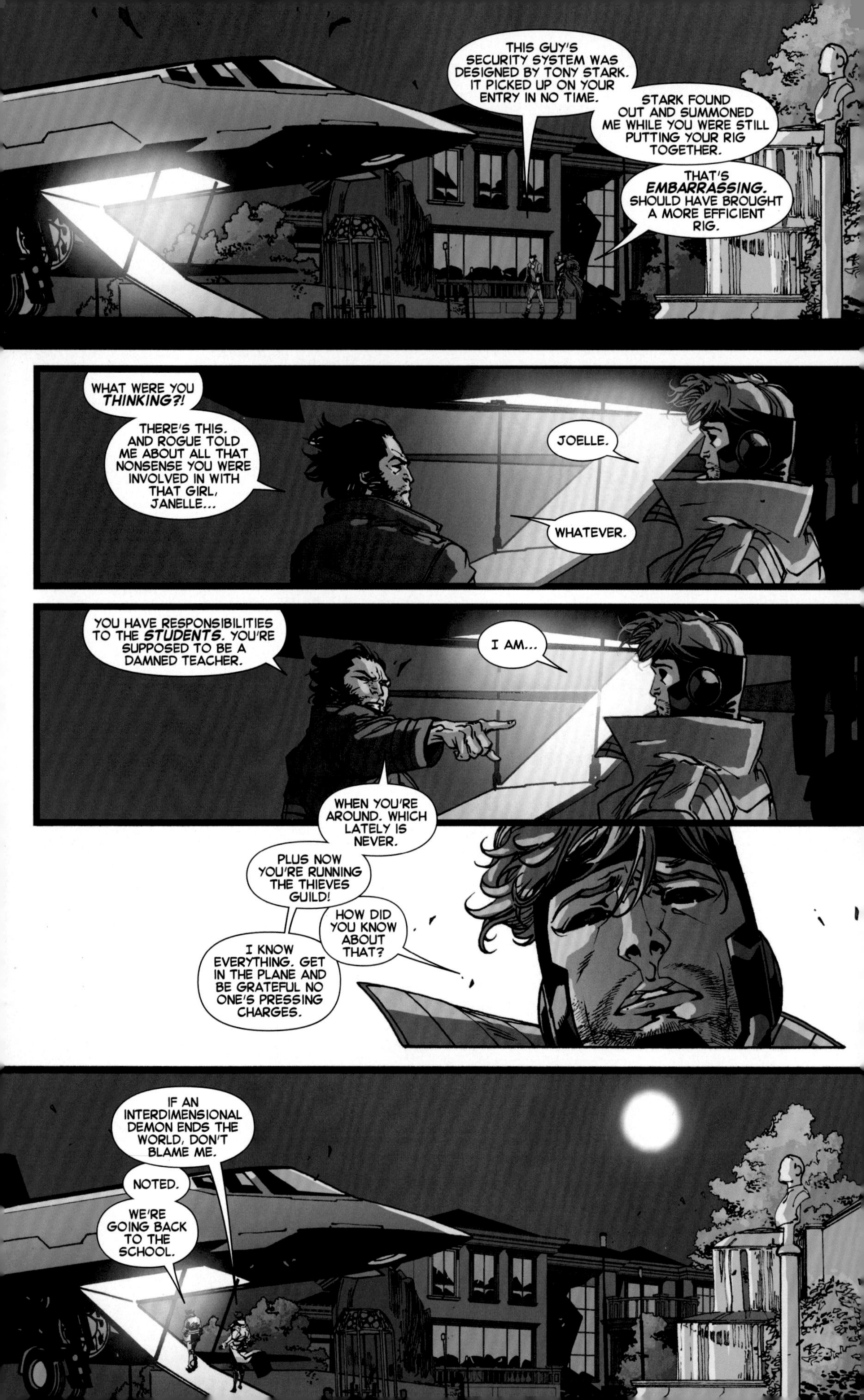
THIS GUY'S SECURITY SYSTEM WAS DESIGNED BY TONY STARK. IT PICKED UP ON YOUR ENTRY IN NO TIME.
STARK FOUND OUT AND SUMMONED ME WHILE YOU WERE STILL PUTTING YOUR RIG TOGETHER.
THAT'S EMBARRASSING. SHOULD HAVE BROUGHT A MORE EFFICIENT RIG.
WHAT WERE YOU THINKING?!
THERE'S THIS. AND ROGUE TOLD ME ABOUT ALL THAT NONSENSE YOU WERE INVOLVED IN WITH THAT GIRL, JANELLE...
JOELLE.
WHATEVER.
YOU HAVE RESPONSIBILITIES TO THE STUDENTS. YOU'RE SUPPOSED TO BE A DAMNED TEACHER.
I AM...
WHEN YOU'RE AROUND. WHICH LATELY IS NEVER.
PLUS NOW YOU'RE RUNNING THE THIEVES GUILD!
HOW DID YOU KNOW ABOUT THAT?
I KNOW EVERYTHING. GET IN THE PLANE AND BE GRATEFUL NO ONE'S PRESSING CHARGES.
IF AN INTERDIMENSIONAL DEMON ENDS THE WORLD, DON'T BLAME ME.
NOTED.
WE'RE GOING BACK TO THE SCHOOL.

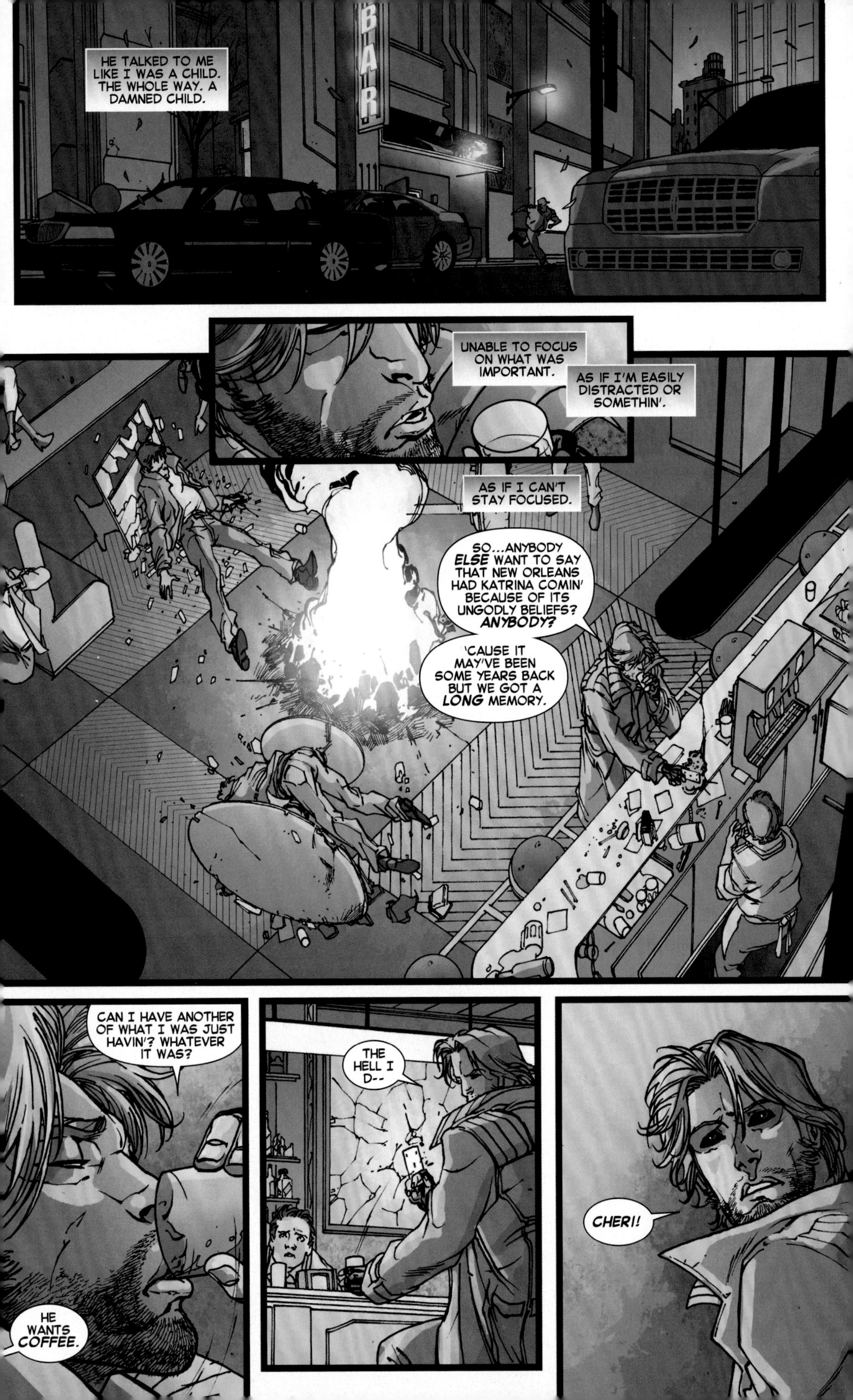
BAR
HE TALKED TO ME LIKE I WAS A CHILD. THE WHOLE WAY. A DAMNED CHILD.
UNABLE TO FOCUS ON WHAT WAS IMPORTANT.
AS IF I'M EASILY DISTRACTED OR SOMETHIN'.
AS IF I CAN'T STAY FOCUSED.
SO...ANYBODY *ELSE* WANT TO SAY THAT NEW ORLEANS HAD KATRINA COMIN' BECAUSE OF ITS UNGODLY BELIEFS? *ANYBODY?*
'CAUSE IT MAY'VE BEEN SOME YEARS BACK BUT WE GOT A *LONG* MEMORY.
CAN I HAVE ANOTHER OF WHAT I WAS JUST HAVIN'? WHATEVER IT WAS?
HE WANTS *COFFEE.*
THE HELL I D--
CHERI!

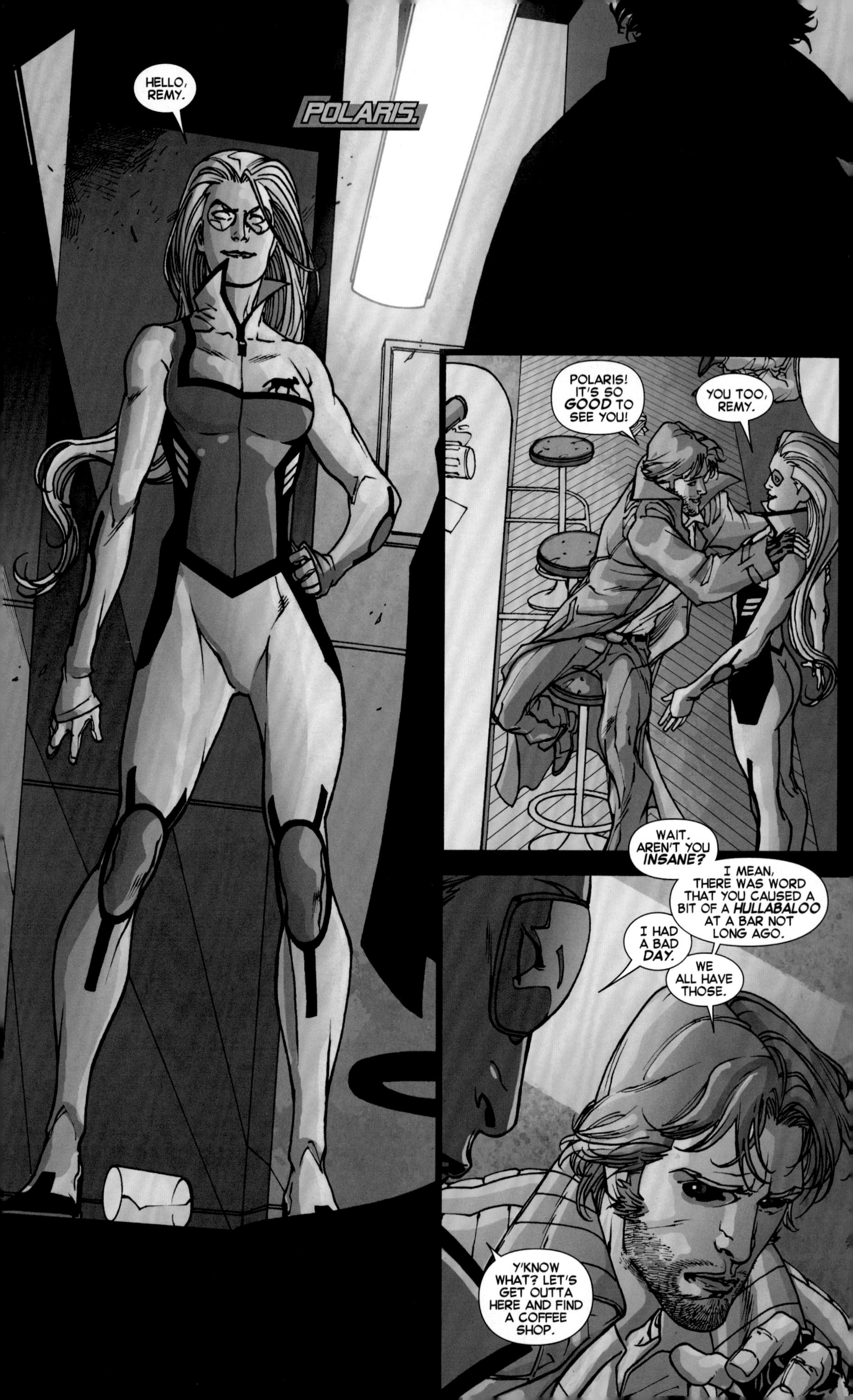
HELLO, REMY.
POLARIS.
POLARIS! IT'S SO *GOOD* TO SEE YOU!
YOU TOO, REMY.
WAIT. AREN'T YOU *INSANE?*
I MEAN, THERE WAS WORD THAT YOU CAUSED A BIT OF A *HULLABALOO* AT A BAR NOT LONG AGO.
I HAD A BAD *DAY.*
WE ALL HAVE THOSE.
Y'KNOW WHAT? LET'S GET OUTTA HERE AND FIND A COFFEE SHOP.

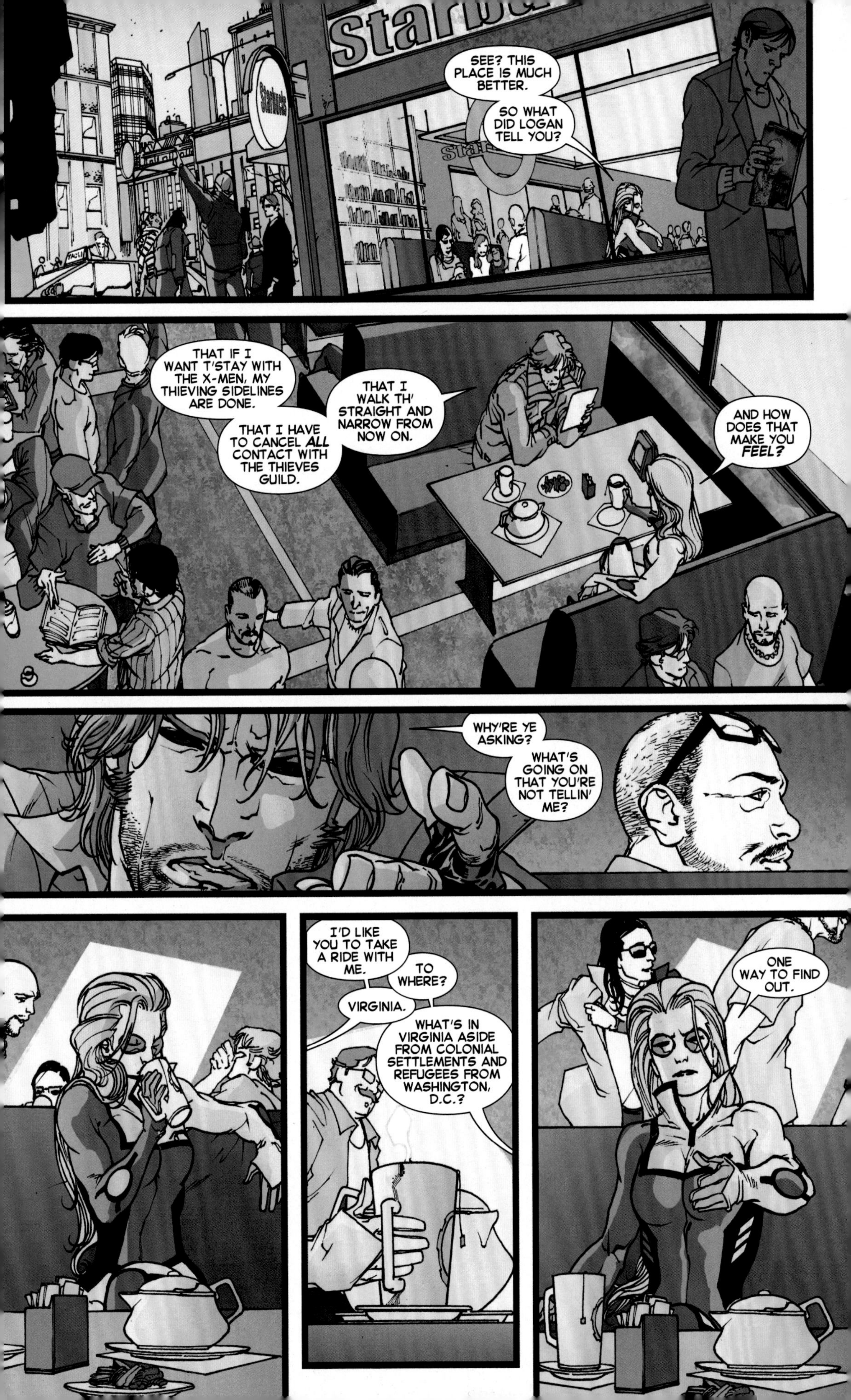
Starbucks
SEE? THIS PLACE IS MUCH BETTER.
SO WHAT DID LOGAN TELL YOU?
THAT IF I WANT T'STAY WITH THE X-MEN, MY THIEVING SIDELINES ARE DONE.
THAT I HAVE TO CANCEL ALL CONTACT WITH THE THIEVES GUILD.
THAT I WALK TH' STRAIGHT AND NARROW FROM NOW ON.
AND HOW DOES THAT MAKE YOU FEEL?
WHY'RE YE ASKING?
WHAT'S GOING ON THAT YOU'RE NOT TELLIN' ME?
I'D LIKE YOU TO TAKE A RIDE WITH ME.
TO WHERE?
VIRGINIA.
WHAT'S IN VIRGINIA ASIDE FROM COLONIAL SETTLEMENTS AND REFUGEES FROM WASHINGTON, D.C.?
ONE WAY TO FIND OUT.

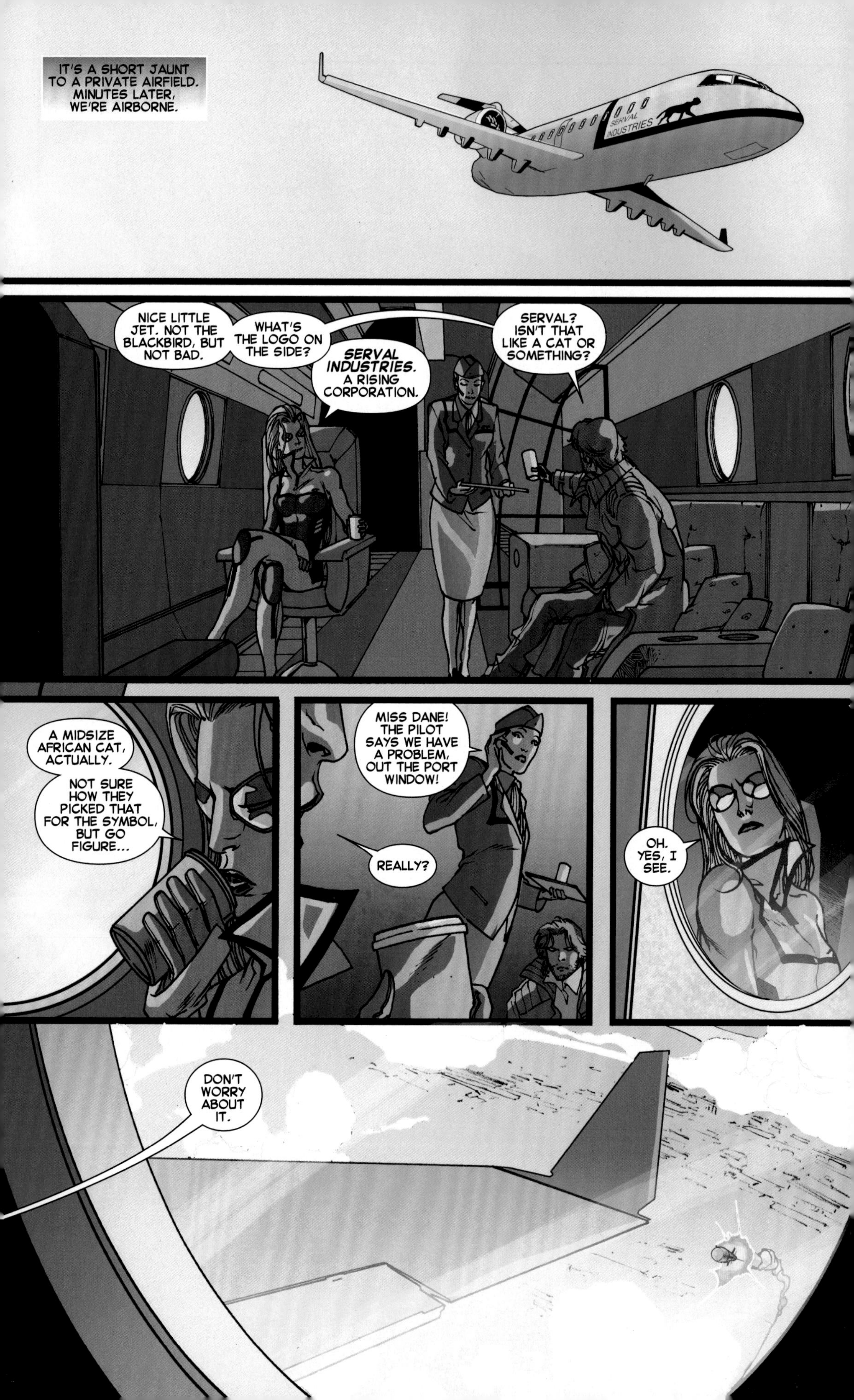
IT'S A SHORT JAUNT TO A PRIVATE AIRFIELD. MINUTES LATER, WE'RE AIRBORNE.
SERVAL INDUSTRIES
NICE LITTLE JET. NOT THE BLACKBIRD, BUT NOT BAD.
WHAT'S THE LOGO ON THE SIDE?
SERVAL INDUSTRIES. A RISING CORPORATION.
SERVAL? ISN'T THAT LIKE A CAT OR SOMETHING?
A MIDSIZE AFRICAN CAT, ACTUALLY.
NOT SURE HOW THEY PICKED THAT FOR THE SYMBOL, BUT GO FIGURE...
MISS DANE! THE PILOT SAYS WE HAVE A PROBLEM, OUT THE PORT WINDOW!
REALLY?
OH. YES, I SEE.
DON'T WORRY ABOUT IT.

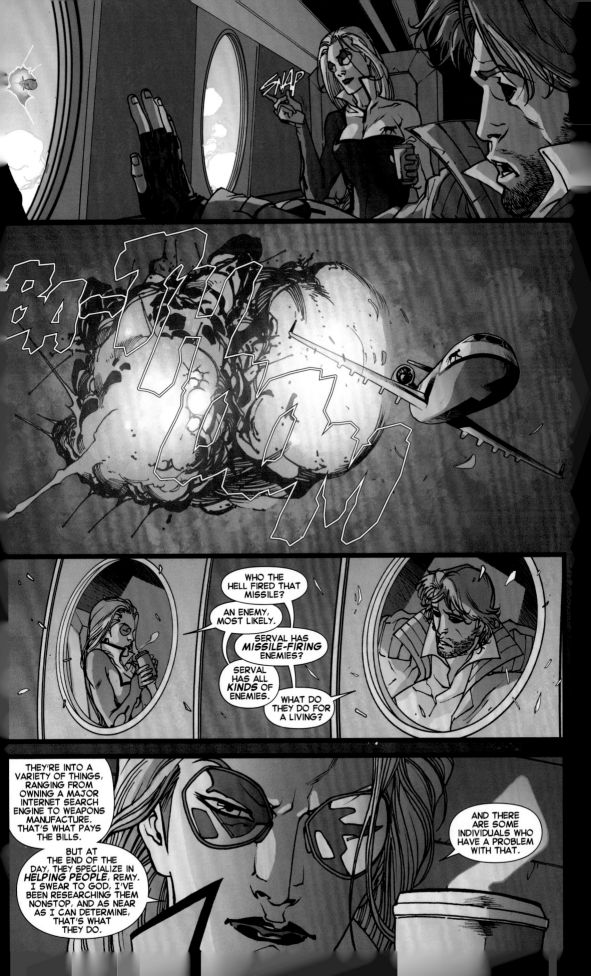

SNAP

BA-THOOOM

WHO THE HELL FIRED THAT MISSILE?

AN ENEMY, MOST LIKELY.

SERVAL HAS *MISSILE-FIRING* ENEMIES?

SERVAL HAS ALL *KINDS* OF ENEMIES.

WHAT DO THEY DO FOR A LIVING?

THEY'RE INTO A VARIETY OF THINGS, RANGING FROM OWNING A MAJOR INTERNET SEARCH ENGINE TO WEAPONS MANUFACTURE. THAT'S WHAT PAYS THE BILLS.

BUT AT THE END OF THE DAY, THEY SPECIALIZE IN *HELPING PEOPLE*, REMY. I SWEAR TO GOD, I'VE BEEN RESEARCHING THEM NONSTOP, AND AS NEAR AS I CAN DETERMINE, THAT'S WHAT THEY DO.

AND THERE ARE SOME INDIVIDUALS WHO HAVE A PROBLEM WITH THAT.

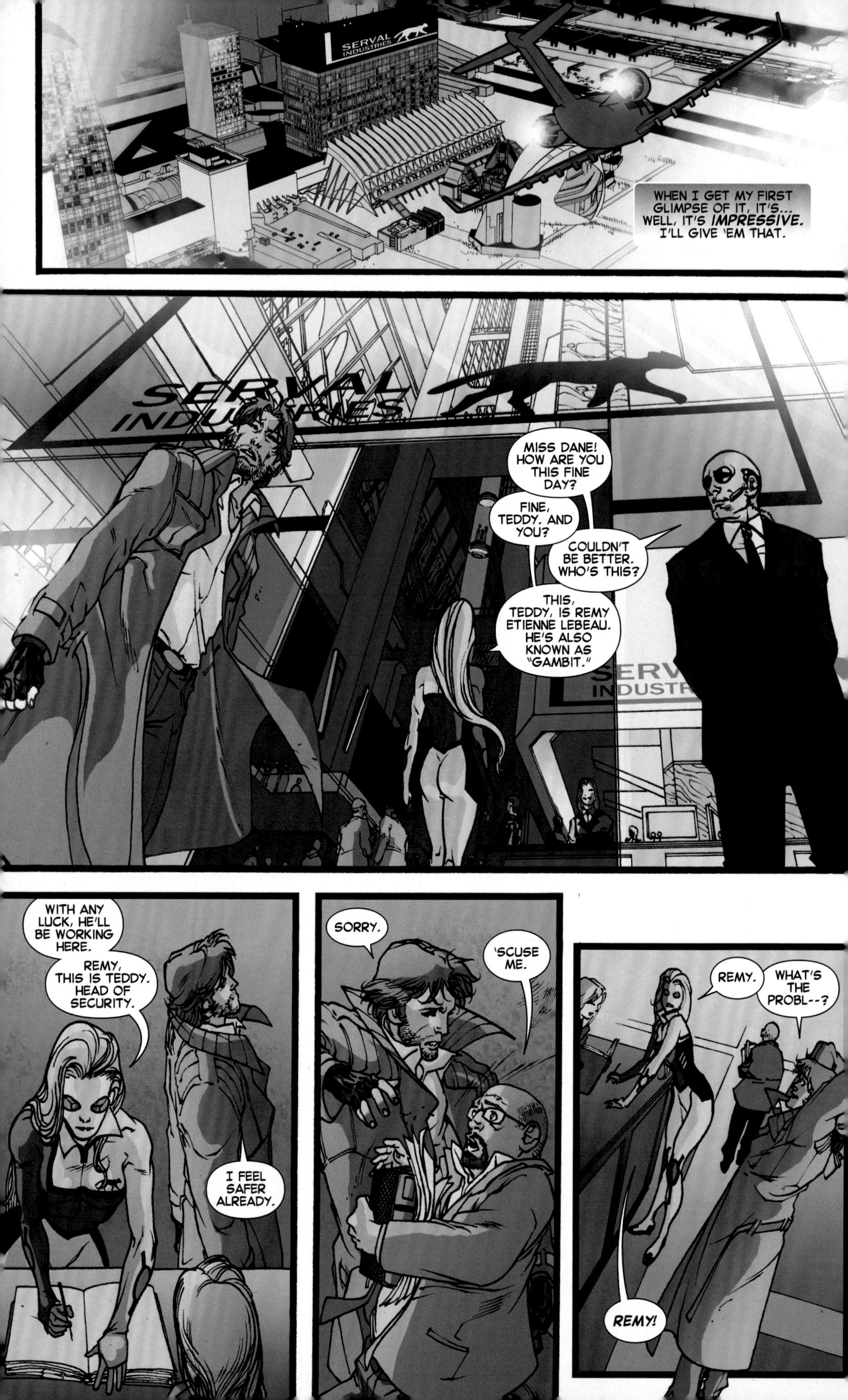
SERVAL INDUSTRIES
WHEN I GET MY FIRST GLIMPSE OF IT, IT'S... WELL, IT'S *IMPRESSIVE.* I'LL GIVE 'EM THAT.
SERVAL INDUSTRIES
MISS DANE! HOW ARE YOU THIS FINE DAY?
FINE, TEDDY. AND YOU?
COULDN'T BE BETTER. WHO'S THIS?
THIS, TEDDY, IS REMY ETIENNE LEBEAU. HE'S ALSO KNOWN AS "GAMBIT."
WITH ANY LUCK, HE'LL BE WORKING HERE.
REMY, THIS IS TEDDY. HEAD OF SECURITY.
I FEEL SAFER ALREADY.
SORRY.
'SCUSE ME.
REMY.
WHAT'S THE PROBL--?
REMY!

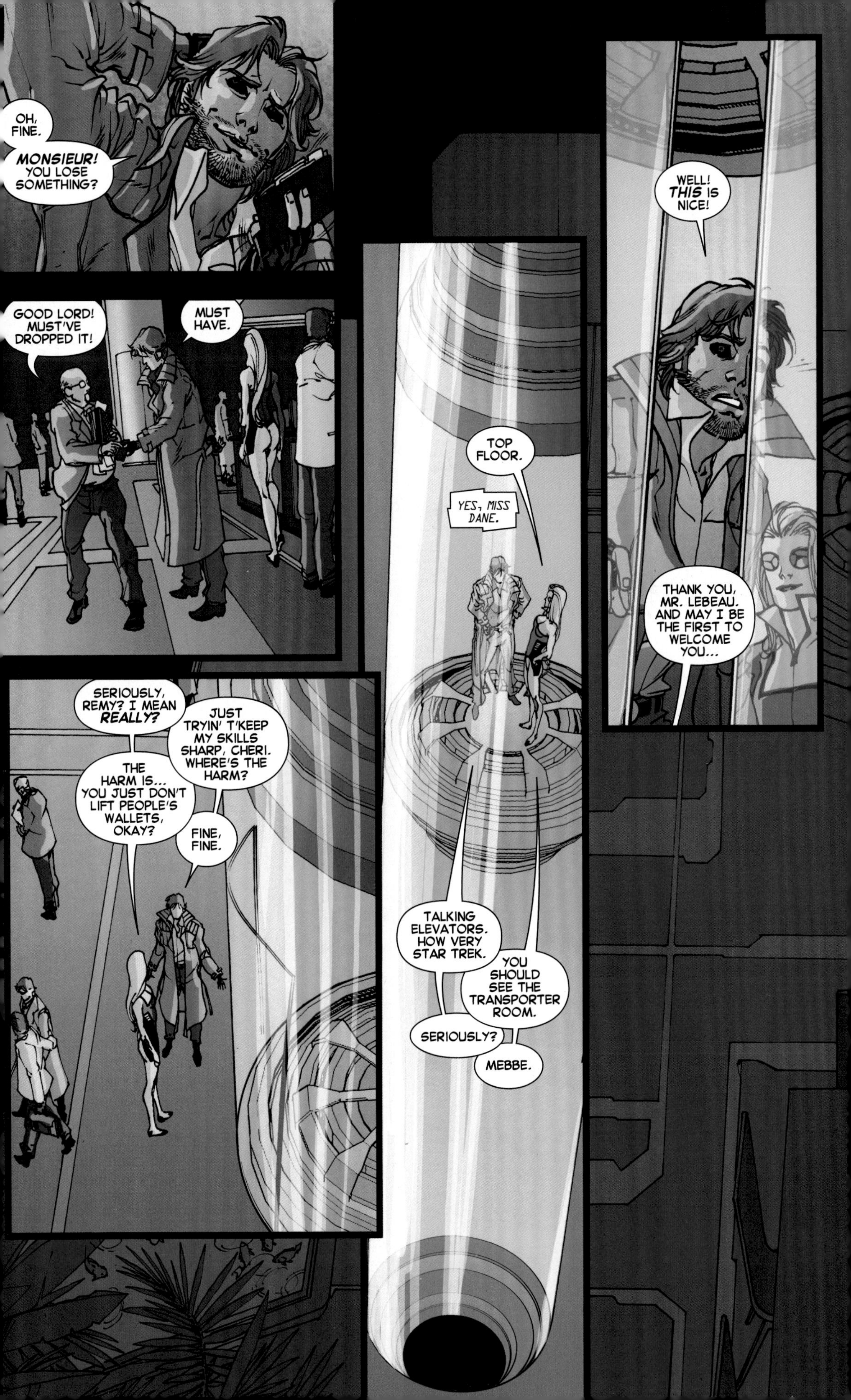
OH, FINE.
MONSIEUR! YOU LOSE SOMETHING?
GOOD LORD! MUST'VE DROPPED IT!
MUST HAVE.
SERIOUSLY, REMY? I MEAN REALLY?
JUST TRYIN' T'KEEP MY SKILLS SHARP, CHERI. WHERE'S THE HARM?
THE HARM IS... YOU JUST DON'T LIFT PEOPLE'S WALLETS, OKAY?
FINE, FINE.
TOP FLOOR.
YES, MISS DANE.
TALKING ELEVATORS. HOW VERY STAR TREK.
YOU SHOULD SEE THE TRANSPORTER ROOM.
SERIOUSLY?
MEBBE.
WELL! THIS IS NICE!
THANK YOU, MR. LEBEAU. AND MAY I BE THE FIRST TO WELCOME YOU...

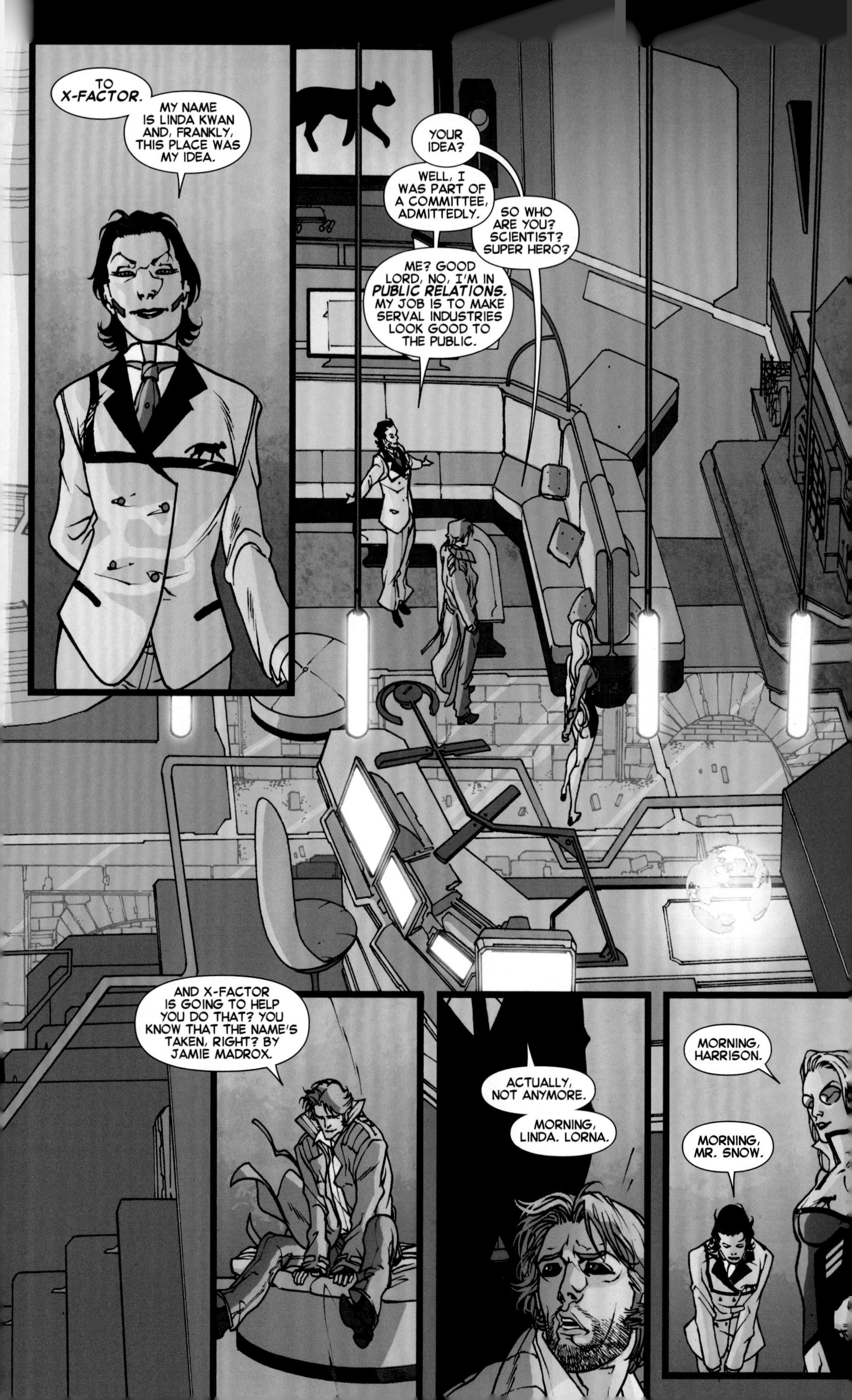
TO X-FACTOR.
MY NAME IS LINDA KWAN AND, FRANKLY, THIS PLACE WAS MY IDEA.
YOUR IDEA?
WELL, I WAS PART OF A COMMITTEE, ADMITTEDLY.
SO WHO ARE YOU? SCIENTIST? SUPER HERO?
ME? GOOD LORD, NO, I'M IN PUBLIC RELATIONS. MY JOB IS TO MAKE SERVAL INDUSTRIES LOOK GOOD TO THE PUBLIC.
AND X-FACTOR IS GOING TO HELP YOU DO THAT? YOU KNOW THAT THE NAME'S TAKEN, RIGHT? BY JAMIE MADROX.
ACTUALLY, NOT ANYMORE.
MORNING, LINDA. LORNA.
MORNING, HARRISON.
MORNING, MR. SNOW.

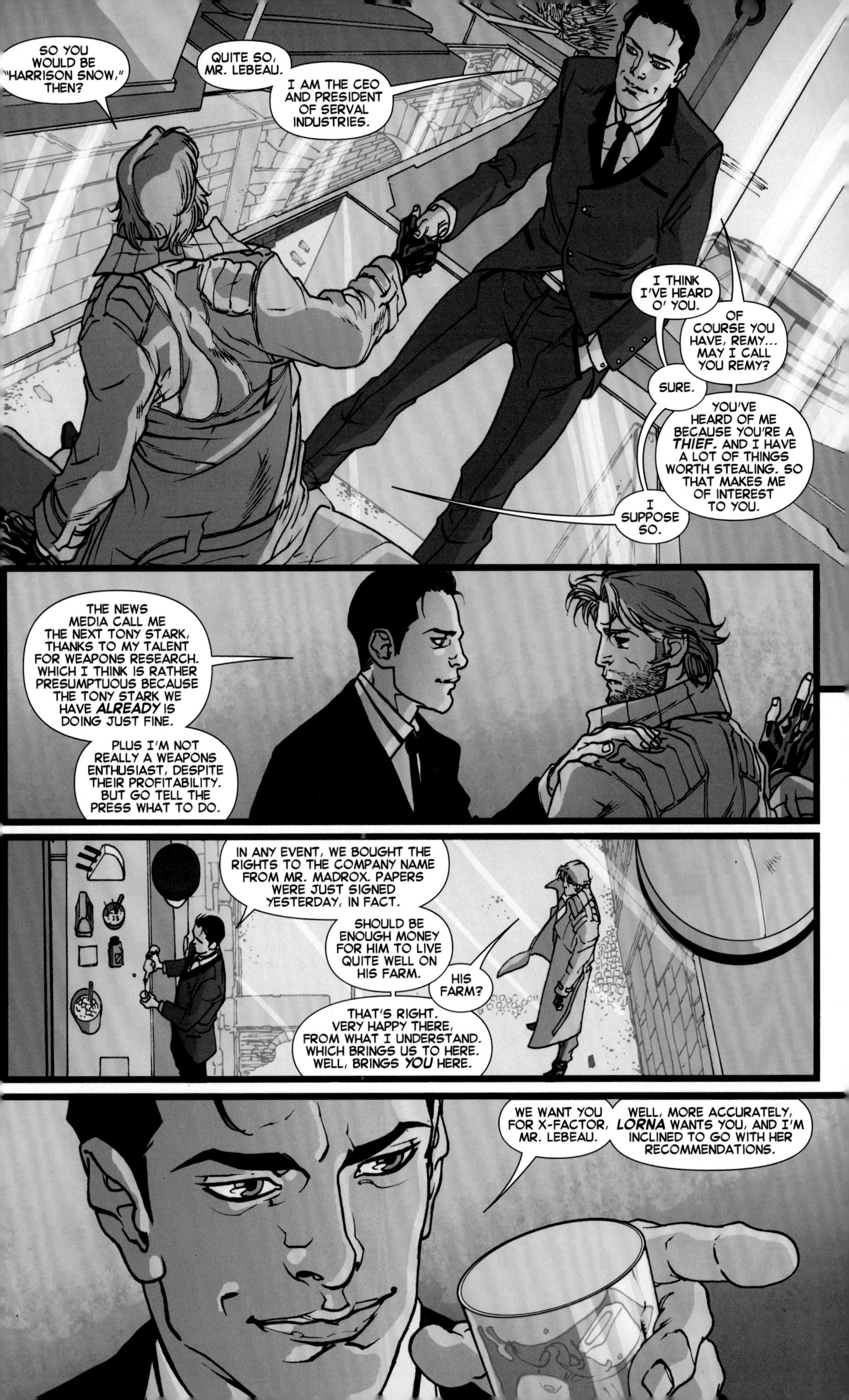

SO YOU WOULD BE "HARRISON SNOW," THEN?
QUITE SO, MR. LEBEAU.
I AM THE CEO AND PRESIDENT OF SERVAL INDUSTRIES.
I THINK I'VE HEARD O' YOU.
OF COURSE YOU HAVE, REMY... MAY I CALL YOU REMY?
SURE.
YOU'VE HEARD OF ME BECAUSE YOU'RE A THIEF. AND I HAVE A LOT OF THINGS WORTH STEALING. SO THAT MAKES ME OF INTEREST TO YOU.
I SUPPOSE SO.
THE NEWS MEDIA CALL ME THE NEXT TONY STARK, THANKS TO MY TALENT FOR WEAPONS RESEARCH. WHICH I THINK IS RATHER PRESUMPTUOUS BECAUSE THE TONY STARK WE HAVE ALREADY IS DOING JUST FINE.
PLUS I'M NOT REALLY A WEAPONS ENTHUSIAST, DESPITE THEIR PROFITABILITY. BUT GO TELL THE PRESS WHAT TO DO.
IN ANY EVENT, WE BOUGHT THE RIGHTS TO THE COMPANY NAME FROM MR. MADROX. PAPERS WERE JUST SIGNED YESTERDAY, IN FACT.
SHOULD BE ENOUGH MONEY FOR HIM TO LIVE QUITE WELL ON HIS FARM.
HIS FARM?
THAT'S RIGHT. VERY HAPPY THERE, FROM WHAT I UNDERSTAND. WHICH BRINGS US TO HERE. WELL, BRINGS YOU HERE.
WE WANT YOU FOR X-FACTOR, MR. LEBEAU.
WELL, MORE ACCURATELY, LORNA WANTS YOU, AND I'M INCLINED TO GO WITH HER RECOMMENDATIONS.

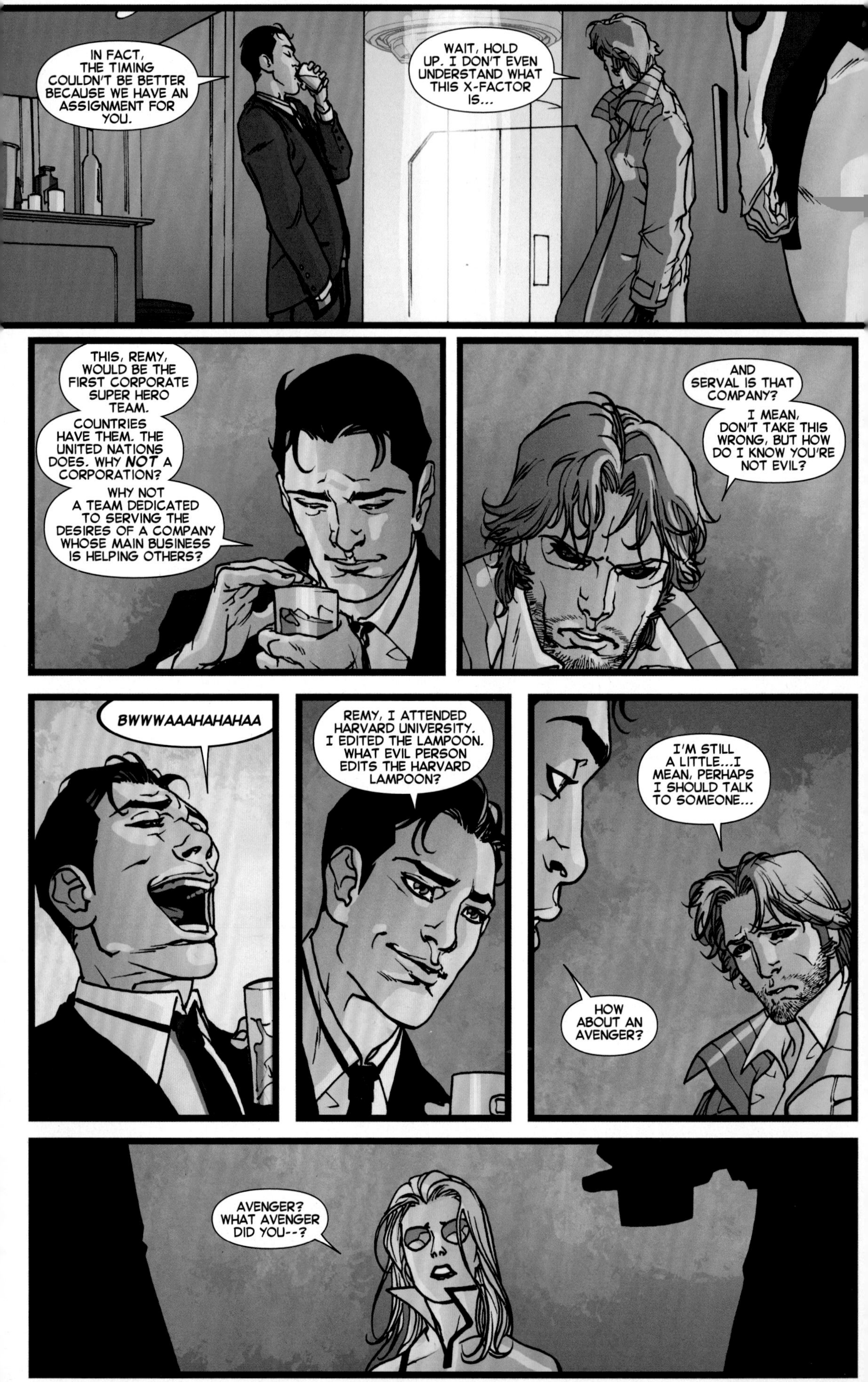
IN FACT, THE TIMING COULDN'T BE BETTER BECAUSE WE HAVE AN ASSIGNMENT FOR YOU.
WAIT, HOLD UP. I DON'T EVEN UNDERSTAND WHAT THIS X-FACTOR IS...
THIS, REMY, WOULD BE THE FIRST CORPORATE SUPER HERO TEAM.
COUNTRIES HAVE THEM. THE UNITED NATIONS DOES. WHY NOT A CORPORATION?
WHY NOT A TEAM DEDICATED TO SERVING THE DESIRES OF A COMPANY WHOSE MAIN BUSINESS IS HELPING OTHERS?
AND SERVAL IS THAT COMPANY?
I MEAN, DON'T TAKE THIS WRONG, BUT HOW DO I KNOW YOU'RE NOT EVIL?
BWWWAAAHAHAHAA
REMY, I ATTENDED HARVARD UNIVERSITY. I EDITED THE LAMPOON. WHAT EVIL PERSON EDITS THE HARVARD LAMPOON?
I'M STILL A LITTLE...I MEAN, PERHAPS I SHOULD TALK TO SOMEONE...
HOW ABOUT AN AVENGER?
AVENGER? WHAT AVENGER DID YOU--?

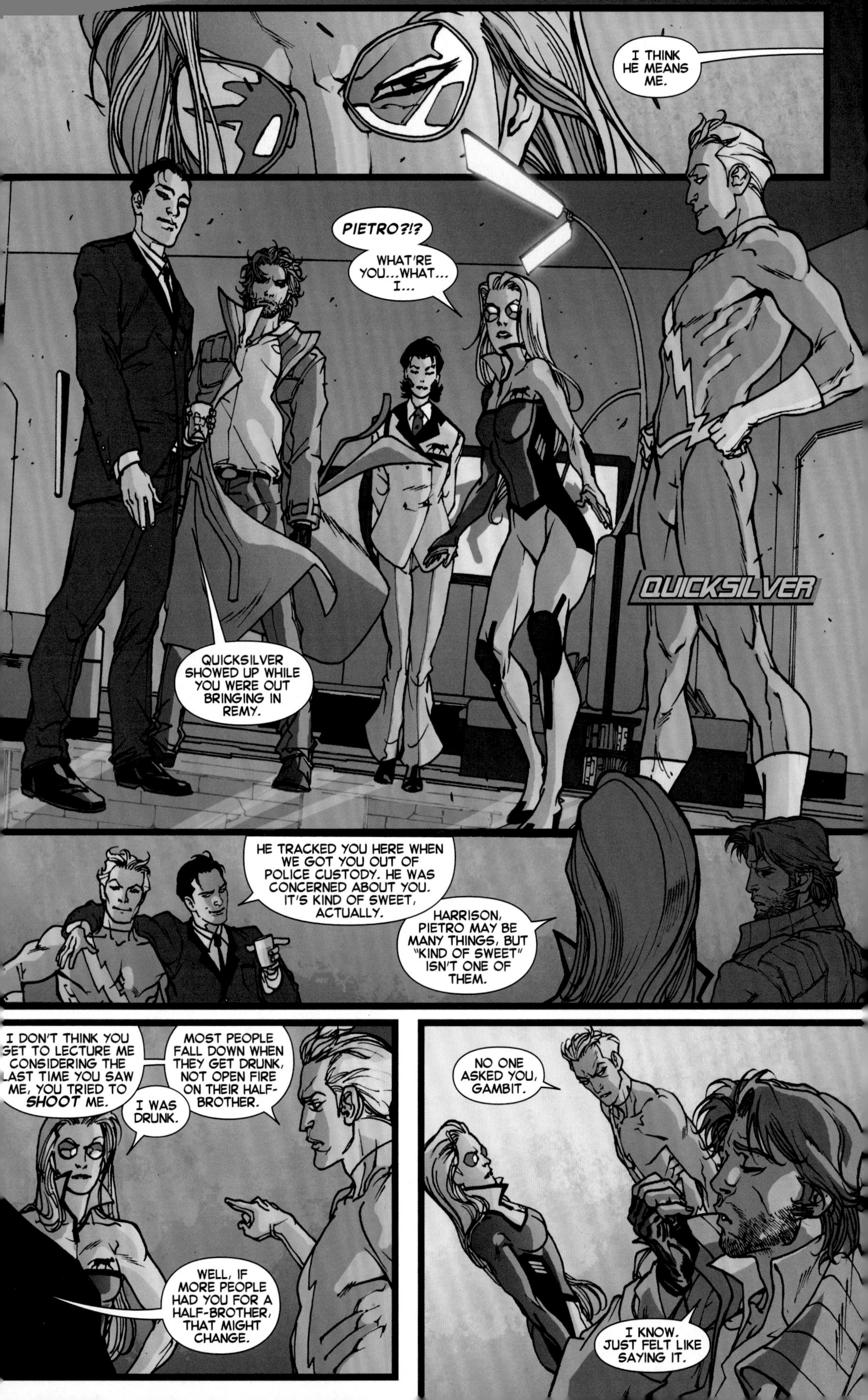
I THINK HE MEANS ME.
PIETRO?!?
WHAT'RE YOU...WHAT... I...
QUICKSILVER
QUICKSILVER SHOWED UP WHILE YOU WERE OUT BRINGING IN REMY.
HE TRACKED YOU HERE WHEN WE GOT YOU OUT OF POLICE CUSTODY. HE WAS CONCERNED ABOUT YOU. IT'S KIND OF SWEET, ACTUALLY.
HARRISON, PIETRO MAY BE MANY THINGS, BUT "KIND OF SWEET" ISN'T ONE OF THEM.
I DON'T THINK YOU GET TO LECTURE ME CONSIDERING THE LAST TIME YOU SAW ME, YOU TRIED TO SHOOT ME.
I WAS DRUNK.
MOST PEOPLE FALL DOWN WHEN THEY GET DRUNK, NOT OPEN FIRE ON THEIR HALF-BROTHER.
WELL, IF MORE PEOPLE HAD YOU FOR A HALF-BROTHER, THAT MIGHT CHANGE.
NO ONE ASKED YOU, GAMBIT.
I KNOW. JUST FELT LIKE SAYING IT.

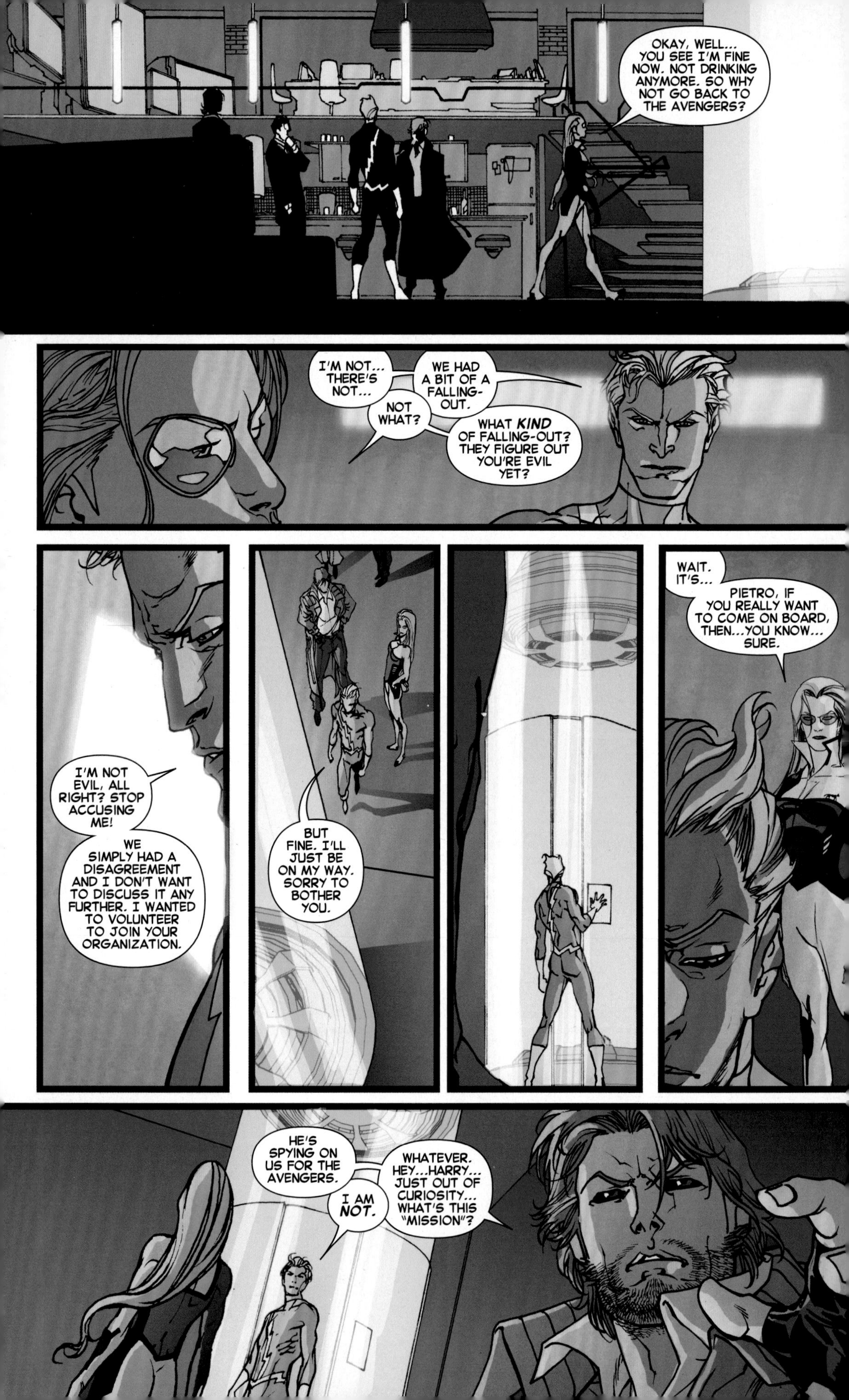
OKAY, WELL... YOU SEE I'M FINE NOW. NOT DRINKING ANYMORE. SO WHY NOT GO BACK TO THE AVENGERS?
I'M NOT... THERE'S NOT...
WE HAD A BIT OF A FALLING-OUT.
NOT WHAT?
WHAT KIND OF FALLING-OUT? THEY FIGURE OUT YOU'RE EVIL YET?
I'M NOT EVIL, ALL RIGHT? STOP ACCUSING ME!
WE SIMPLY HAD A DISAGREEMENT AND I DON'T WANT TO DISCUSS IT ANY FURTHER. I WANTED TO VOLUNTEER TO JOIN YOUR ORGANIZATION.
BUT FINE. I'LL JUST BE ON MY WAY. SORRY TO BOTHER YOU.
WAIT. IT'S...
PIETRO, IF YOU REALLY WANT TO COME ON BOARD, THEN...YOU KNOW... SURE.
HE'S SPYING ON US FOR THE AVENGERS.
I AM NOT.
WHATEVER. HEY...HARRY... JUST OUT OF CURIOSITY... WHAT'S THIS "MISSION"?

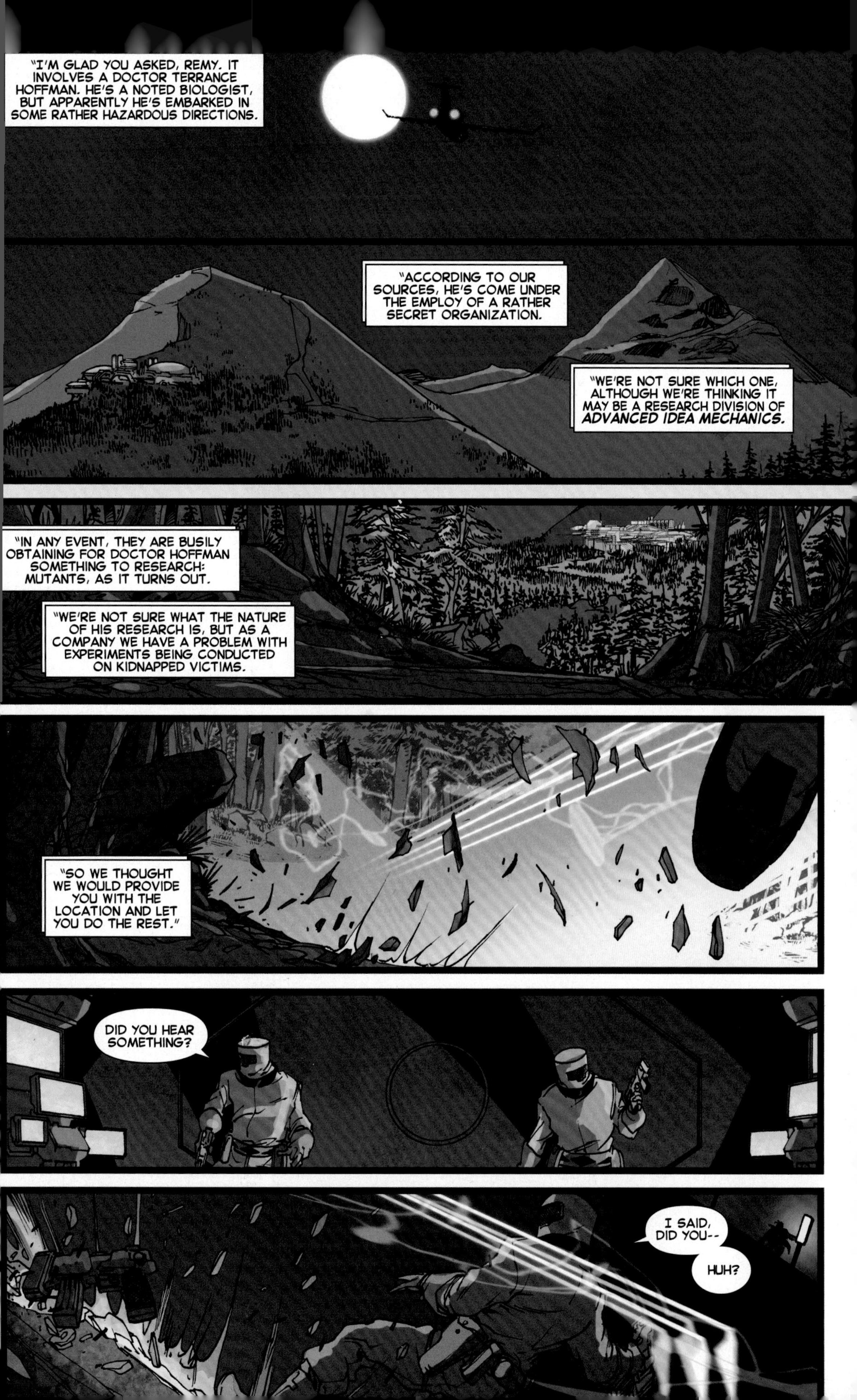
"I'M GLAD YOU ASKED, REMY. IT INVOLVES A DOCTOR TERRANCE HOFFMAN. HE'S A NOTED BIOLOGIST, BUT APPARENTLY HE'S EMBARKED IN SOME RATHER HAZARDOUS DIRECTIONS.
"ACCORDING TO OUR SOURCES, HE'S COME UNDER THE EMPLOY OF A RATHER SECRET ORGANIZATION.
"WE'RE NOT SURE WHICH ONE, ALTHOUGH WE'RE THINKING IT MAY BE A RESEARCH DIVISION OF *ADVANCED IDEA MECHANICS.*
"IN ANY EVENT, THEY ARE BUSILY OBTAINING FOR DOCTOR HOFFMAN SOMETHING TO RESEARCH: MUTANTS, AS IT TURNS OUT.
"WE'RE NOT SURE WHAT THE NATURE OF HIS RESEARCH IS, BUT AS A COMPANY WE HAVE A PROBLEM WITH EXPERIMENTS BEING CONDUCTED ON KIDNAPPED VICTIMS.
"SO WE THOUGHT WE WOULD PROVIDE YOU WITH THE LOCATION AND LET YOU DO THE REST."
DID YOU HEAR SOMETHING?
I SAID, DID YOU--
HUH?

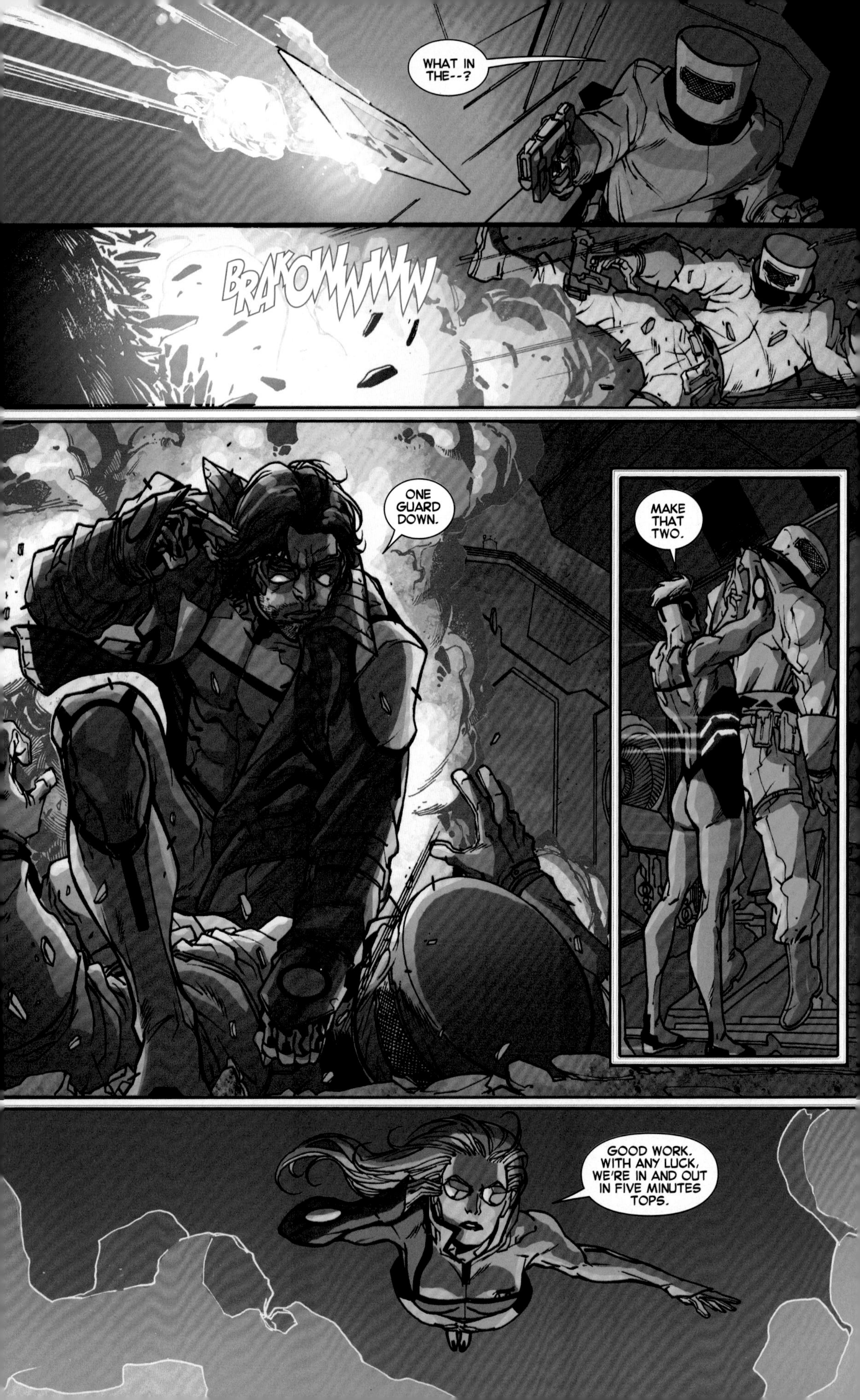
WHAT IN THE--?
BRAKOWWWW
ONE GUARD DOWN.
MAKE THAT TWO.
GOOD WORK. WITH ANY LUCK, WE'RE IN AND OUT IN FIVE MINUTES TOPS.

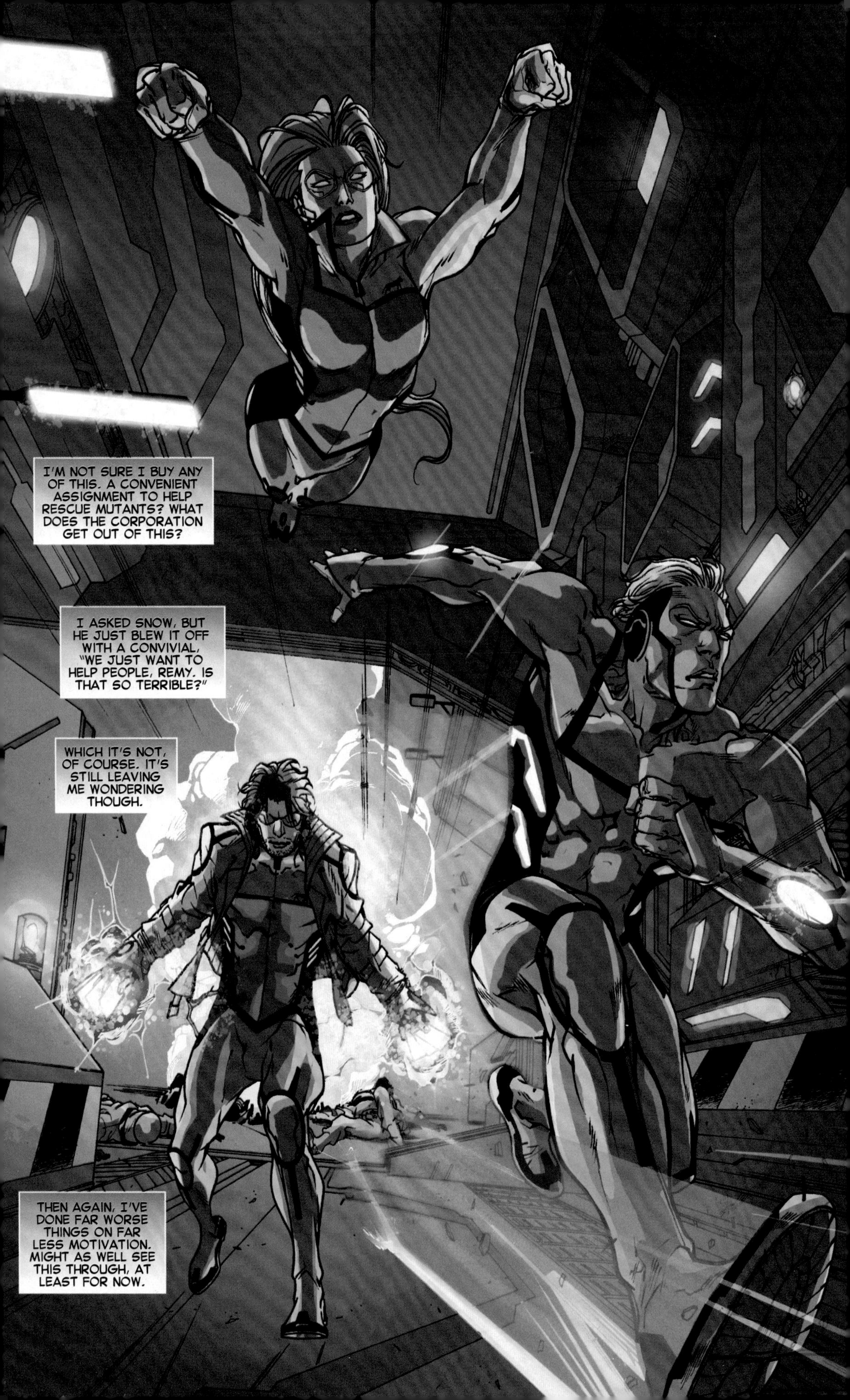
I'M NOT SURE I BUY ANY OF THIS. A CONVENIENT ASSIGNMENT TO HELP RESCUE MUTANTS? WHAT DOES THE CORPORATION GET OUT OF THIS?
I ASKED SNOW, BUT HE JUST BLEW IT OFF WITH A CONVIVIAL, "WE JUST WANT TO HELP PEOPLE, REMY. IS THAT SO TERRIBLE?"
WHICH IT'S NOT, OF COURSE. IT'S STILL LEAVING ME WONDERING THOUGH.
THEN AGAIN, I'VE DONE FAR WORSE THINGS ON FAR LESS MOTIVATION. MIGHT AS WELL SEE THIS THROUGH, AT LEAST FOR NOW.

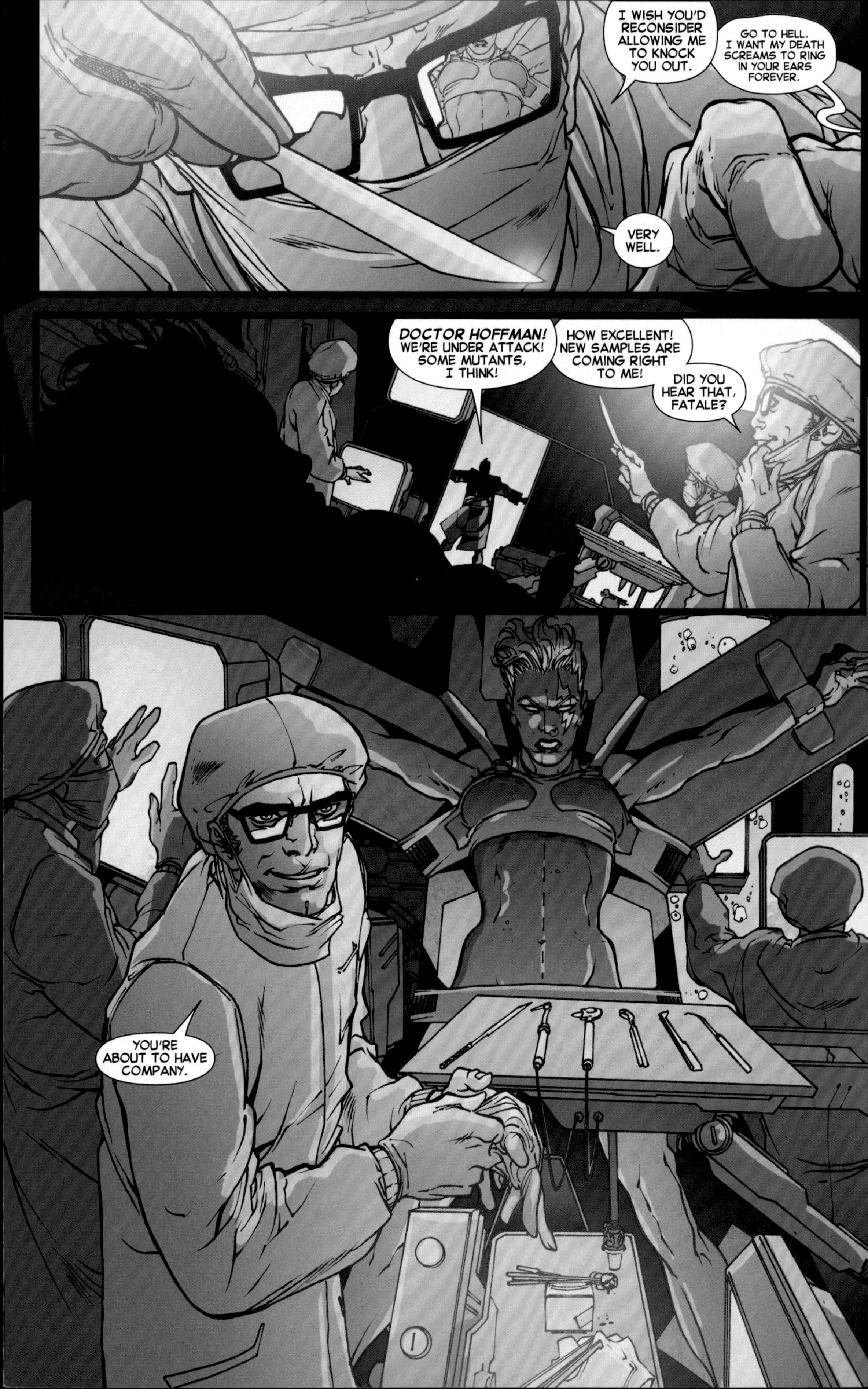
I WISH YOU'D RECONSIDER ALLOWING ME TO KNOCK YOU OUT.
GO TO HELL. I WANT MY DEATH SCREAMS TO RING IN YOUR EARS FOREVER.
VERY WELL.
DOCTOR HOFFMAN! WE'RE UNDER ATTACK! SOME MUTANTS, I THINK!
HOW EXCELLENT! NEW SAMPLES ARE COMING RIGHT TO ME!
DID YOU HEAR THAT, FATALE?
YOU'RE ABOUT TO HAVE COMPANY.

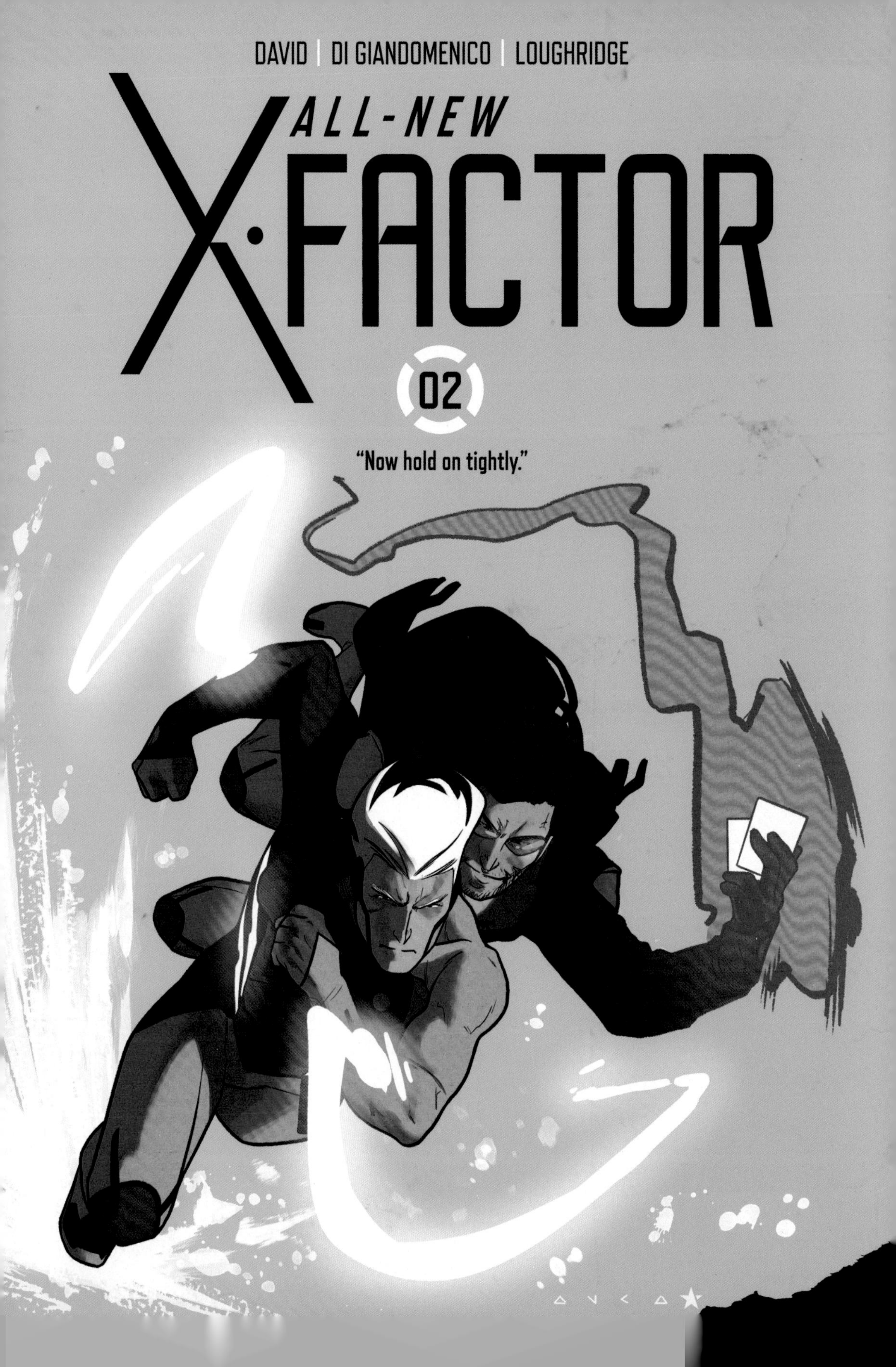
DAVID | DI GIANDOMENICO | LOUGHRIDGE
ALL-NEW
X-FACTOR
02
"Now hold on tightly."

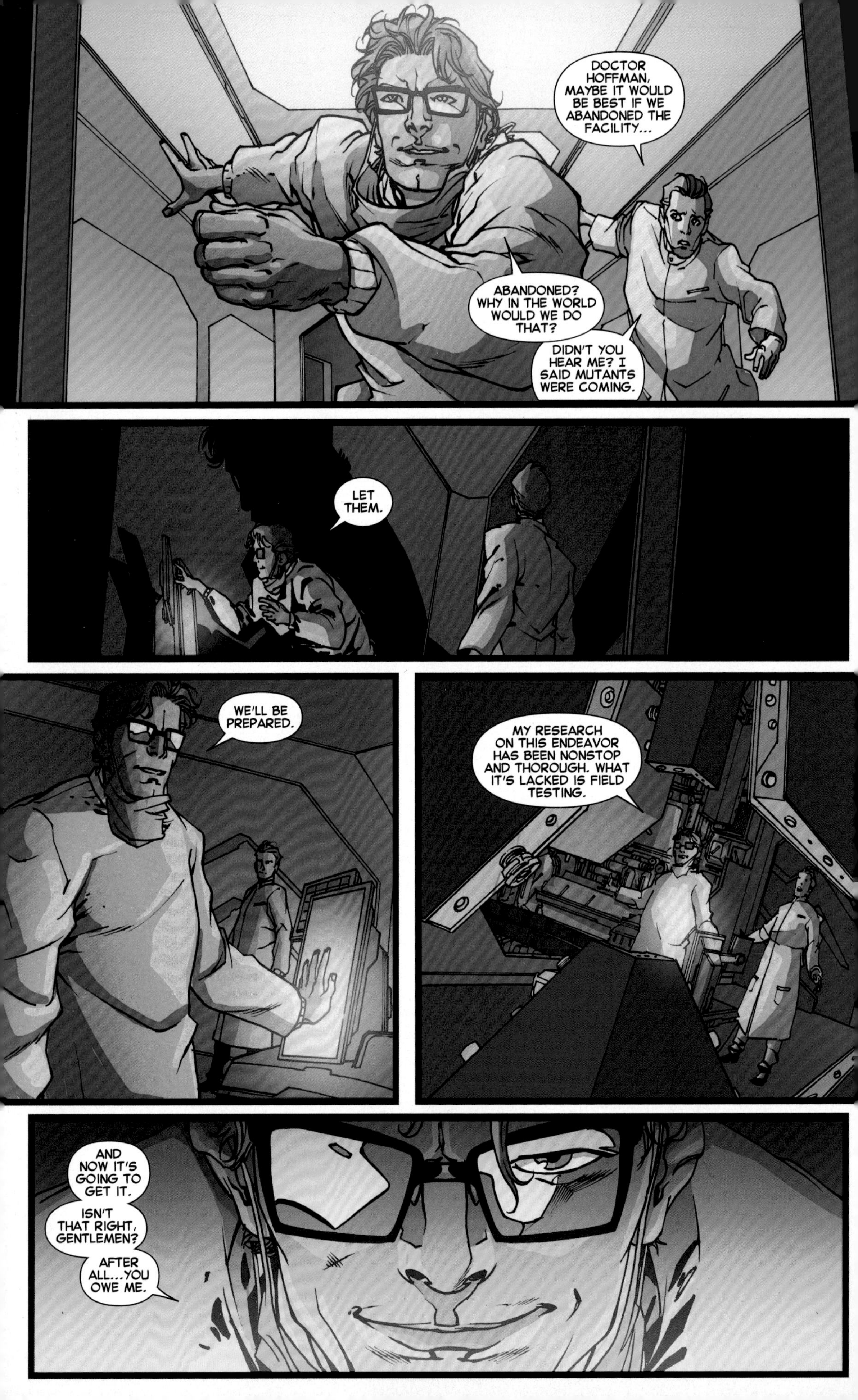
DOCTOR HOFFMAN, MAYBE IT WOULD BE BEST IF WE ABANDONED THE FACILITY...
ABANDONED? WHY IN THE WORLD WOULD WE DO THAT?
DIDN'T YOU HEAR ME? I SAID MUTANTS WERE COMING.
LET THEM.
WE'LL BE PREPARED.
MY RESEARCH ON THIS ENDEAVOR HAS BEEN NONSTOP AND THOROUGH. WHAT IT'S LACKED IS FIELD TESTING.
AND NOW IT'S GOING TO GET IT.
ISN'T THAT RIGHT, GENTLEMEN?
AFTER ALL...YOU OWE ME.

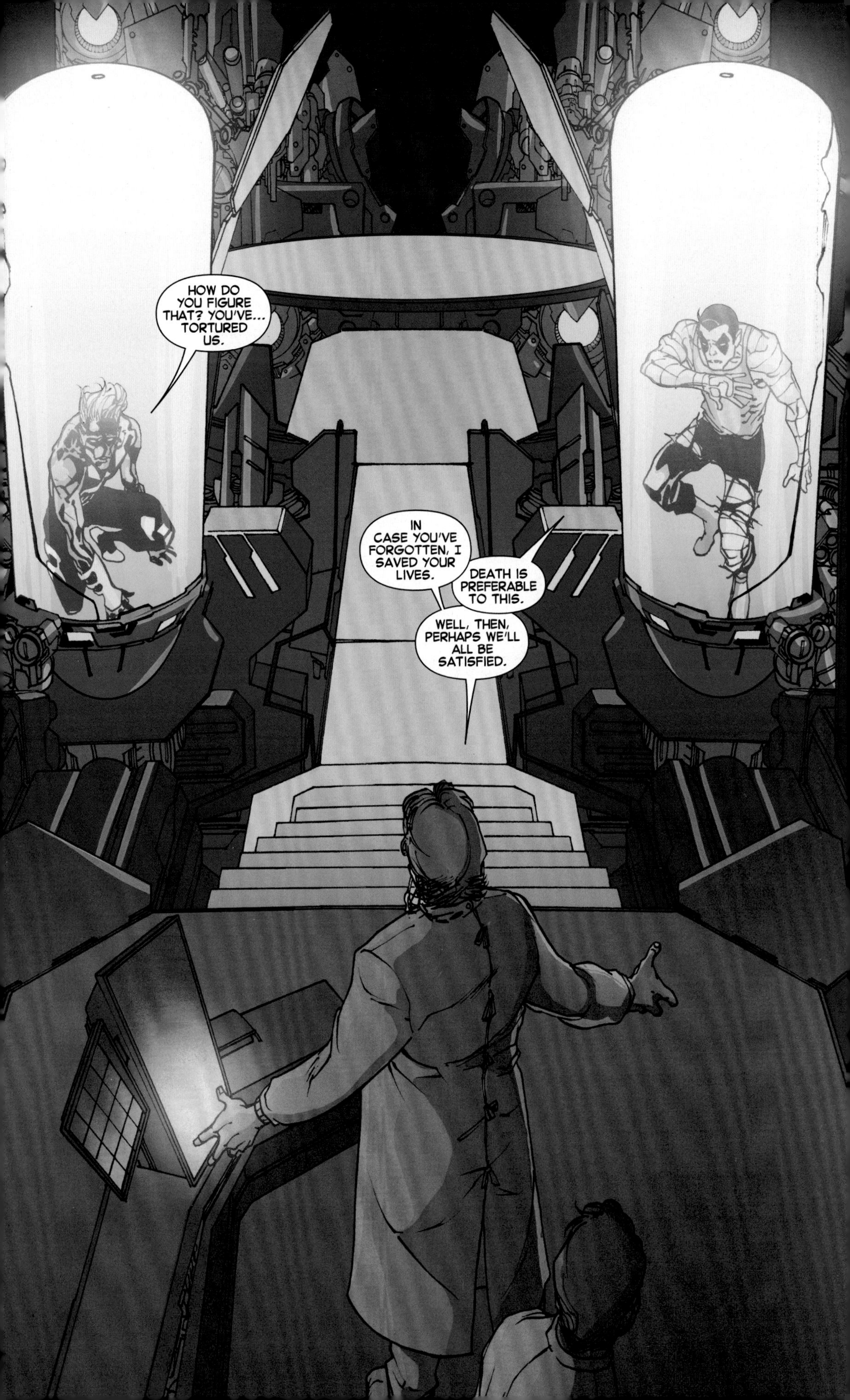

HOW DO YOU FIGURE THAT? YOU'VE... TORTURED US.
IN CASE YOU'VE FORGOTTEN, I SAVED YOUR LIVES.
DEATH IS PREFERABLE TO THIS.
WELL, THEN, PERHAPS WE'LL ALL BE SATISFIED.

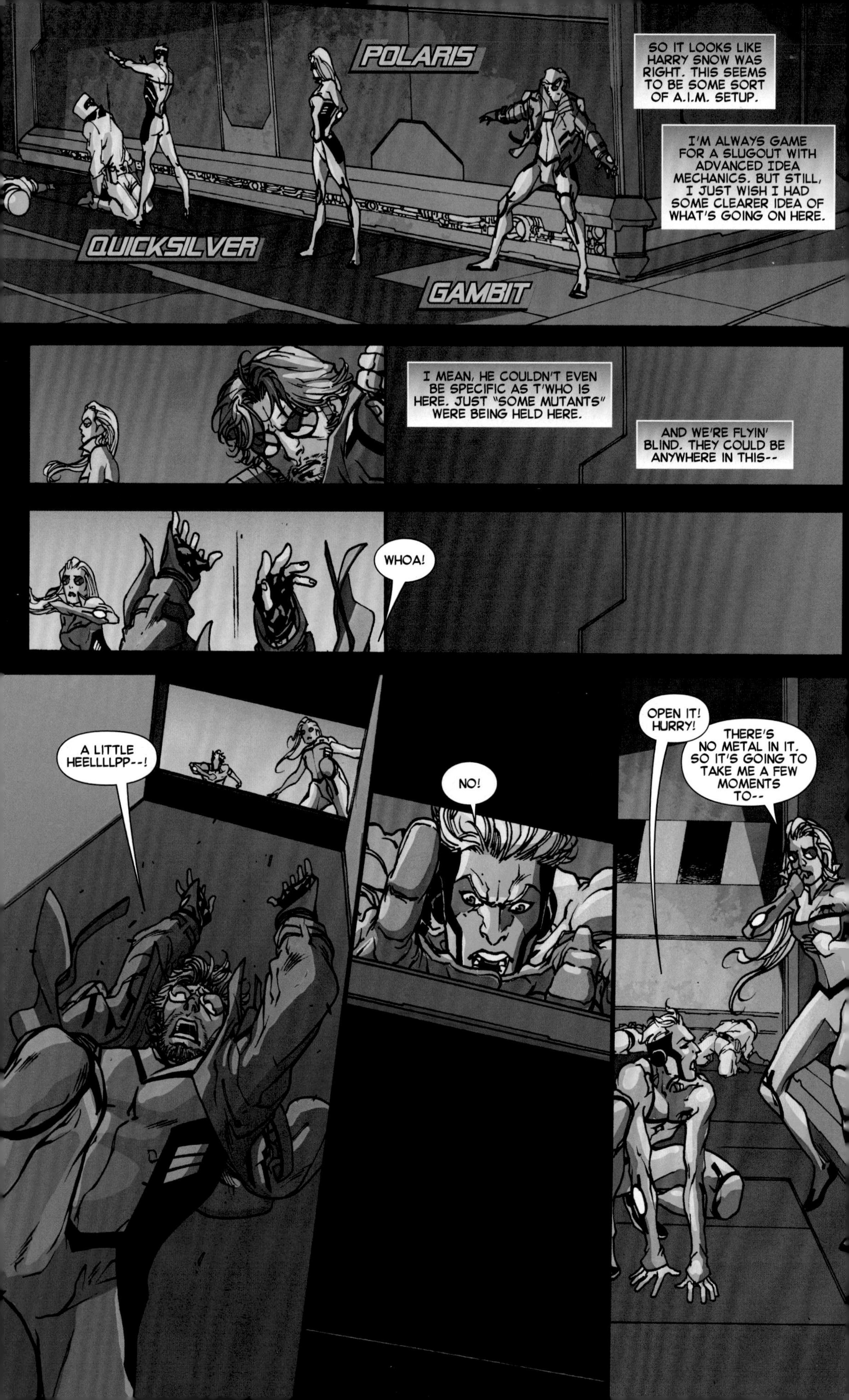
POLARIS
SO IT LOOKS LIKE HARRY SNOW WAS RIGHT. THIS SEEMS TO BE SOME SORT OF A.I.M. SETUP.
I'M ALWAYS GAME FOR A SLUGOUT WITH ADVANCED IDEA MECHANICS. BUT STILL, I JUST WISH I HAD SOME CLEARER IDEA OF WHAT'S GOING ON HERE.
QUICKSILVER
GAMBIT
I MEAN, HE COULDN'T EVEN BE SPECIFIC AS T'WHO IS HERE. JUST "SOME MUTANTS" WERE BEING HELD HERE.
AND WE'RE FLYIN' BLIND. THEY COULD BE ANYWHERE IN THIS--
WHOA!
A LITTLE HEELLLLPP--!
NO!
OPEN IT! HURRY!
THERE'S NO METAL IN IT. SO IT'S GOING TO TAKE ME A FEW MOMENTS TO--

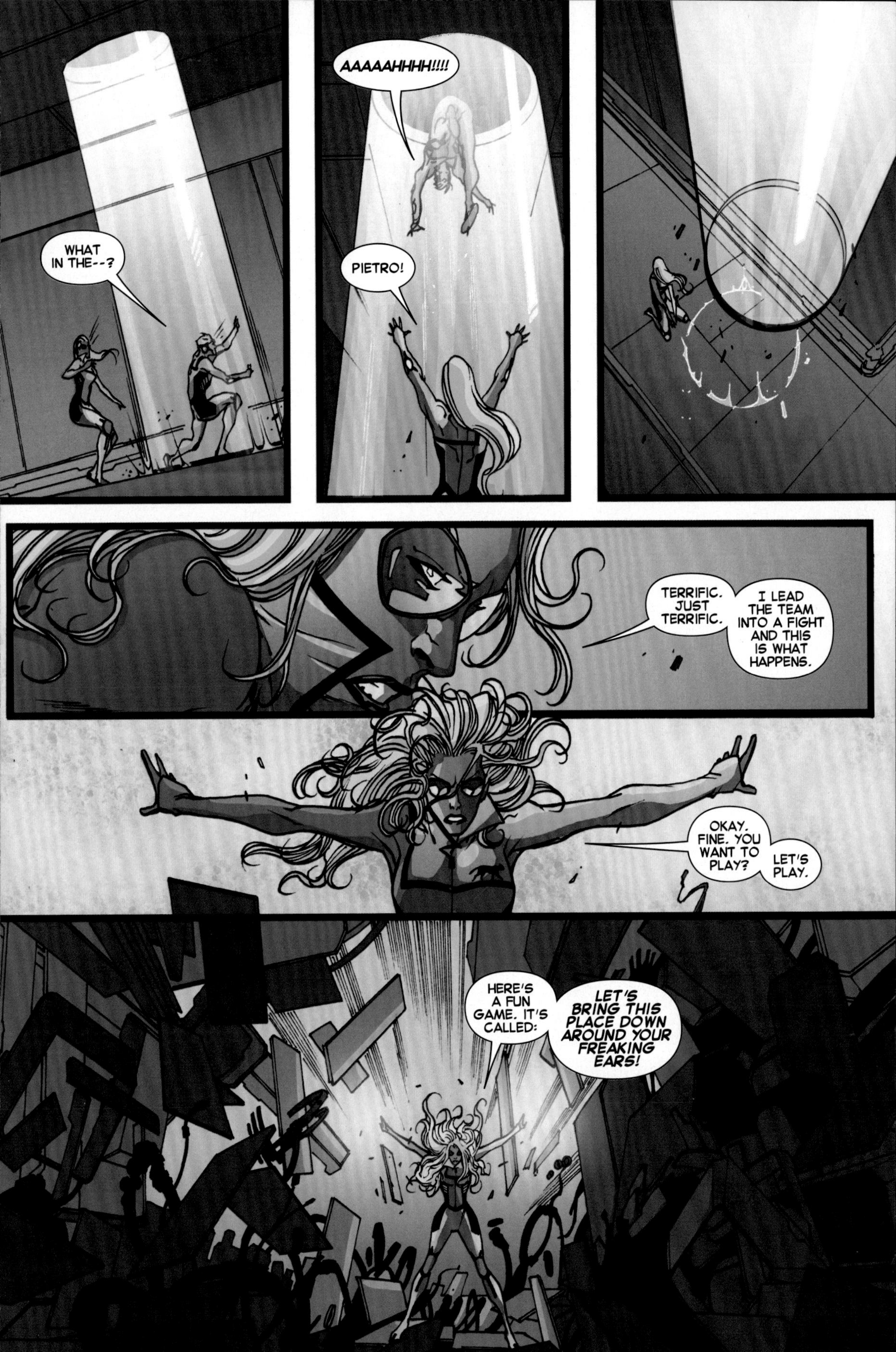
WHAT IN THE--?
AAAAAHHHH!!!!
PIETRO!
TERRIFIC. JUST TERRIFIC.
I LEAD THE TEAM INTO A FIGHT AND THIS IS WHAT HAPPENS.
OKAY. FINE. YOU WANT TO PLAY?
LET'S PLAY.
HERE'S A FUN GAME. IT'S CALLED:
LET'S BRING THIS PLACE DOWN AROUND YOUR FREAKING EARS!

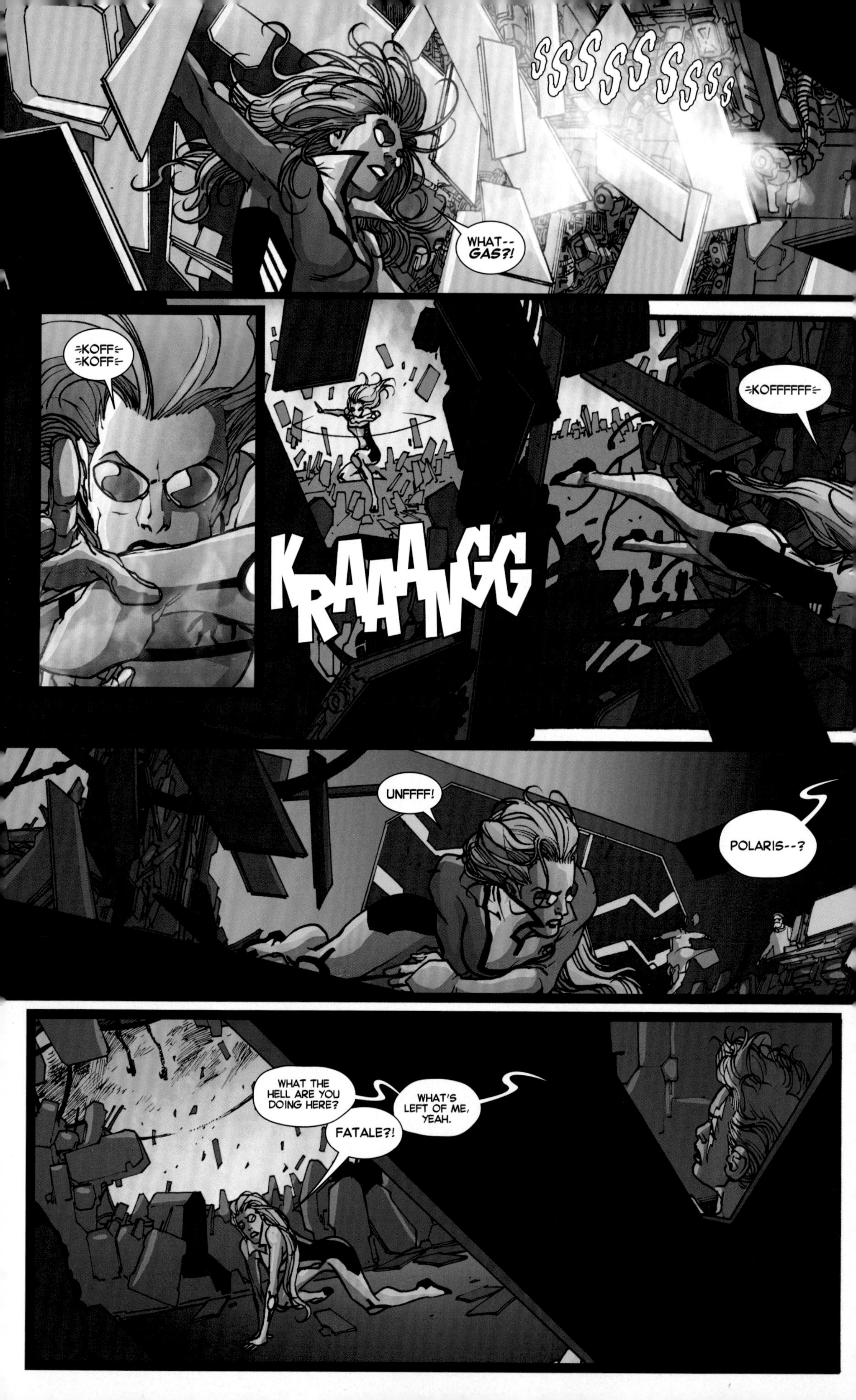
SSSSSSSSs
WHAT-- GAS?!
KOFF KOFF
KRAAAANGG
KOFFFFFFF
UNFFFF!
POLARIS--?
WHAT THE HELL ARE YOU DOING HERE?
FATALE?!
WHAT'S LEFT OF ME, YEAH.

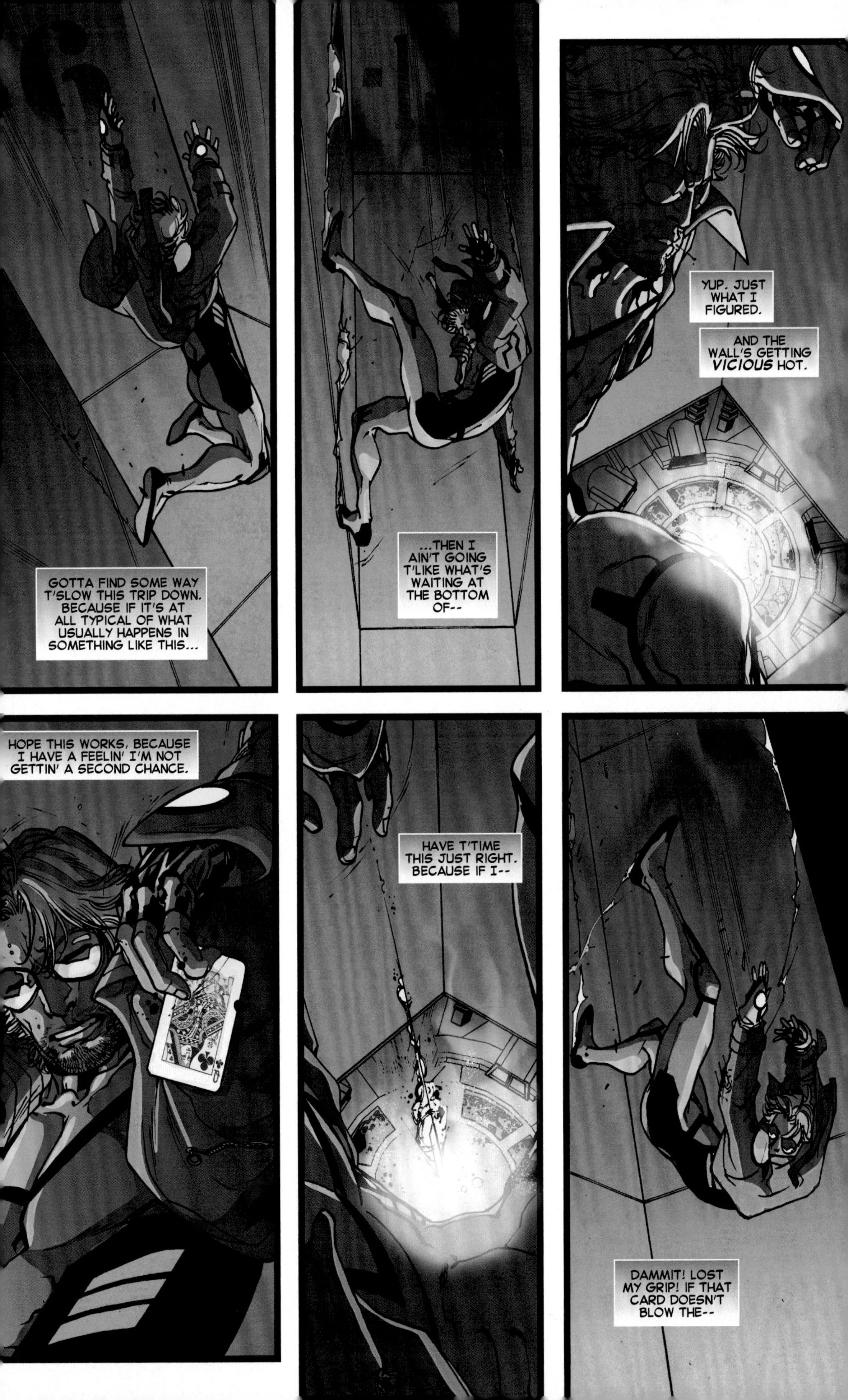
GOTTA FIND SOME WAY T'SLOW THIS TRIP DOWN. BECAUSE IF IT'S AT ALL TYPICAL OF WHAT USUALLY HAPPENS IN SOMETHING LIKE THIS...
...THEN I AIN'T GOING T'LIKE WHAT'S WAITING AT THE BOTTOM OF--
YUP. JUST WHAT I FIGURED.
AND THE WALL'S GETTING *VICIOUS* HOT.
HOPE THIS WORKS, BECAUSE I HAVE A FEELIN' I'M NOT GETTIN' A SECOND CHANCE.
HAVE T'TIME THIS JUST RIGHT. BECAUSE IF I--
DAMMIT! LOST MY GRIP! IF THAT CARD DOESN'T BLOW THE--

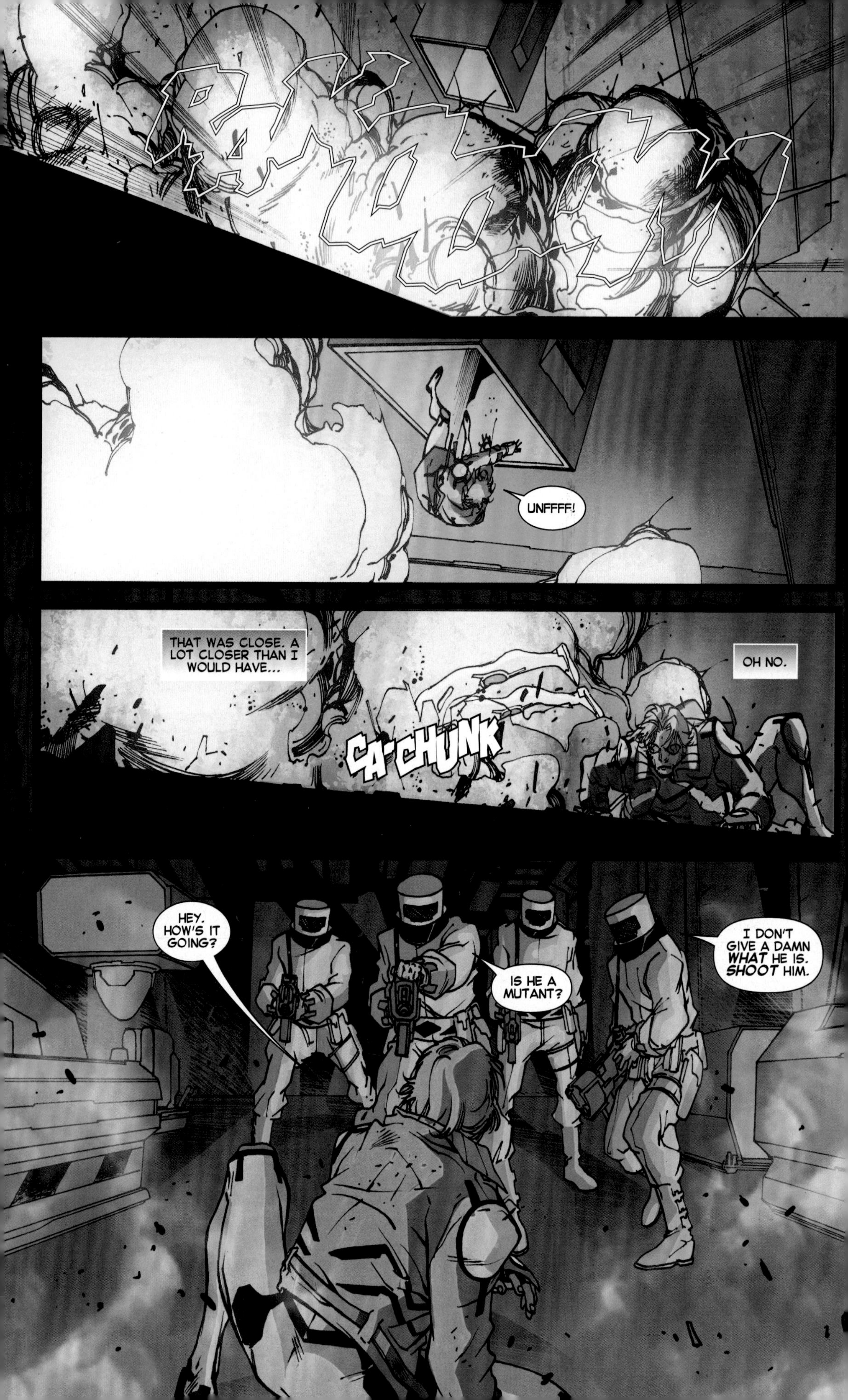
UNFFFF!
THAT WAS CLOSE. A LOT CLOSER THAN I WOULD HAVE...
OH NO.
CA-CHUNK
HEY. HOW'S IT GOING?
IS HE A MUTANT?
I DON'T GIVE A DAMN *WHAT* HE IS. ***SHOOT*** HIM.

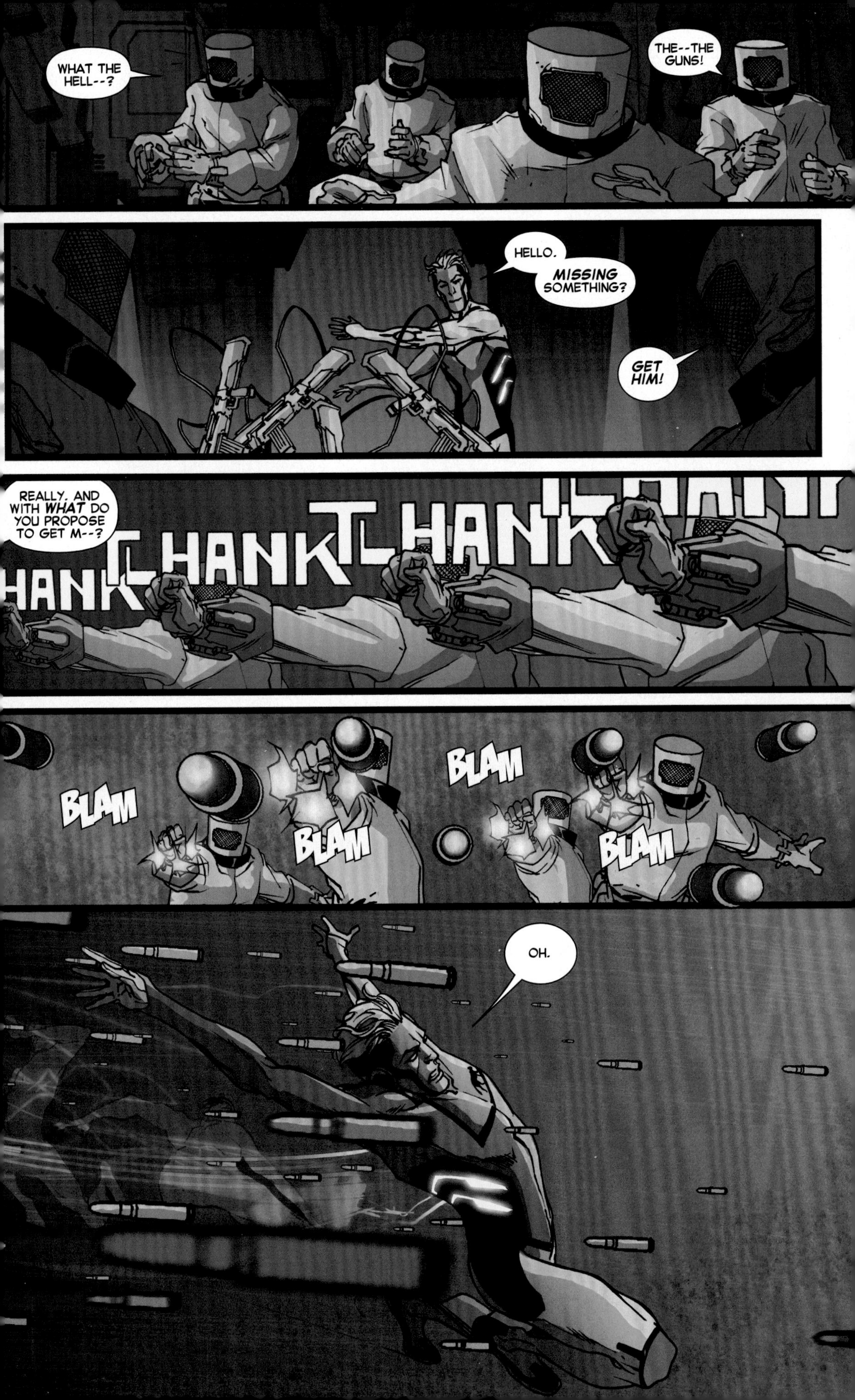
WHAT THE HELL--?
THE--THE GUNS!
HELLO. MISSING SOMETHING?
GET HIM!
REALLY. AND WITH WHAT DO YOU PROPOSE TO GET M--?
HANK
CHANK
CHANK
BLAM
BLAM
BLAM
BLAM
OH.

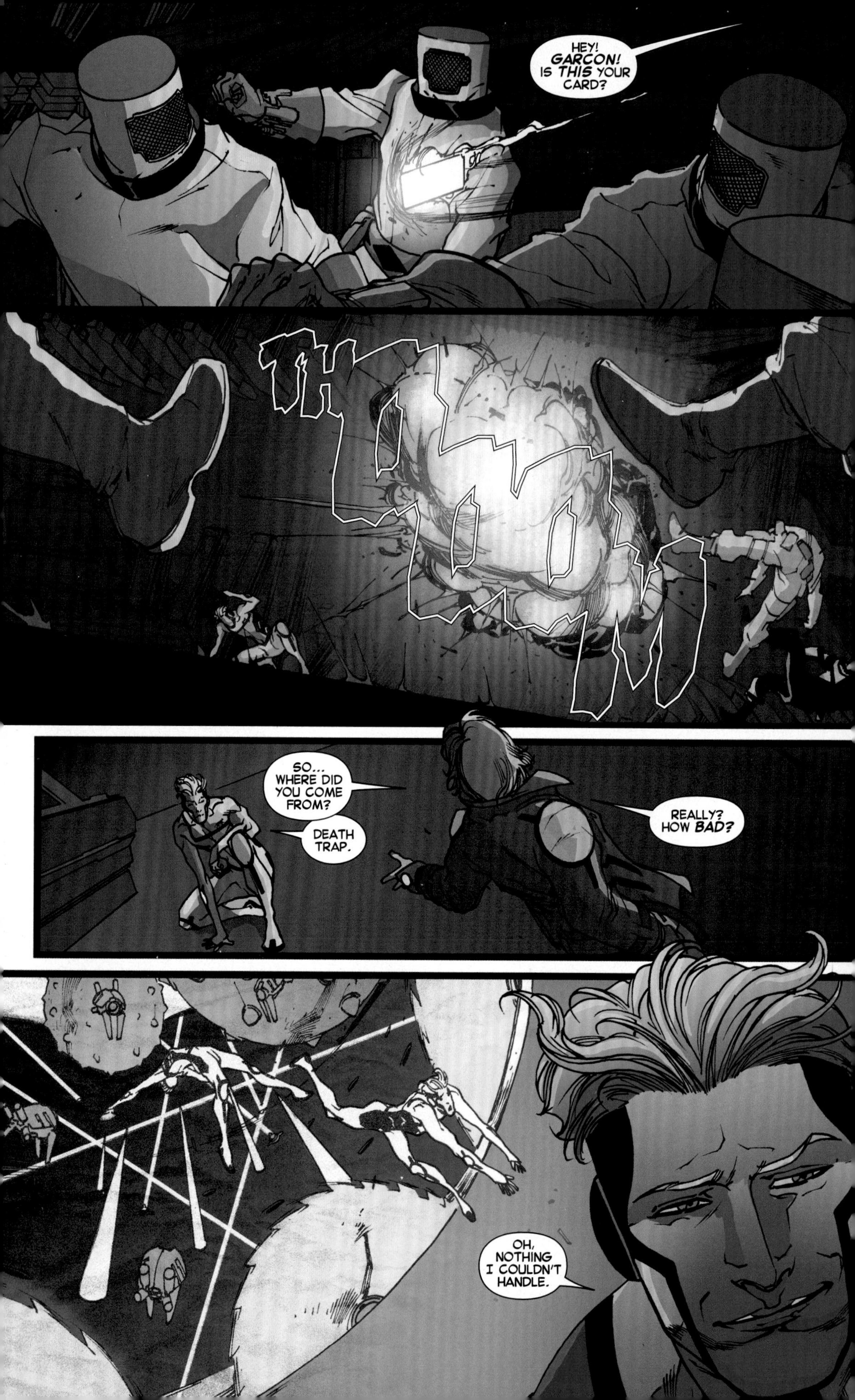
HEY! GARCON! IS THIS YOUR CARD?
THOOOM
SO... WHERE DID YOU COME FROM?
DEATH TRAP.
REALLY? HOW BAD?
OH, NOTHING I COULDN'T HANDLE.

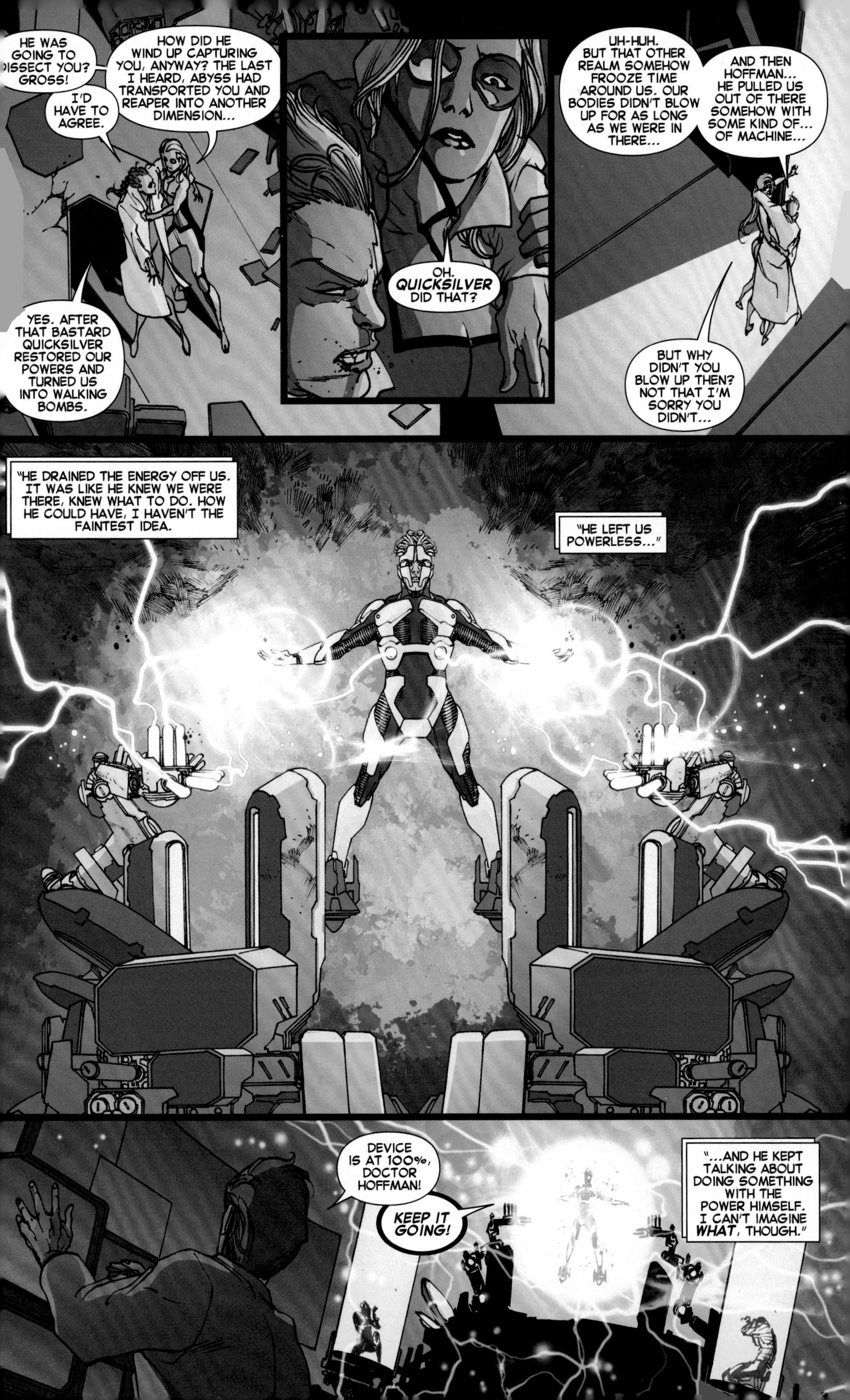
HE WAS GOING TO DISSECT YOU? GROSS!
I'D HAVE TO AGREE.
HOW DID HE WIND UP CAPTURING YOU, ANYWAY? THE LAST I HEARD, ABYSS HAD TRANSPORTED YOU AND REAPER INTO ANOTHER DIMENSION...
YES. AFTER THAT BASTARD QUICKSILVER RESTORED OUR POWERS AND TURNED US INTO WALKING BOMBS.
OH. QUICKSILVER DID THAT?
UH-HUH. BUT THAT OTHER REALM SOMEHOW FROOZE TIME AROUND US. OUR BODIES DIDN'T BLOW UP FOR AS LONG AS WE WERE IN THERE...
AND THEN HOFFMAN... HE PULLED US OUT OF THERE SOMEHOW WITH SOME KIND OF... OF MACHINE...
BUT WHY DIDN'T YOU BLOW UP THEN? NOT THAT I'M SORRY YOU DIDN'T...
"HE DRAINED THE ENERGY OFF US. IT WAS LIKE HE KNEW WE WERE THERE, KNEW WHAT TO DO. HOW HE COULD HAVE, I HAVEN'T THE FAINTEST IDEA.
"HE LEFT US POWERLESS..."
DEVICE IS AT 100%, DOCTOR HOFFMAN!
KEEP IT GOING!
"...AND HE KEPT TALKING ABOUT DOING SOMETHING WITH THE POWER HIMSELF. I CAN'T IMAGINE WHAT, THOUGH."

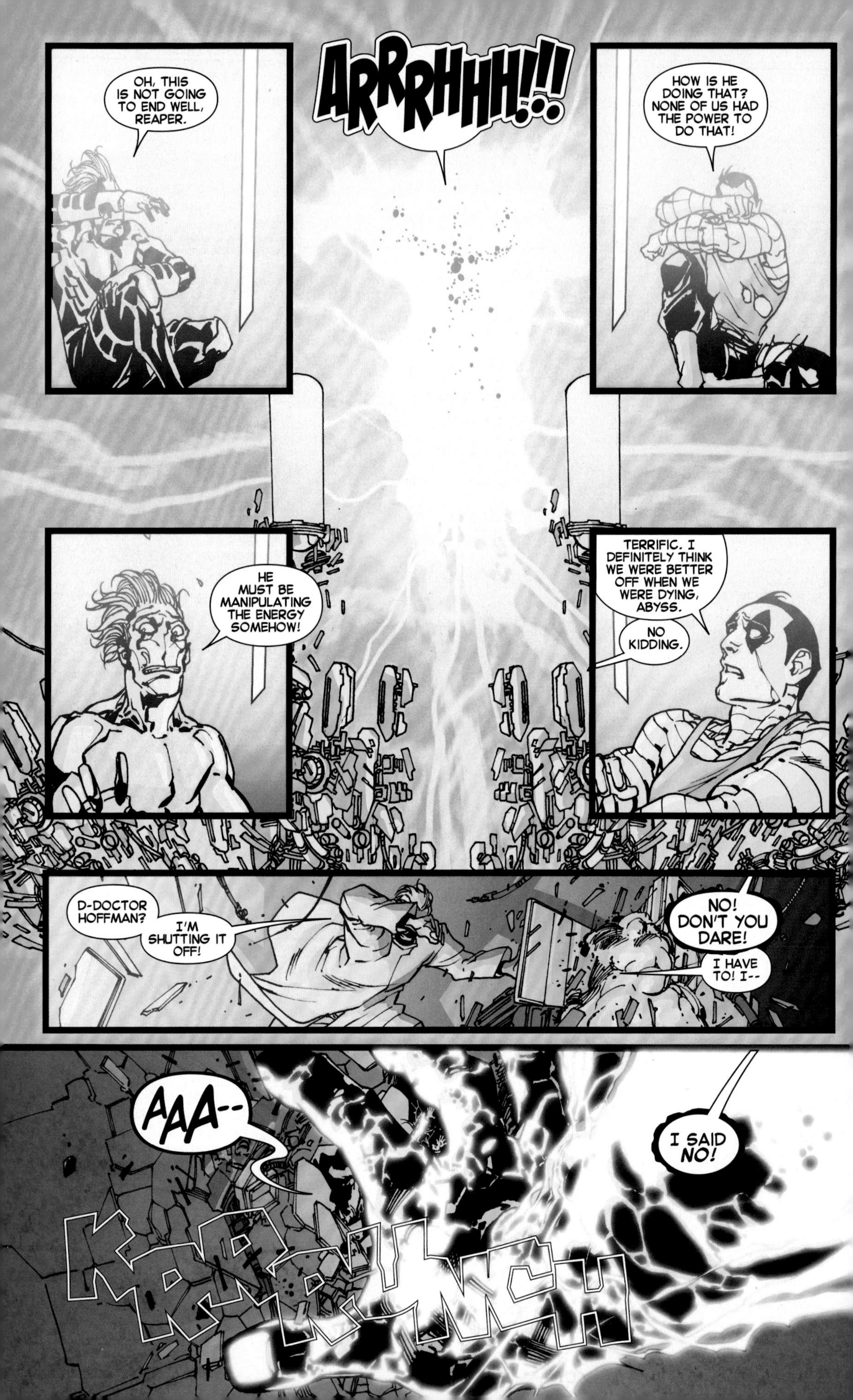
OH, THIS IS NOT GOING TO END WELL, REAPER.
ARRRHHH!!!
HOW IS HE DOING THAT? NONE OF US HAD THE POWER TO DO THAT!
HE MUST BE MANIPULATING THE ENERGY SOMEHOW!
TERRIFIC. I DEFINITELY THINK WE WERE BETTER OFF WHEN WE WERE DYING, ABYSS.
NO KIDDING.
D-DOCTOR HOFFMAN?
I'M SHUTTING IT OFF!
NO! DON'T YOU DARE!
I HAVE TO! I--
AAA--
I SAID NO!
KRRUNCH

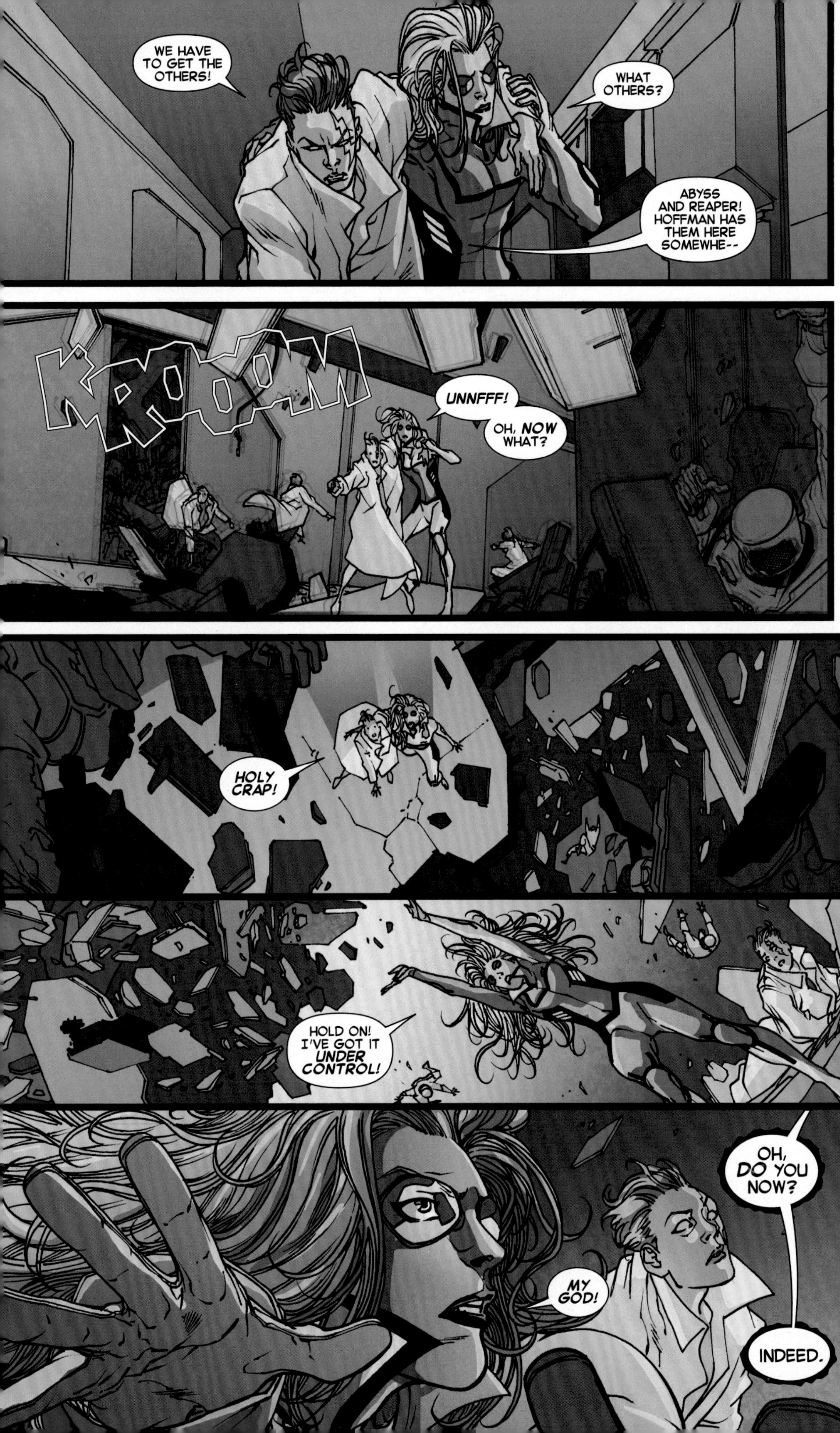
WE HAVE TO GET THE OTHERS!
WHAT OTHERS?
ABYSS AND REAPER! HOFFMAN HAS THEM HERE SOMEWHE--
KROOOM
UNNFFF!
OH, NOW WHAT?
HOLY CRAP!
HOLD ON! I'VE GOT IT UNDER CONTROL!
OH, DO YOU NOW?
MY GOD!
INDEED.

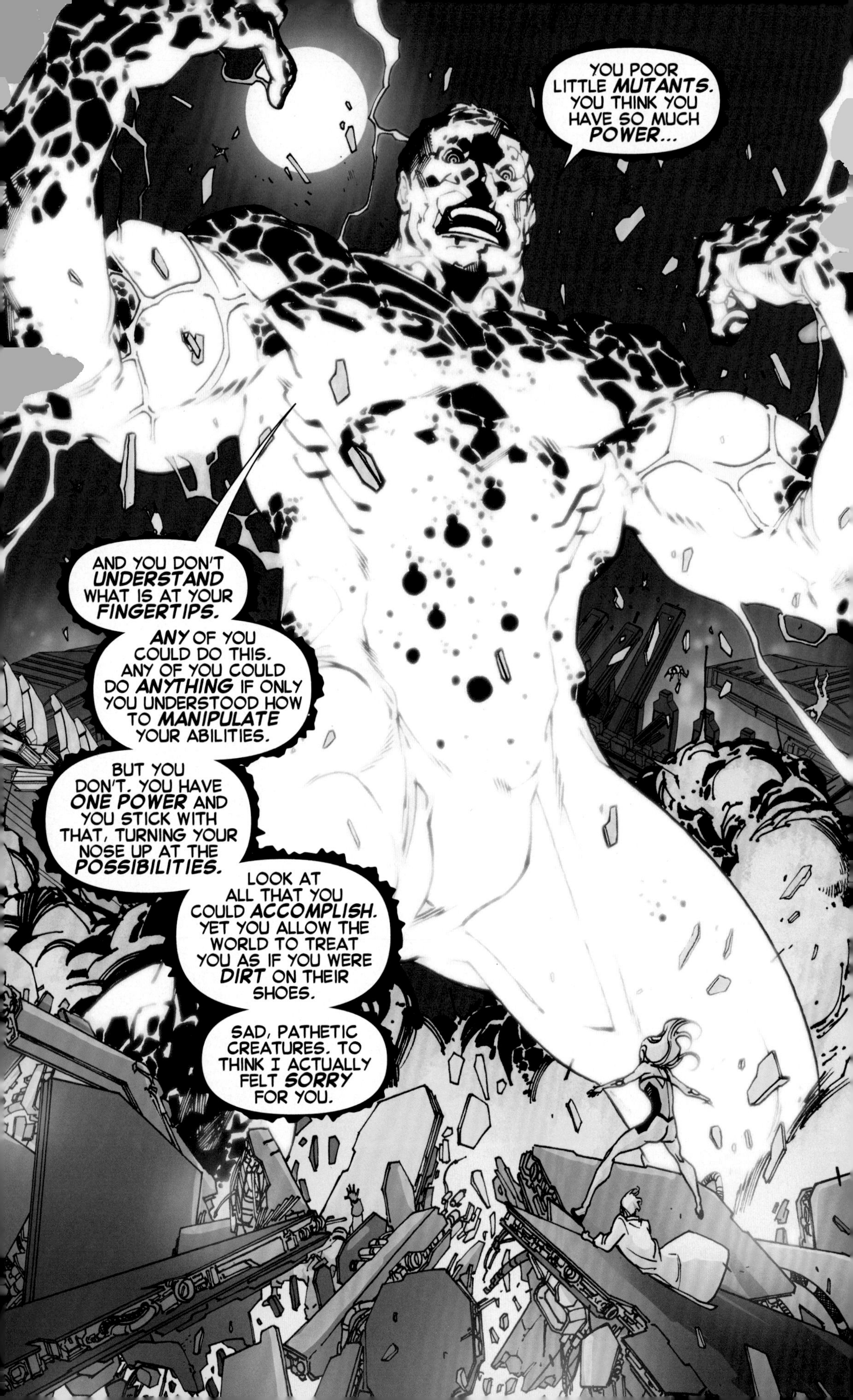
YOU POOR LITTLE MUTANTS. YOU THINK YOU HAVE SO MUCH POWER...
AND YOU DON'T UNDERSTAND WHAT IS AT YOUR FINGERTIPS.
ANY OF YOU COULD DO THIS. ANY OF YOU COULD DO ANYTHING IF ONLY YOU UNDERSTOOD HOW TO MANIPULATE YOUR ABILITIES.
BUT YOU DON'T. YOU HAVE ONE POWER AND YOU STICK WITH THAT, TURNING YOUR NOSE UP AT THE POSSIBILITIES.
LOOK AT ALL THAT YOU COULD ACCOMPLISH. YET YOU ALLOW THE WORLD TO TREAT YOU AS IF YOU WERE DIRT ON THEIR SHOES.
SAD, PATHETIC CREATURES. TO THINK I ACTUALLY FELT SORRY FOR YOU.

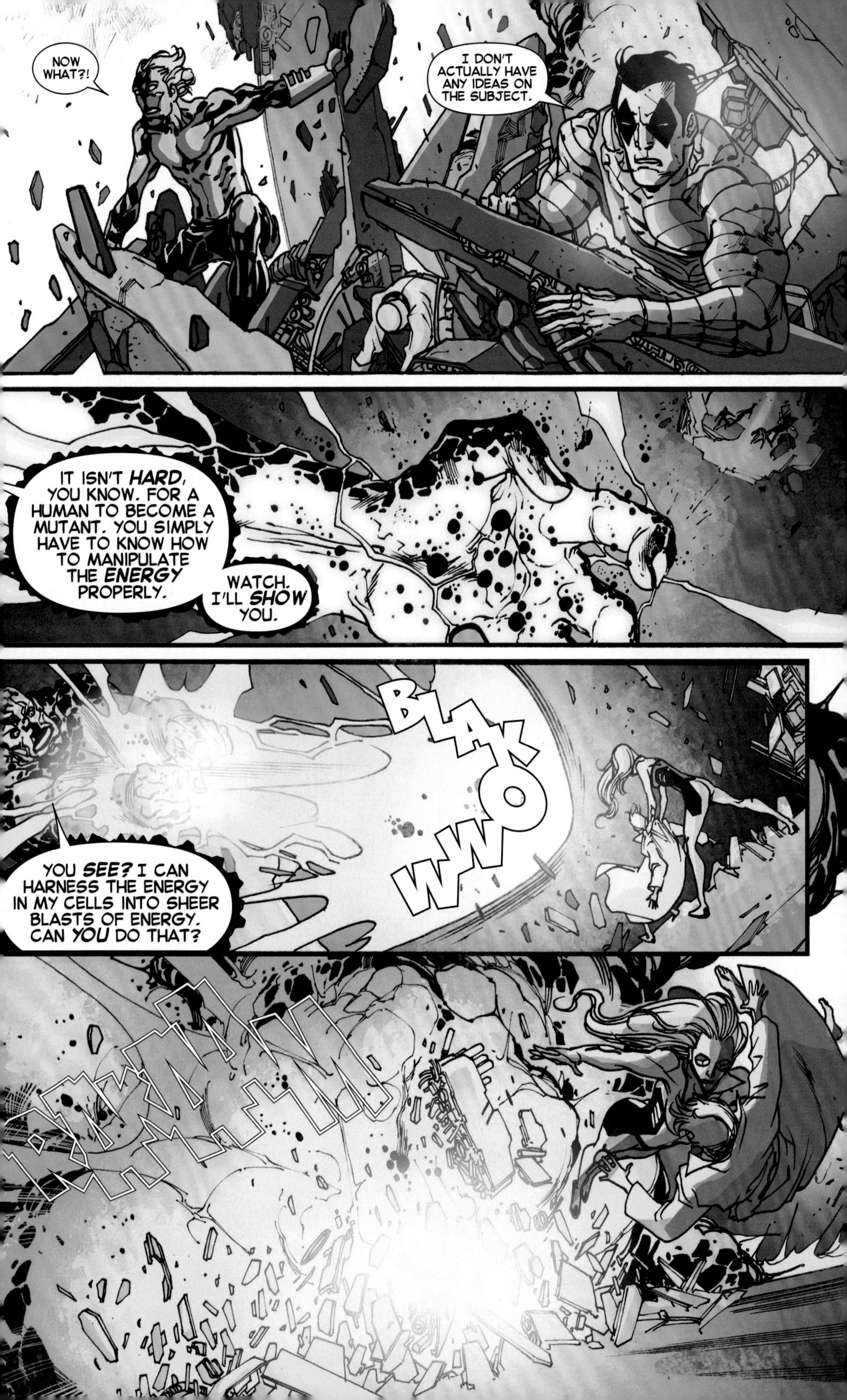
NOW WHAT?!
I DON'T ACTUALLY HAVE ANY IDEAS ON THE SUBJECT.
IT ISN'T HARD, YOU KNOW. FOR A HUMAN TO BECOME A MUTANT. YOU SIMPLY HAVE TO KNOW HOW TO MANIPULATE THE ENERGY PROPERLY.
WATCH. I'LL SHOW YOU.
BLAKOWW
YOU SEE? I CAN HARNESS THE ENERGY IN MY CELLS INTO SHEER BLASTS OF ENERGY. CAN YOU DO THAT?

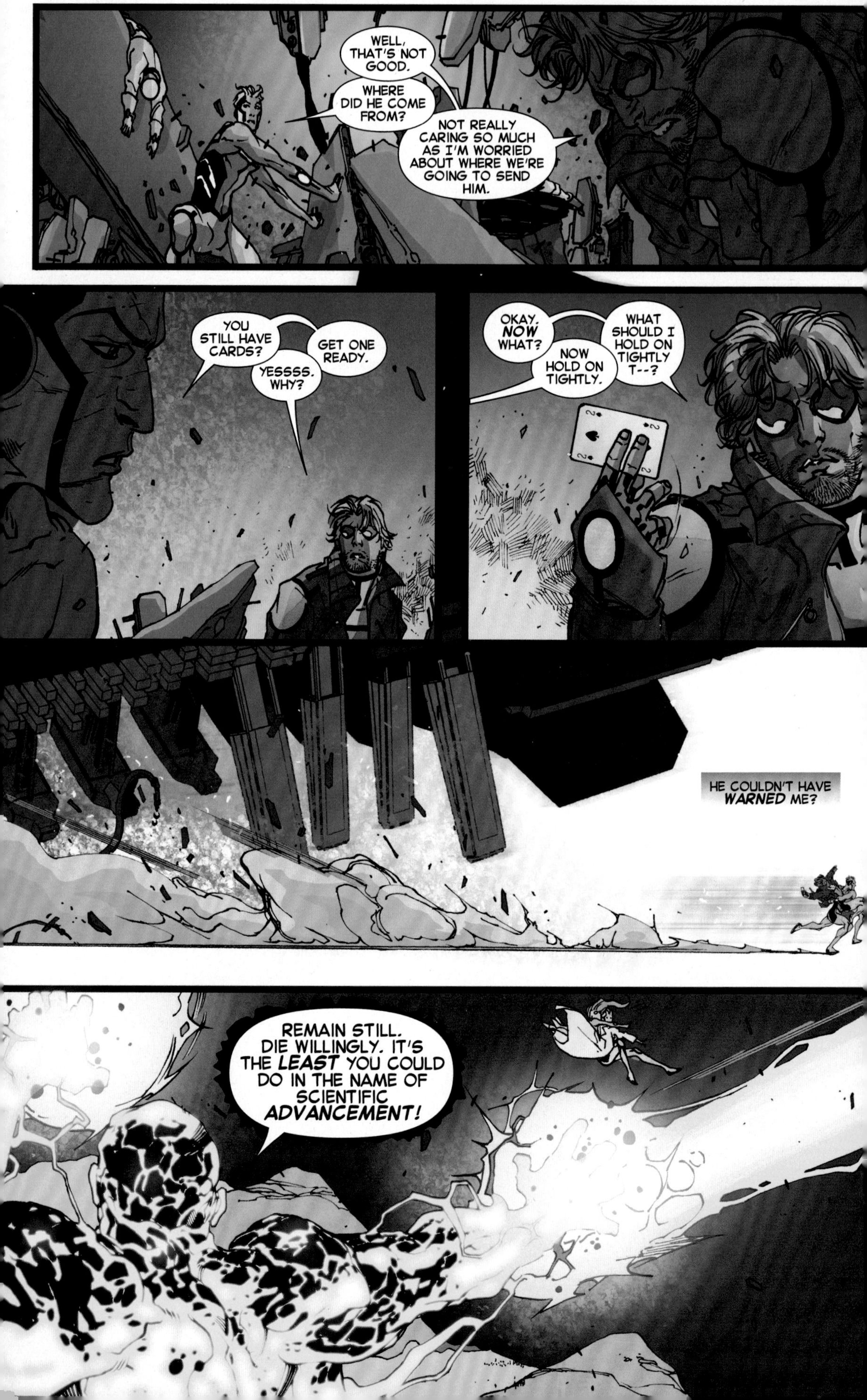
WELL, THAT'S NOT GOOD.
WHERE DID HE COME FROM?
NOT REALLY CARING SO MUCH AS I'M WORRIED ABOUT WHERE WE'RE GOING TO SEND HIM.
YOU STILL HAVE CARDS?
YESSSS. WHY?
GET ONE READY.
OKAY. NOW WHAT?
NOW HOLD ON TIGHTLY.
WHAT SHOULD I HOLD ON TIGHTLY T--?
HE COULDN'T HAVE WARNED ME?
REMAIN STILL. DIE WILLINGLY. IT'S THE LEAST YOU COULD DO IN THE NAME OF SCIENTIFIC ADVANCEMENT!

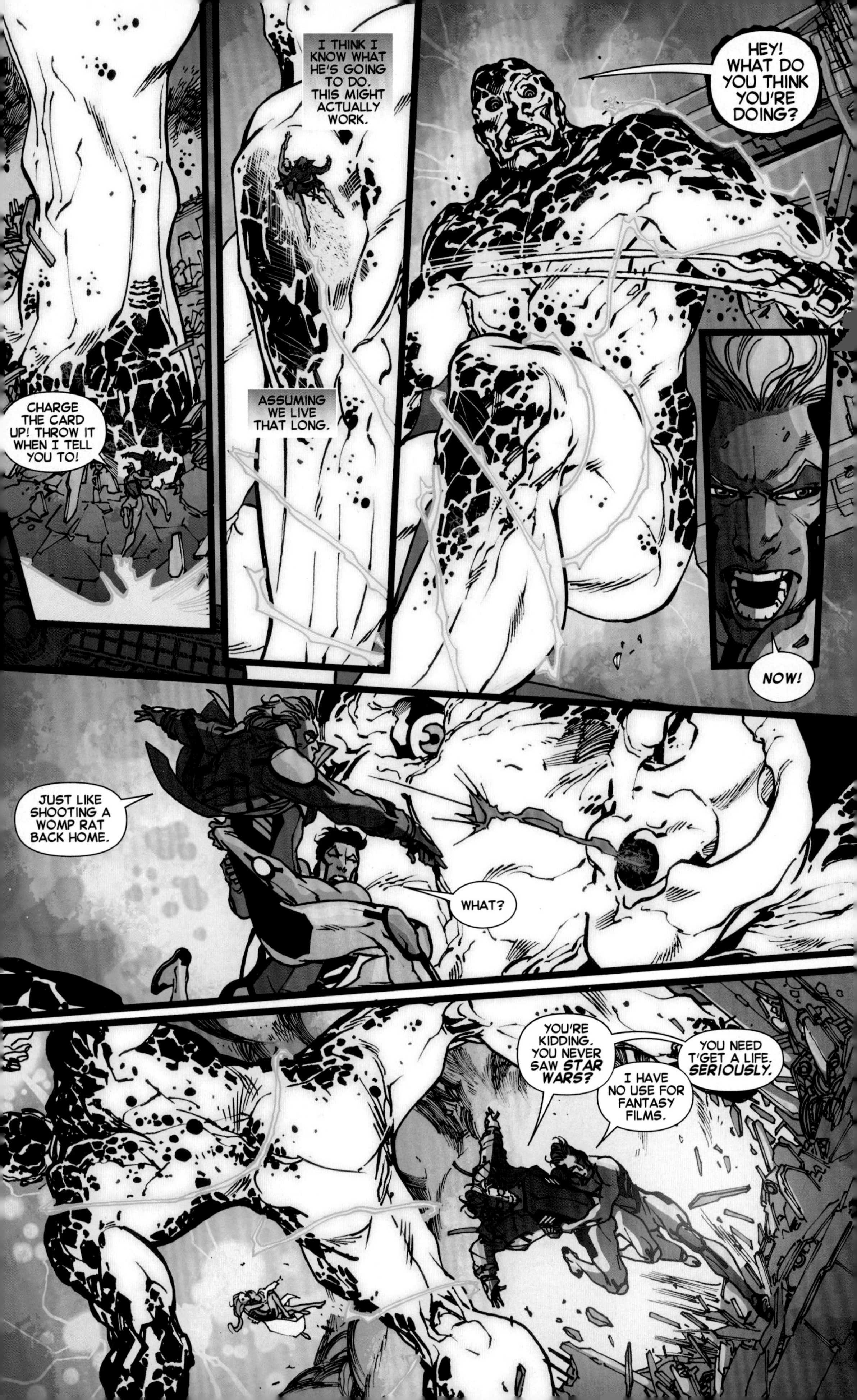
I THINK I KNOW WHAT HE'S GOING TO DO. THIS MIGHT ACTUALLY WORK.
HEY! WHAT DO YOU THINK YOU'RE DOING?
CHARGE THE CARD UP! THROW IT WHEN I TELL YOU TO!
ASSUMING WE LIVE THAT LONG.
NOW!
JUST LIKE SHOOTING A WOMP RAT BACK HOME.
WHAT?
YOU'RE KIDDING. YOU NEVER SAW STAR WARS?
I HAVE NO USE FOR FANTASY FILMS.
YOU NEED T'GET A LIFE. SERIOUSLY.

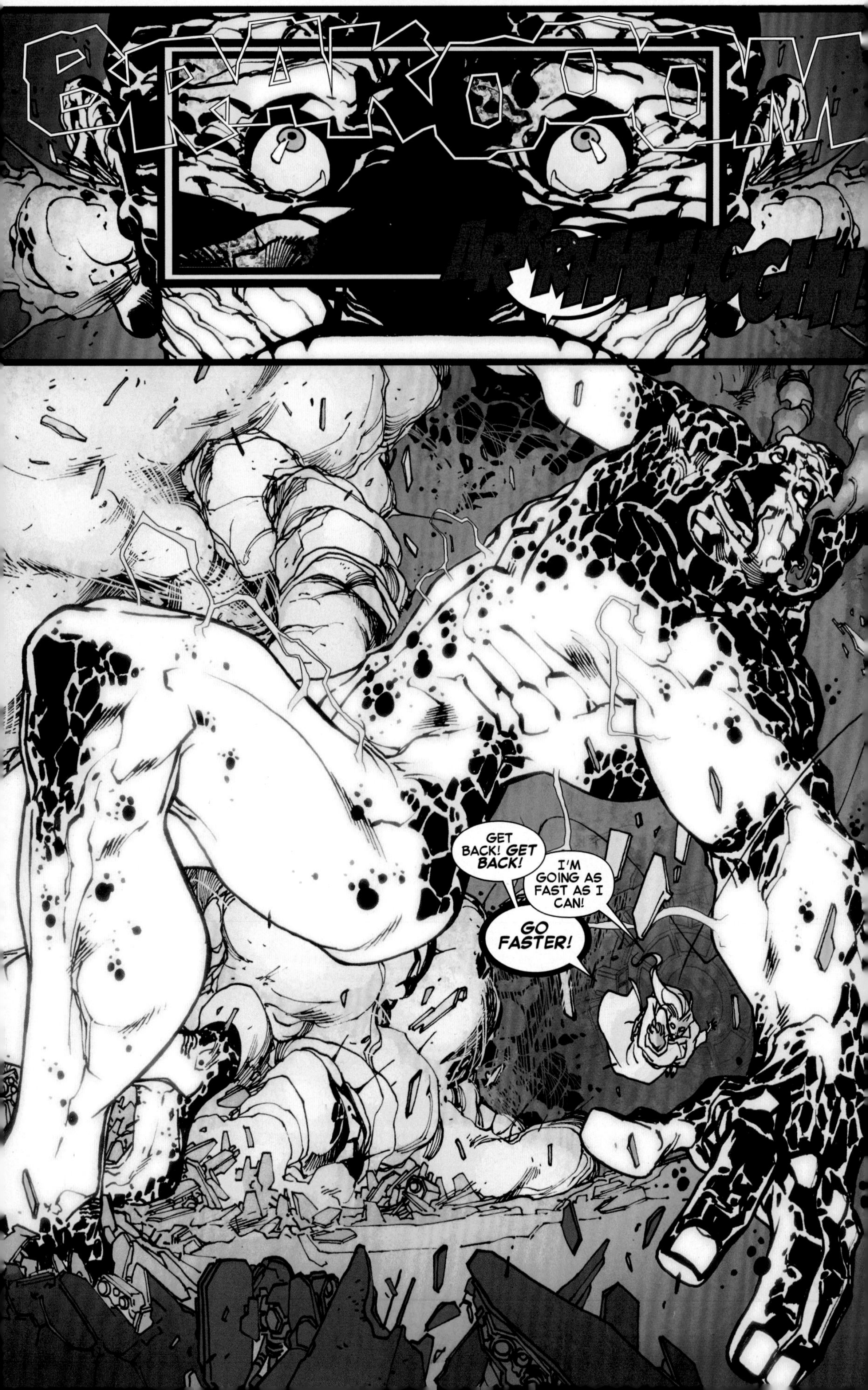
GET BACK! GET BACK!
I'M GOING AS FAST AS I CAN!
GO FASTER!

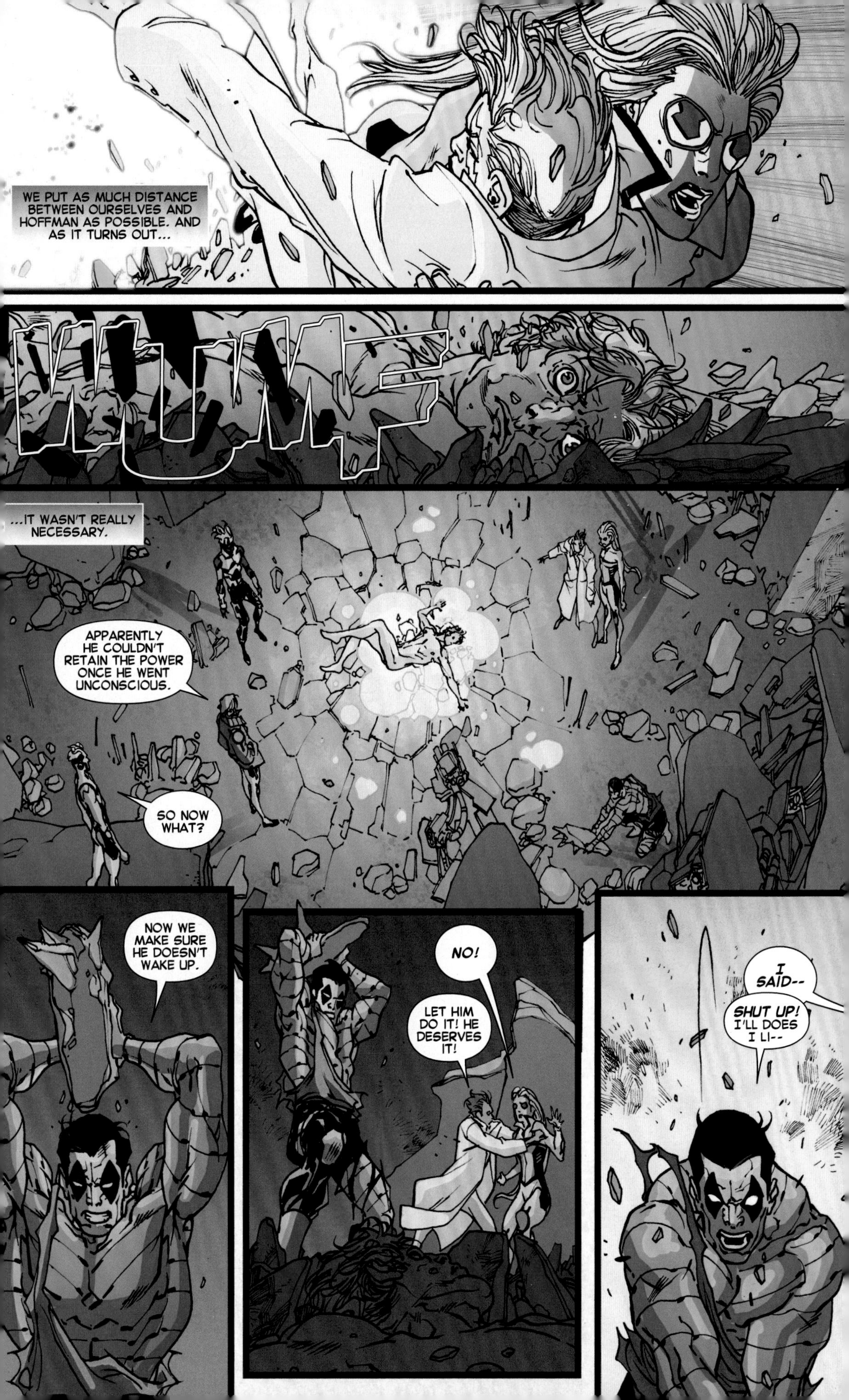
WE PUT AS MUCH DISTANCE BETWEEN OURSELVES AND HOFFMAN AS POSSIBLE. AND AS IT TURNS OUT...
WUMF
...IT WASN'T REALLY NECESSARY.
APPARENTLY HE COULDN'T RETAIN THE POWER ONCE HE WENT UNCONSCIOUS.
SO NOW WHAT?
NOW WE MAKE SURE HE DOESN'T WAKE UP.
NO!
LET HIM DO IT! HE DESERVES IT!
I SAID--
SHUT UP! I'LL DOES I LI--

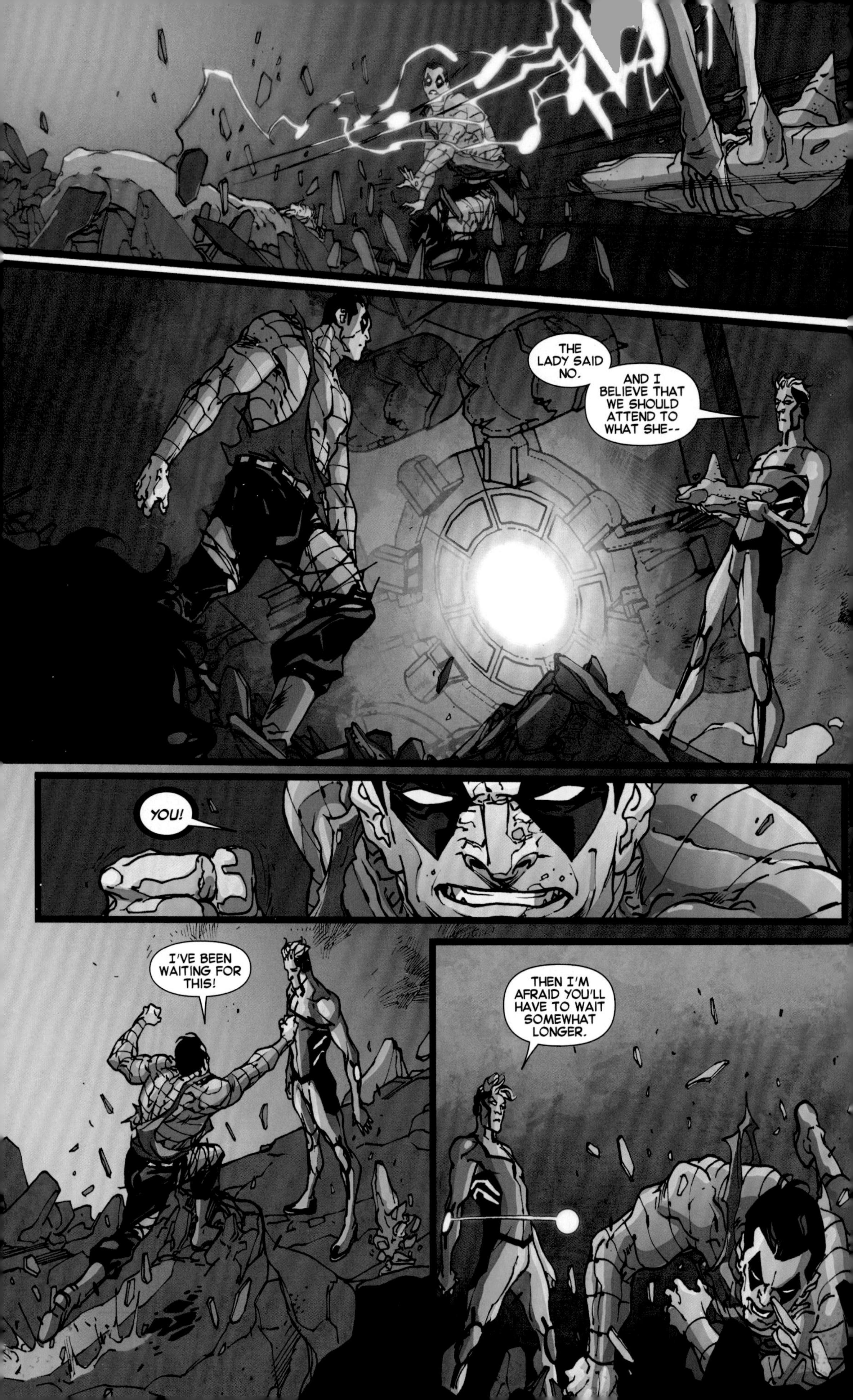
THE LADY SAID NO.
AND I BELIEVE THAT WE SHOULD ATTEND TO WHAT SHE--
YOU!
I'VE BEEN WAITING FOR THIS!
THEN I'M AFRAID YOU'LL HAVE TO WAIT SOMEWHAT LONGER.

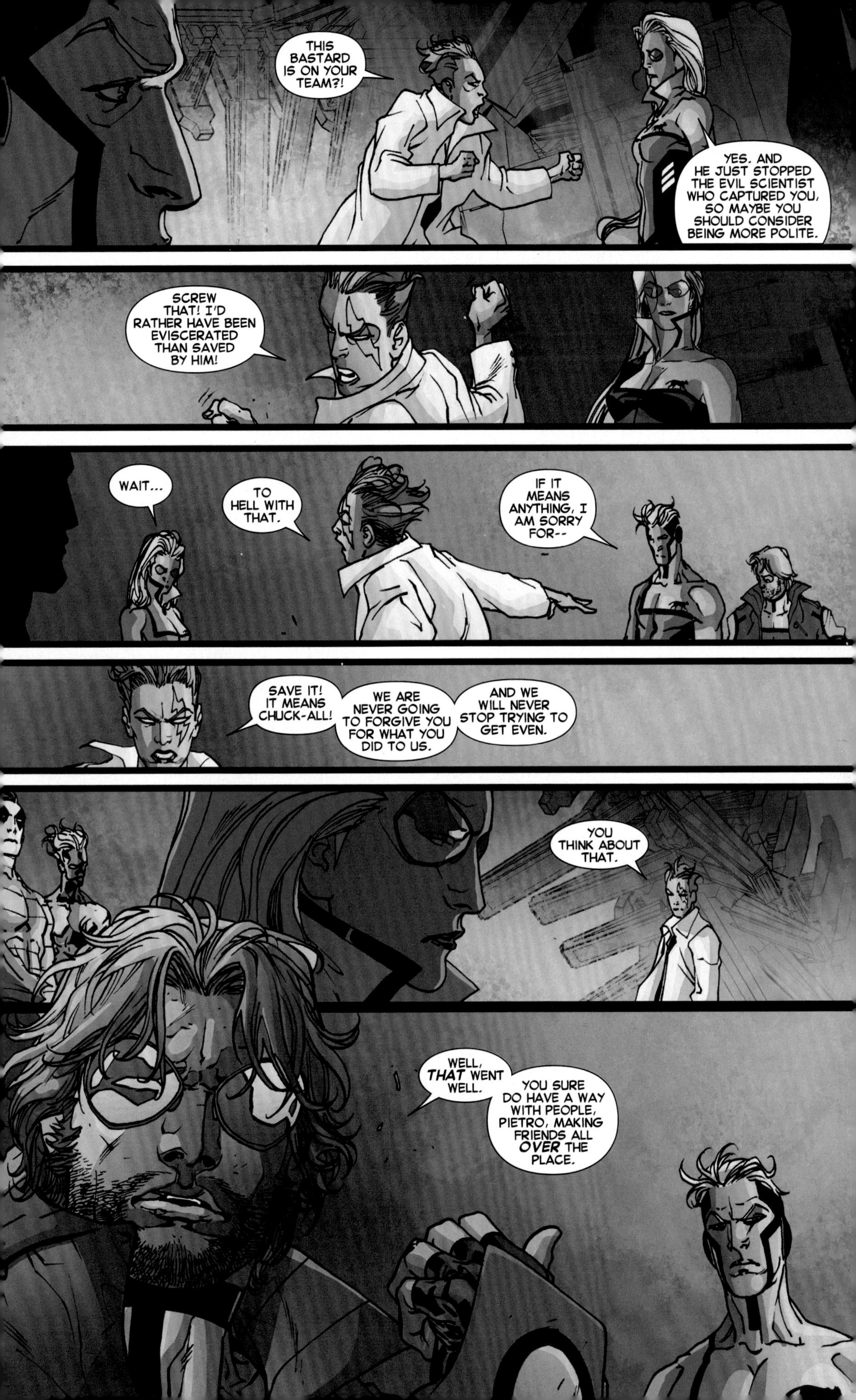
THIS BASTARD IS ON YOUR TEAM?!
YES. AND HE JUST STOPPED THE EVIL SCIENTIST WHO CAPTURED YOU, SO MAYBE YOU SHOULD CONSIDER BEING MORE POLITE.
SCREW THAT! I'D RATHER HAVE BEEN EVISCERATED THAN SAVED BY HIM!
WAIT...
TO HELL WITH THAT.
IF IT MEANS ANYTHING, I AM SORRY FOR--
SAVE IT! IT MEANS CHUCK-ALL!
WE ARE NEVER GOING TO FORGIVE YOU FOR WHAT YOU DID TO US.
AND WE WILL NEVER STOP TRYING TO GET EVEN.
YOU THINK ABOUT THAT.
WELL, *THAT* WENT WELL.
YOU SURE DO HAVE A WAY WITH PEOPLE, PIETRO, MAKING FRIENDS ALL *OVER* THE PLACE.

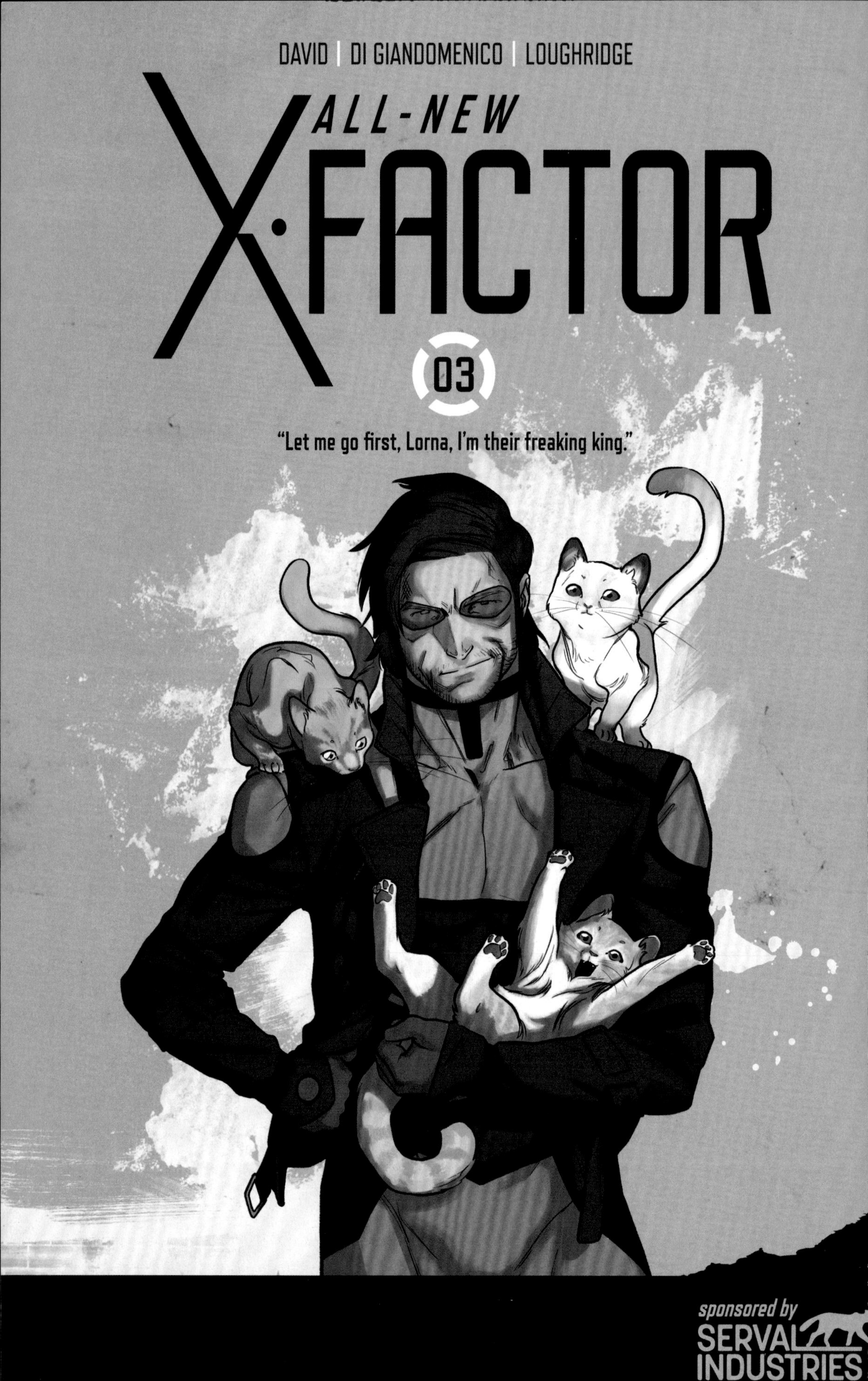
DAVID | DI GIANDOMENICO | LOUGHRIDGE
ALL-NEW
X-FACTOR
03
"Let me go first, Lorna, I'm their freaking king."
sponsored by
SERVAL
INDUSTRIES

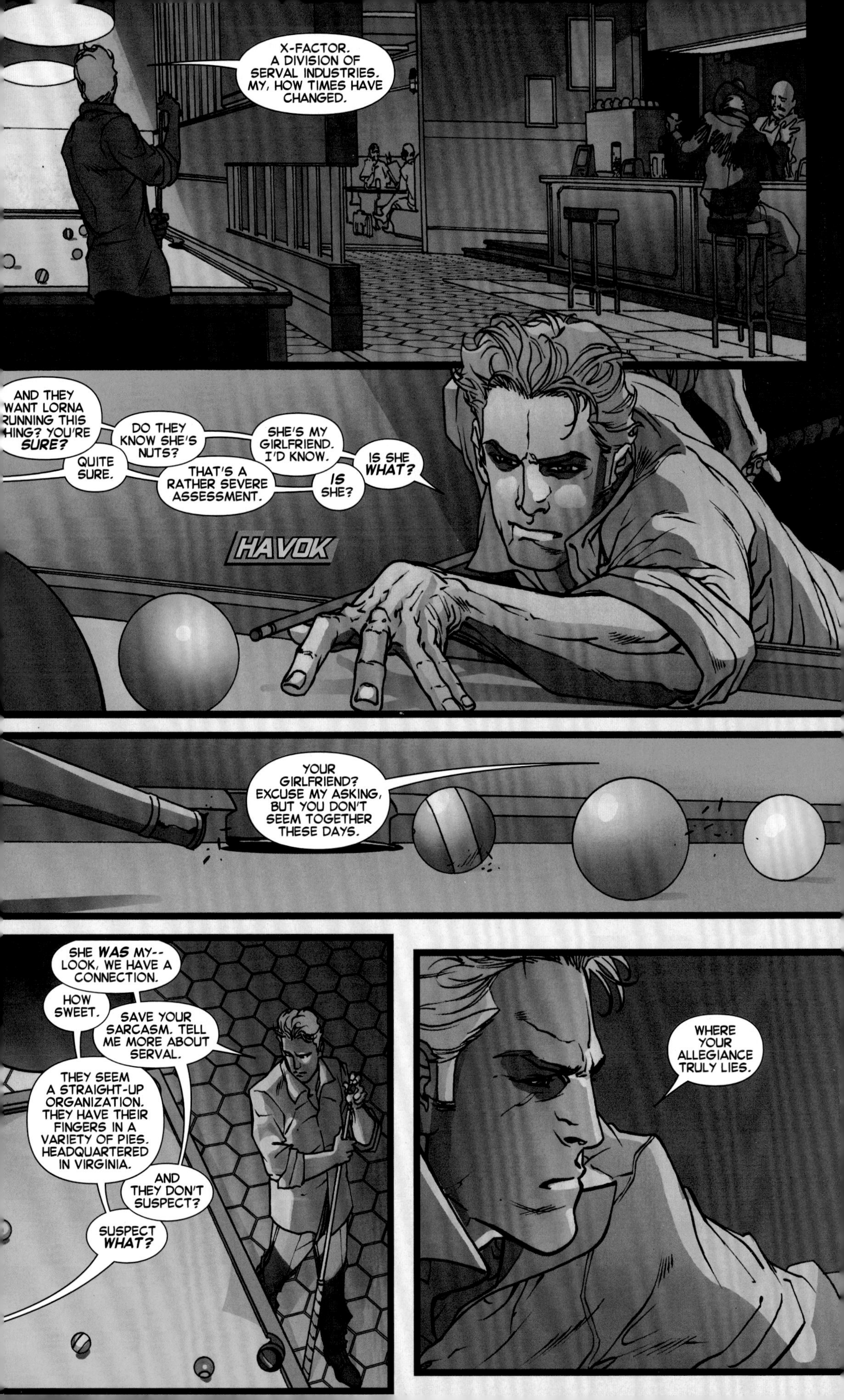
X-FACTOR. A DIVISION OF SERVAL INDUSTRIES. MY, HOW TIMES HAVE CHANGED.
AND THEY WANT LORNA RUNNING THIS THING? YOU'RE SURE?
QUITE SURE.
DO THEY KNOW SHE'S NUTS?
THAT'S A RATHER SEVERE ASSESSMENT.
SHE'S MY GIRLFRIEND. I'D KNOW.
IS SHE?
IS SHE WHAT?
HAVOK
YOUR GIRLFRIEND? EXCUSE MY ASKING, BUT YOU DON'T SEEM TOGETHER THESE DAYS.
SHE WAS MY-- LOOK, WE HAVE A CONNECTION.
HOW SWEET.
SAVE YOUR SARCASM. TELL ME MORE ABOUT SERVAL.
THEY SEEM A STRAIGHT-UP ORGANIZATION. THEY HAVE THEIR FINGERS IN A VARIETY OF PIES. HEADQUARTERED IN VIRGINIA.
AND THEY DON'T SUSPECT?
SUSPECT WHAT?
WHERE YOUR ALLEGIANCE TRULY LIES.

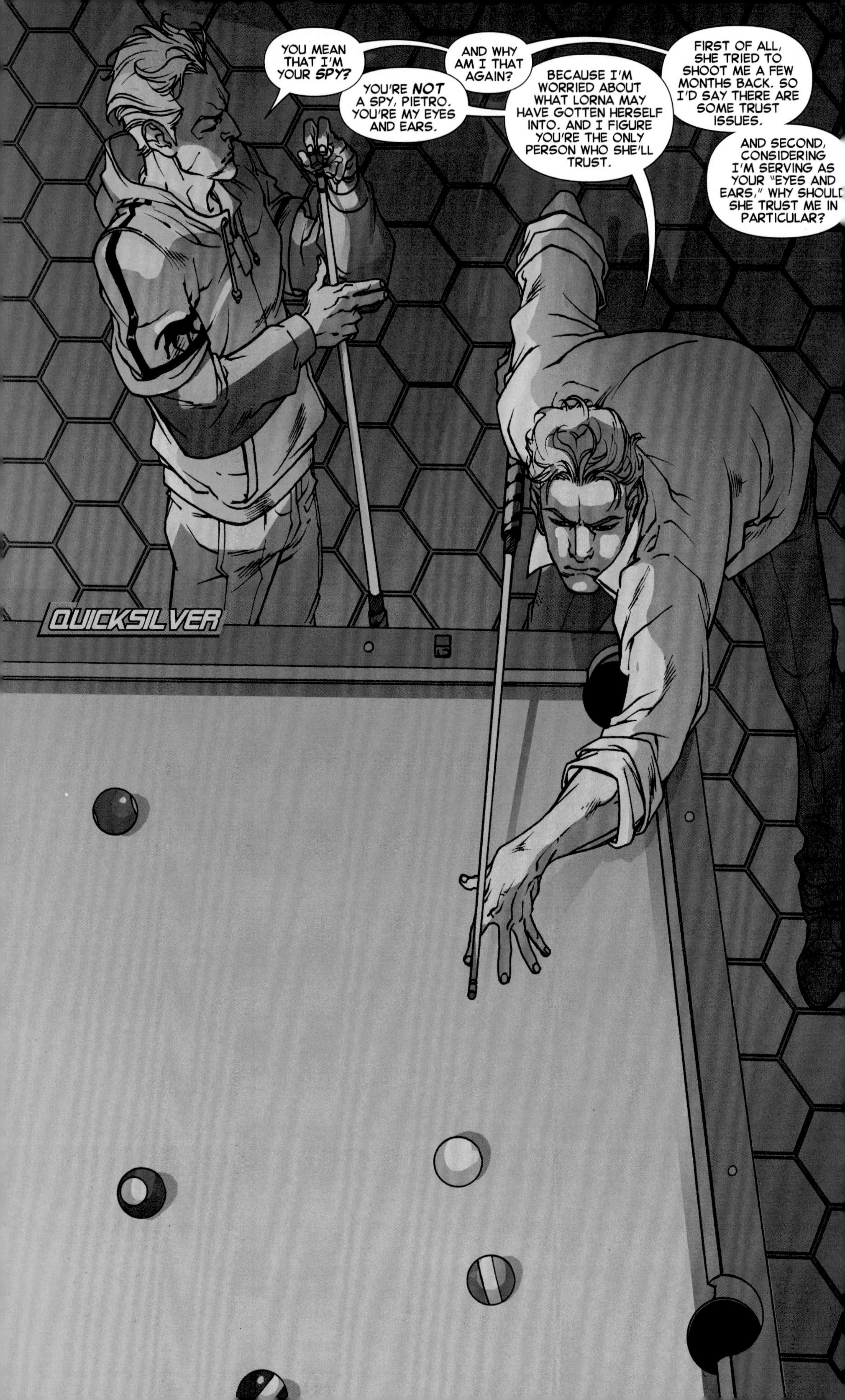
YOU MEAN THAT I'M YOUR SPY?
AND WHY AM I THAT AGAIN?
YOU'RE NOT A SPY, PIETRO. YOU'RE MY EYES AND EARS.
BECAUSE I'M WORRIED ABOUT WHAT LORNA MAY HAVE GOTTEN HERSELF INTO. AND I FIGURE YOU'RE THE ONLY PERSON WHO SHE'LL TRUST.
FIRST OF ALL, SHE TRIED TO SHOOT ME A FEW MONTHS BACK. SO I'D SAY THERE ARE SOME TRUST ISSUES.
AND SECOND, CONSIDERING I'M SERVING AS YOUR "EYES AND EARS," WHY SHOULD SHE TRUST ME IN PARTICULAR?
QUICKSILVER

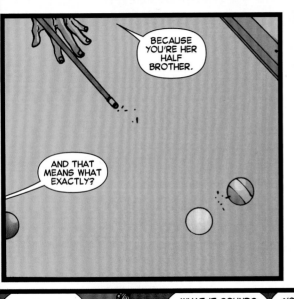

BECAUSE YOU'RE HER HALF BROTHER.

AND THAT MEANS WHAT EXACTLY?

IT MEANS WHATEVER YOU *MAKE* IT MEAN. DAMN. YOUR SHOT.

FRANKLY, I'M NOT SURE *WHAT* IT MEANS, MUCH LESS WHAT TO MAKE IT.

WHAT IT SOUNDS LIKE TO ME, ALEX, IS THAT YOU WANT ME TO MANIPULATE IT SOMEHOW.

YOU'RE COMPLETELY MISREADING IT. I JUST WANT YOU TO CONTINUE WITH HER AND KEEP AN EYE ON HER.

FOR HOW LONG?

UNTIL I'M SATISFIED SHE'S OKAY.

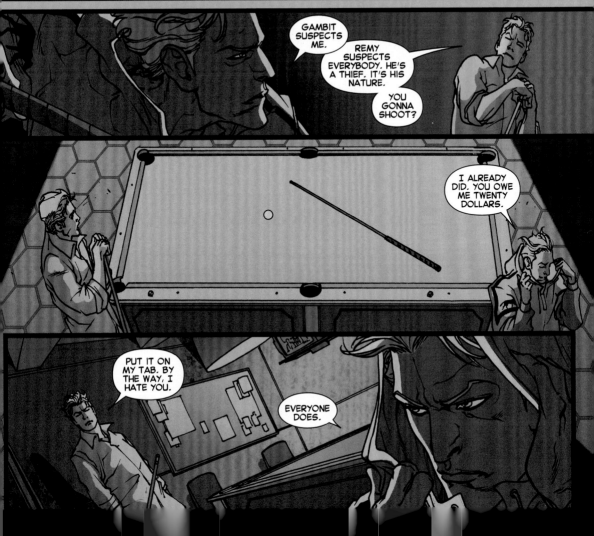

GAMBIT SUSPECTS ME.

REMY SUSPECTS EVERYBODY. HE'S A THIEF. IT'S HIS NATURE.

YOU GONNA SHOOT?

I ALREADY DID. YOU OWE ME TWENTY DOLLARS.

PUT IT ON MY TAB. BY THE WAY, I HATE YOU.

EVERYONE DOES.

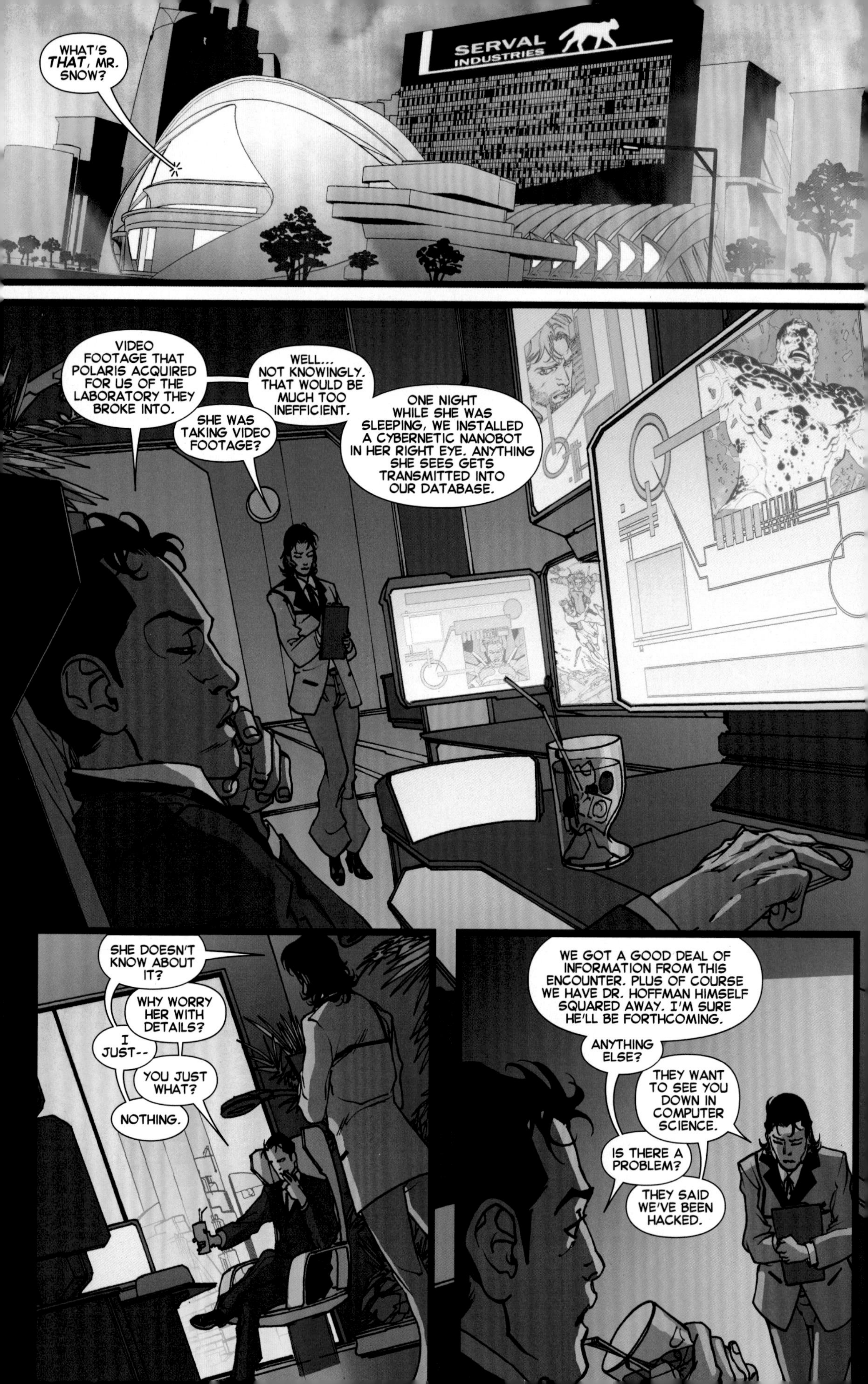
SERVAL INDUSTRIES
WHAT'S *THAT*, MR. SNOW?
VIDEO FOOTAGE THAT POLARIS ACQUIRED FOR US OF THE LABORATORY THEY BROKE INTO.
SHE WAS TAKING VIDEO FOOTAGE?
WELL... NOT KNOWINGLY. THAT WOULD BE MUCH TOO INEFFICIENT.
ONE NIGHT WHILE SHE WAS SLEEPING, WE INSTALLED A CYBERNETIC NANOBOT IN HER RIGHT EYE. ANYTHING SHE SEES GETS TRANSMITTED INTO OUR DATABASE.
SHE DOESN'T KNOW ABOUT IT?
WHY WORRY HER WITH DETAILS?
I JUST--
YOU JUST WHAT?
NOTHING.
WE GOT A GOOD DEAL OF INFORMATION FROM THIS ENCOUNTER. PLUS OF COURSE WE HAVE DR. HOFFMAN HIMSELF SQUARED AWAY. I'M SURE HE'LL BE FORTHCOMING.
ANYTHING ELSE?
THEY WANT TO SEE YOU DOWN IN COMPUTER SCIENCE.
IS THERE A PROBLEM?
THEY SAID WE'VE BEEN HACKED.

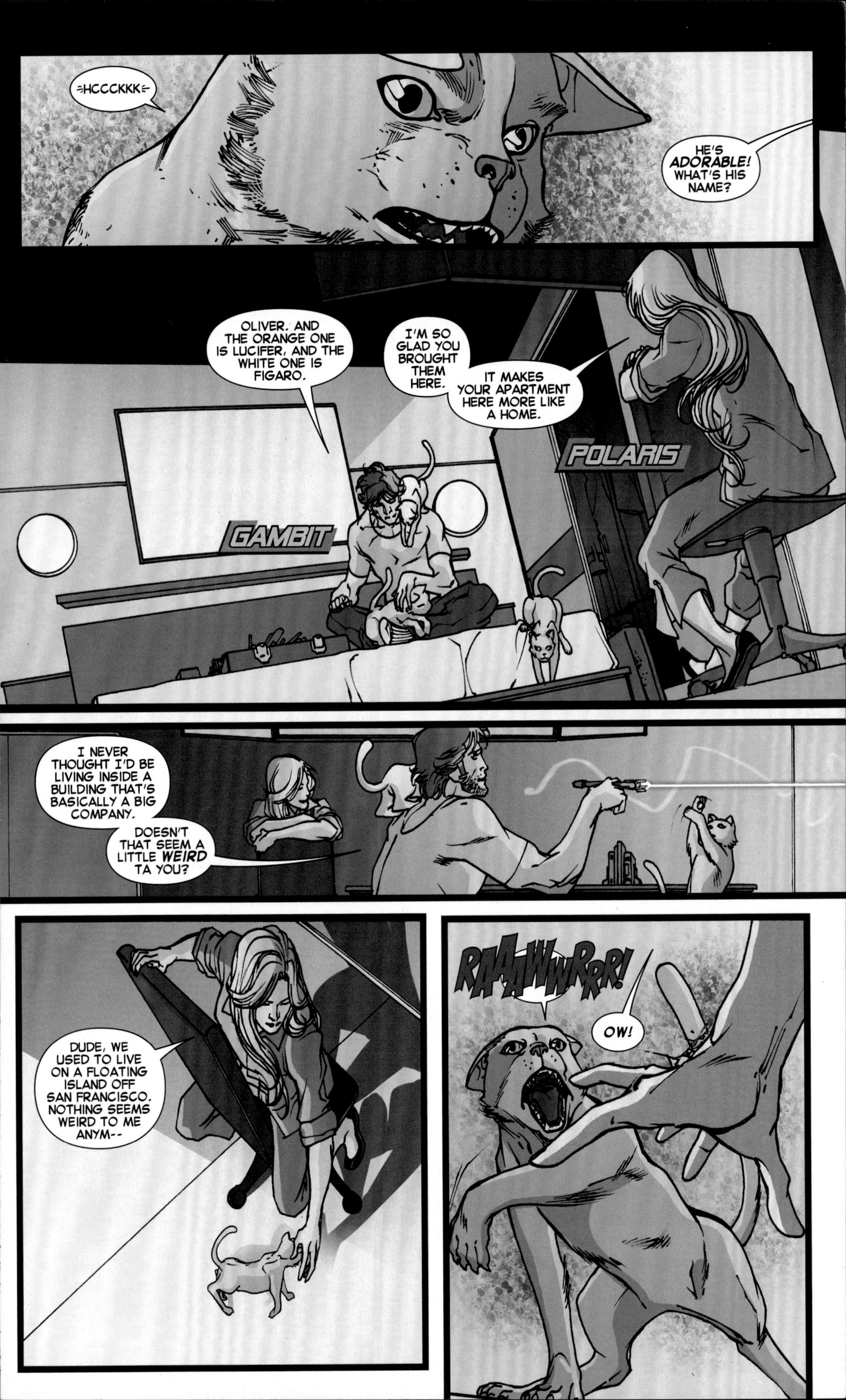

=HCCCKKK=
HE'S ADORABLE! WHAT'S HIS NAME?
OLIVER. AND THE ORANGE ONE IS LUCIFER, AND THE WHITE ONE IS FIGARO.
I'M SO GLAD YOU BROUGHT THEM HERE.
IT MAKES YOUR APARTMENT HERE MORE LIKE A HOME.
POLARIS
GAMBIT
I NEVER THOUGHT I'D BE LIVING INSIDE A BUILDING THAT'S BASICALLY A BIG COMPANY.
DOESN'T THAT SEEM A LITTLE WEIRD TA YOU?
DUDE, WE USED TO LIVE ON A FLOATING ISLAND OFF SAN FRANCISCO. NOTHING SEEMS WEIRD TO ME ANYM--
RAAAWWRRR!
OW!

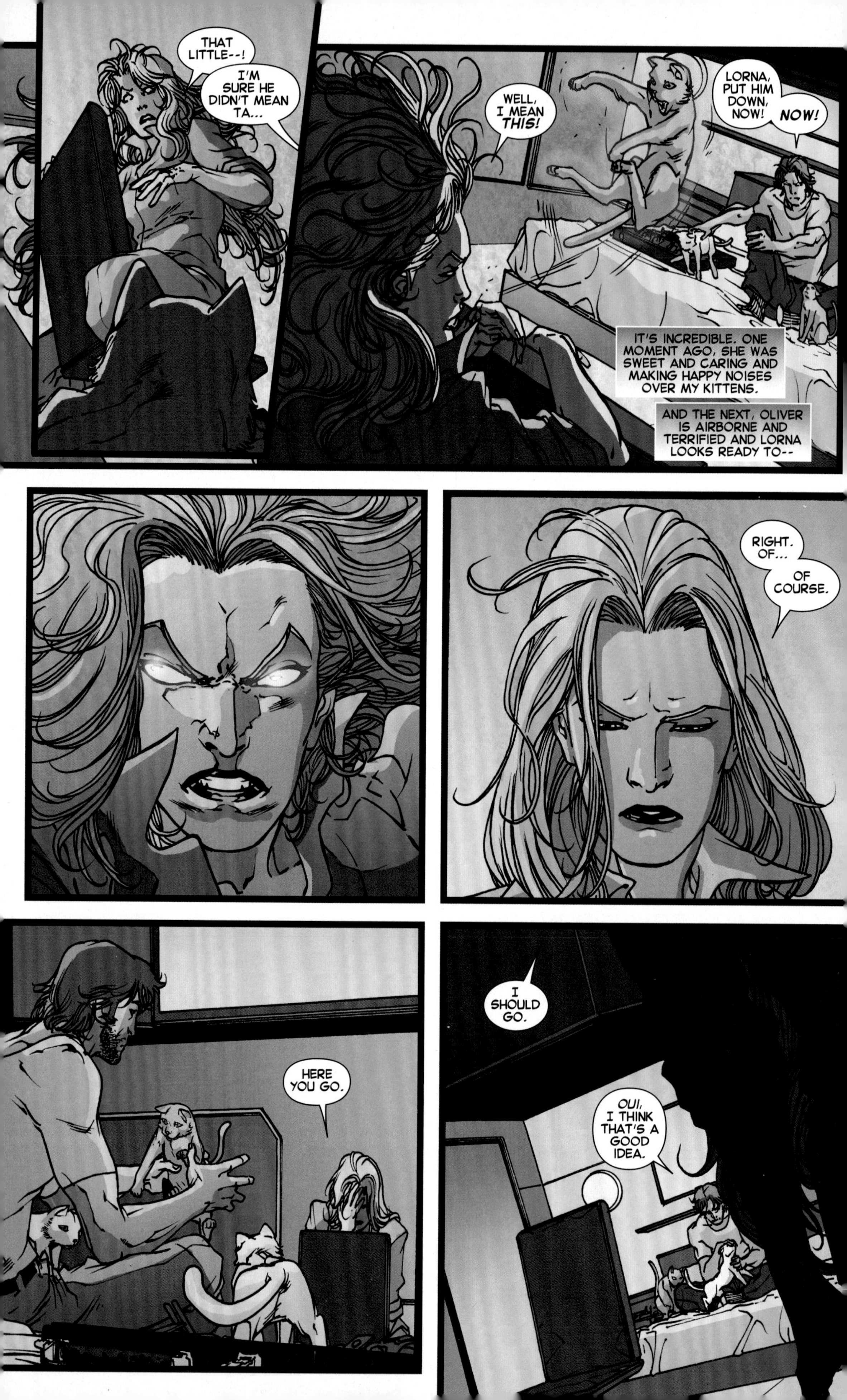
THAT LITTLE--!
I'M SURE HE DIDN'T MEAN TA...
WELL, I MEAN THIS!
LORNA, PUT HIM DOWN, NOW!
NOW!
IT'S INCREDIBLE. ONE MOMENT AGO, SHE WAS SWEET AND CARING AND MAKING HAPPY NOISES OVER MY KITTENS.
AND THE NEXT, OLIVER IS AIRBORNE AND TERRIFIED AND LORNA LOOKS READY TO--
RIGHT. OF...
OF COURSE.
HERE YOU GO.
I SHOULD GO.
OUI, I THINK THAT'S A GOOD IDEA.

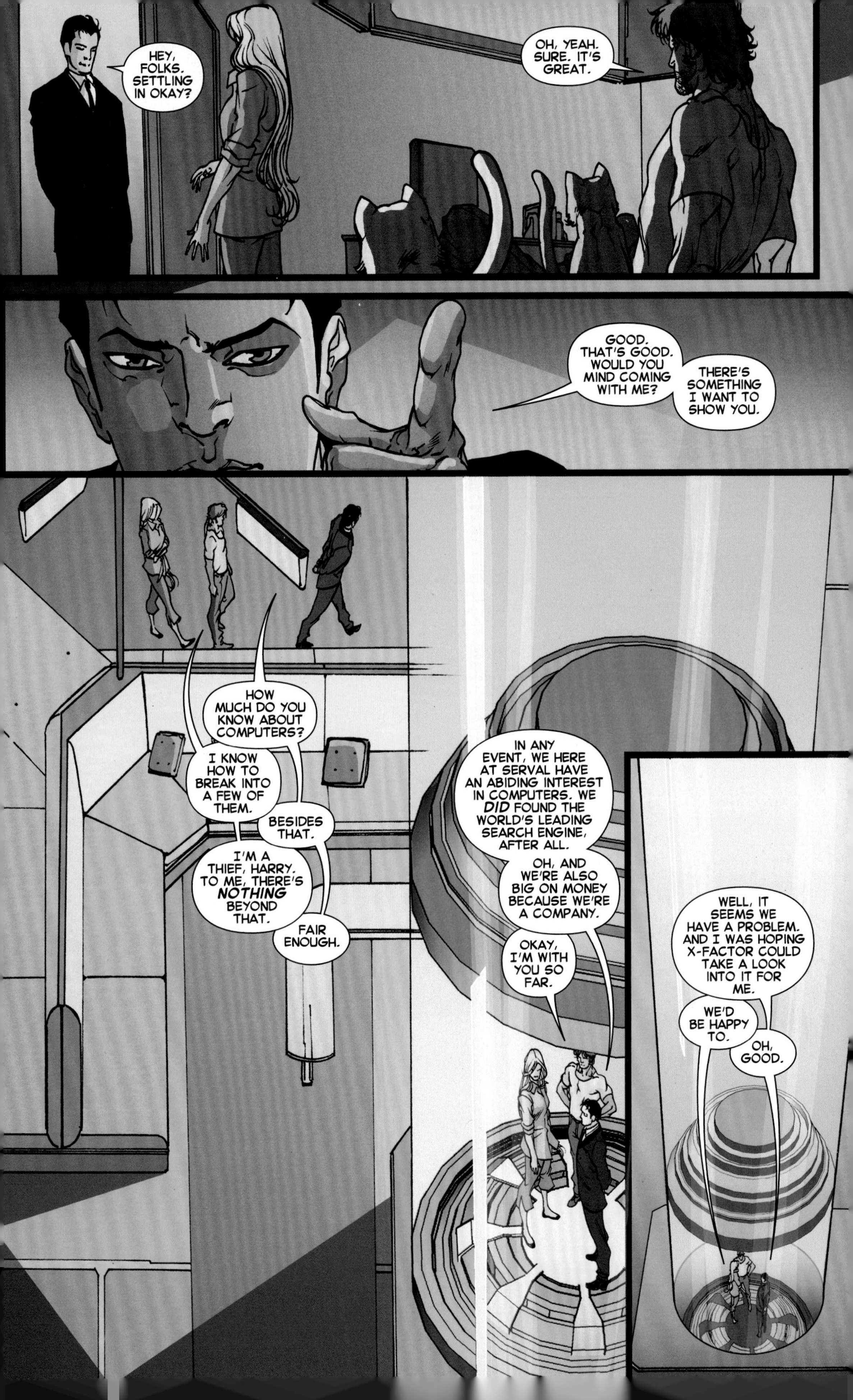
HEY, FOLKS. SETTLING IN OKAY?
OH, YEAH. SURE. IT'S GREAT.
GOOD. THAT'S GOOD. WOULD YOU MIND COMING WITH ME?
THERE'S SOMETHING I WANT TO SHOW YOU.
HOW MUCH DO YOU KNOW ABOUT COMPUTERS?
I KNOW HOW TO BREAK INTO A FEW OF THEM.
BESIDES THAT.
I'M A THIEF, HARRY. TO ME, THERE'S NOTHING BEYOND THAT.
FAIR ENOUGH.
IN ANY EVENT, WE HERE AT SERVAL HAVE AN ABIDING INTEREST IN COMPUTERS. WE DID FOUND THE WORLD'S LEADING SEARCH ENGINE, AFTER ALL.
OH, AND WE'RE ALSO BIG ON MONEY BECAUSE WE'RE A COMPANY.
OKAY, I'M WITH YOU SO FAR.
WELL, IT SEEMS WE HAVE A PROBLEM. AND I WAS HOPING X-FACTOR COULD TAKE A LOOK INTO IT FOR ME.
WE'D BE HAPPY TO.
OH, GOOD.

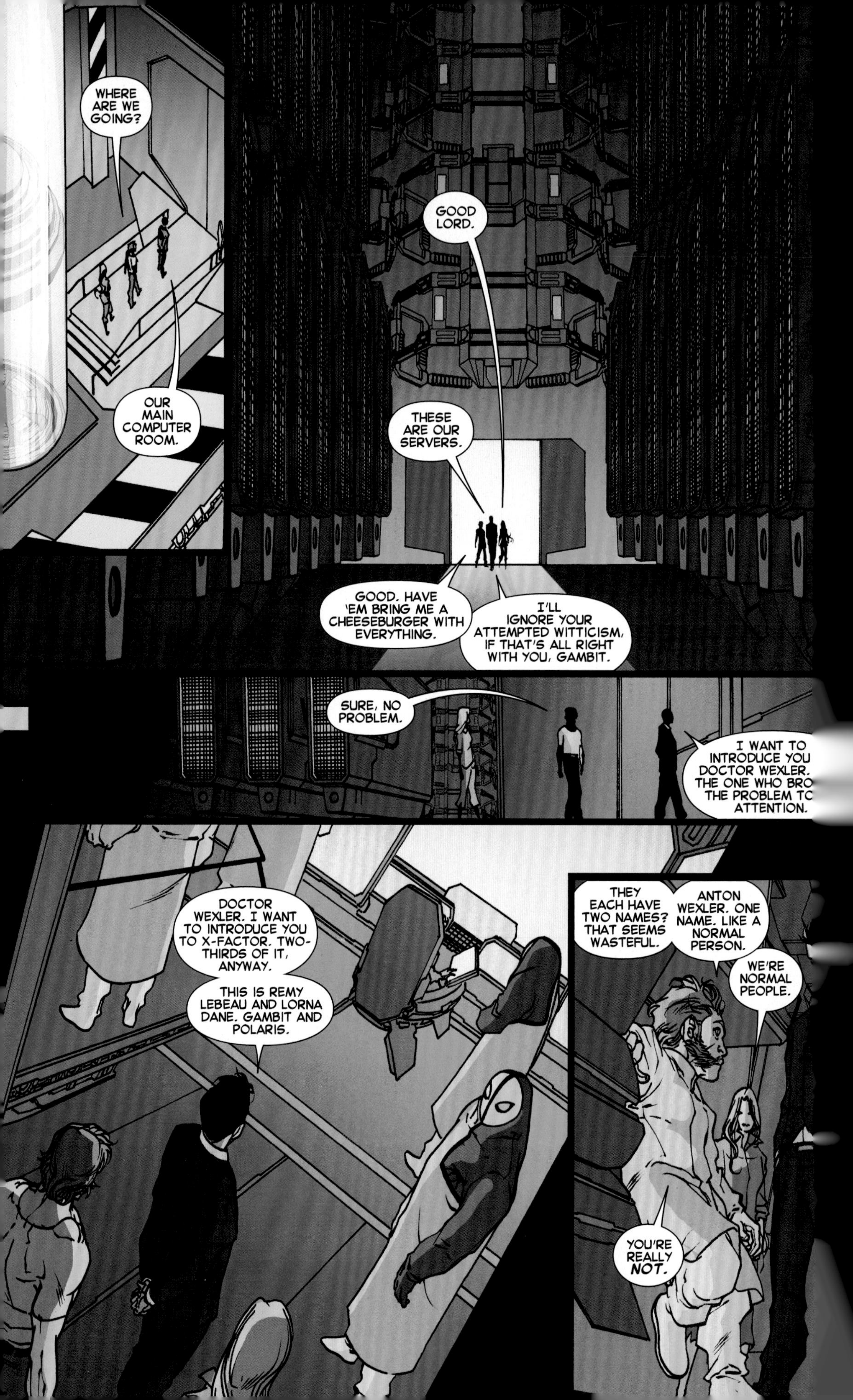
WHERE ARE WE GOING?
OUR MAIN COMPUTER ROOM.
GOOD LORD.
THESE ARE OUR SERVERS.
GOOD. HAVE 'EM BRING ME A CHEESEBURGER WITH EVERYTHING.
I'LL IGNORE YOUR ATTEMPTED WITTICISM, IF THAT'S ALL RIGHT WITH YOU, GAMBIT.
SURE, NO PROBLEM.
I WANT TO INTRODUCE YOU DOCTOR WEXLER. THE ONE WHO BRO THE PROBLEM TO ATTENTION.
DOCTOR WEXLER. I WANT TO INTRODUCE YOU TO X-FACTOR. TWO-THIRDS OF IT, ANYWAY.
THIS IS REMY LEBEAU AND LORNA DANE. GAMBIT AND POLARIS.
THEY EACH HAVE TWO NAMES? THAT SEEMS WASTEFUL.
ANTON WEXLER. ONE NAME. LIKE A NORMAL PERSON.
WE'RE NORMAL PEOPLE.
YOU'RE REALLY NOT.

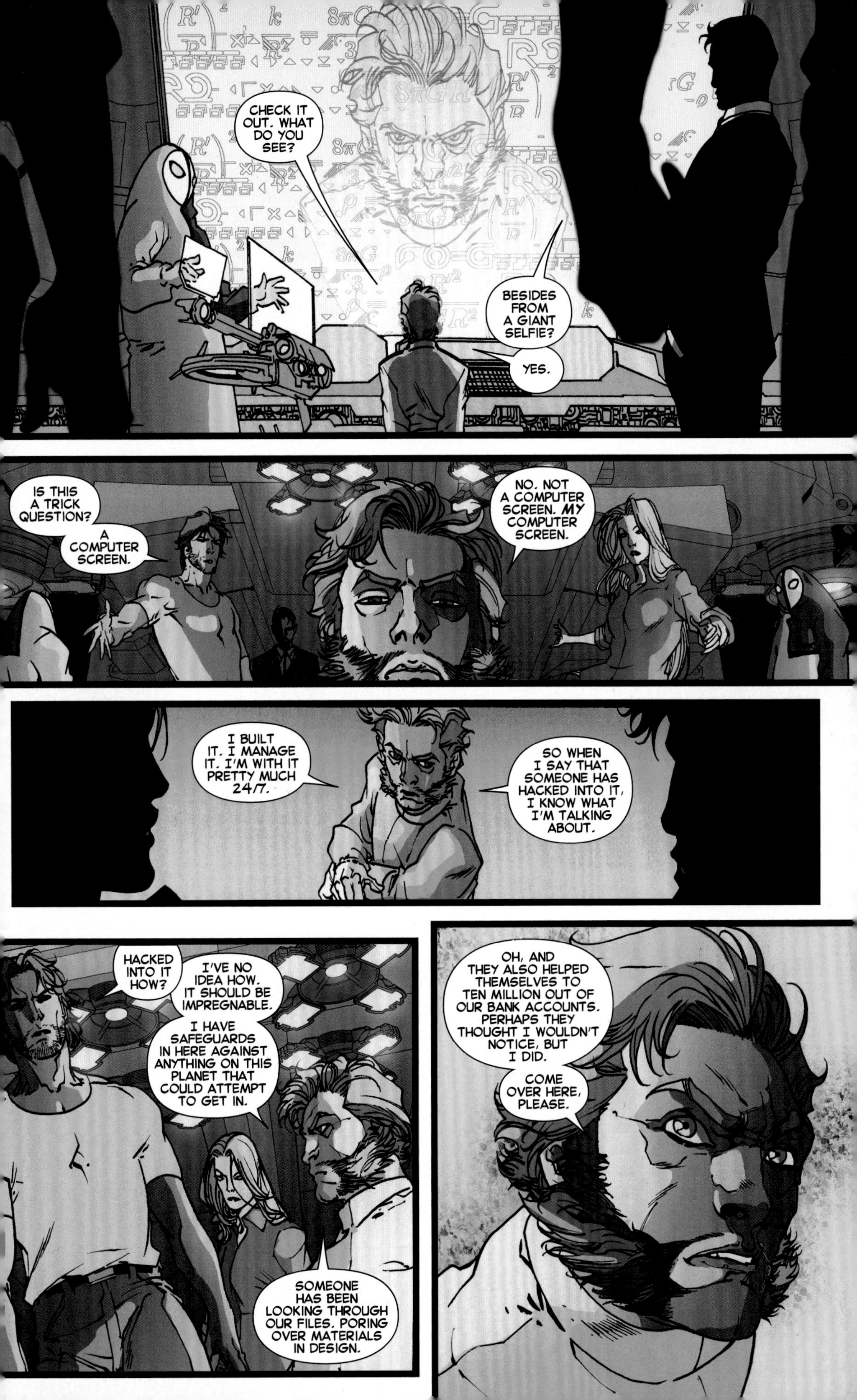

CHECK IT OUT. WHAT DO YOU SEE?
BESIDES FROM A GIANT SELFIE?
YES.
IS THIS A TRICK QUESTION?
A COMPUTER SCREEN.
NO. NOT A COMPUTER SCREEN. MY COMPUTER SCREEN.
I BUILT IT. I MANAGE IT. I'M WITH IT PRETTY MUCH 24/7.
SO WHEN I SAY THAT SOMEONE HAS HACKED INTO IT, I KNOW WHAT I'M TALKING ABOUT.
HACKED INTO IT HOW?
I'VE NO IDEA HOW. IT SHOULD BE IMPREGNABLE.
I HAVE SAFEGUARDS IN HERE AGAINST ANYTHING ON THIS PLANET THAT COULD ATTEMPT TO GET IN.
SOMEONE HAS BEEN LOOKING THROUGH OUR FILES. PORING OVER MATERIALS IN DESIGN.
OH, AND THEY ALSO HELPED THEMSELVES TO TEN MILLION OUT OF OUR BANK ACCOUNTS. PERHAPS THEY THOUGHT I WOULDN'T NOTICE, BUT I DID.
COME OVER HERE, PLEASE.

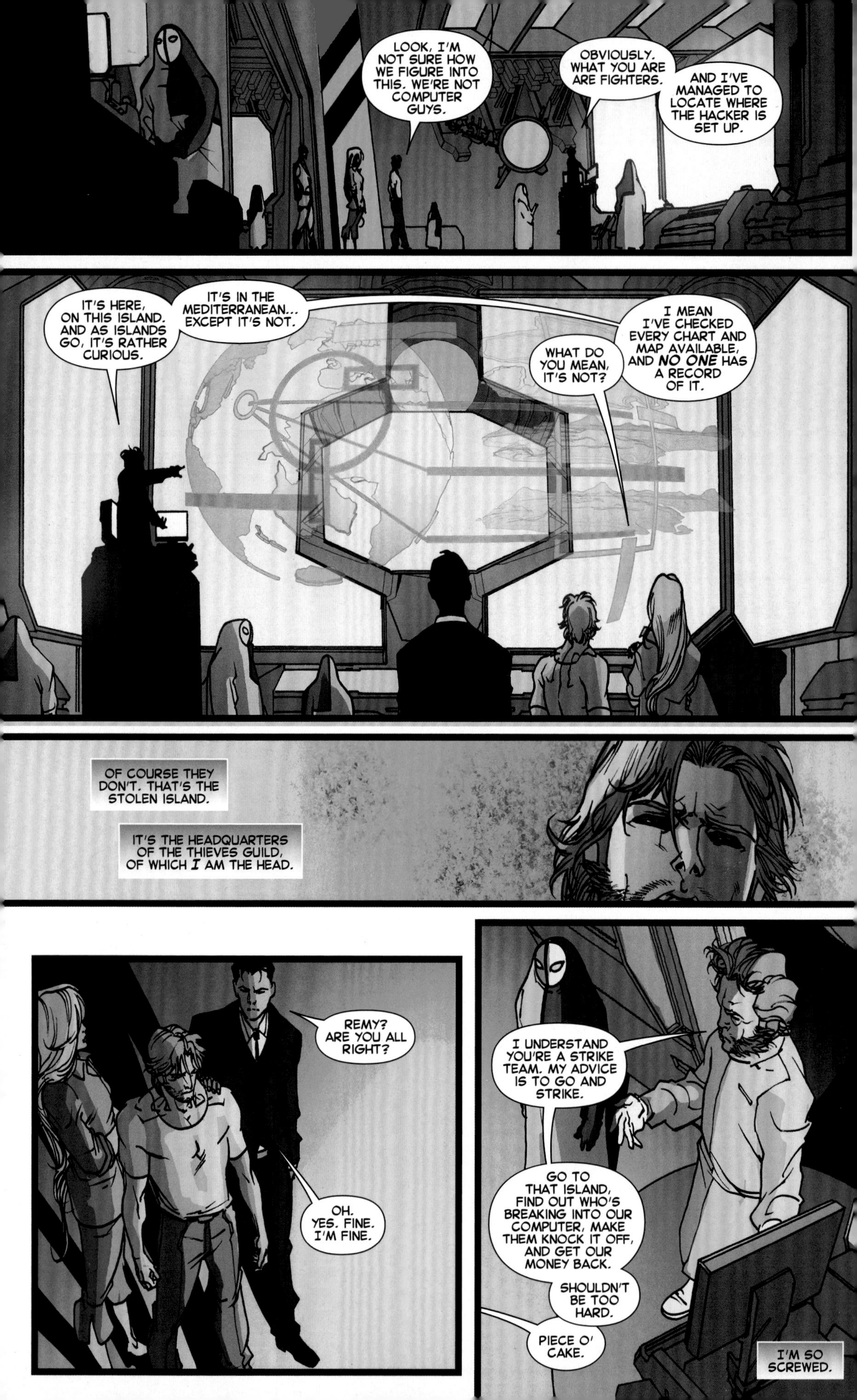
LOOK, I'M NOT SURE HOW WE FIGURE INTO THIS. WE'RE NOT COMPUTER GUYS.
OBVIOUSLY. WHAT YOU ARE ARE FIGHTERS.
AND I'VE MANAGED TO LOCATE WHERE THE HACKER IS SET UP.
IT'S HERE, ON THIS ISLAND. AND AS ISLANDS GO, IT'S RATHER CURIOUS.
IT'S IN THE MEDITERRANEAN... EXCEPT IT'S NOT.
WHAT DO YOU MEAN, IT'S NOT?
I MEAN I'VE CHECKED EVERY CHART AND MAP AVAILABLE, AND NO ONE HAS A RECORD OF IT.
OF COURSE THEY DON'T. THAT'S THE STOLEN ISLAND.
IT'S THE HEADQUARTERS OF THE THIEVES GUILD, OF WHICH I AM THE HEAD.
REMY? ARE YOU ALL RIGHT?
OH. YES. FINE. I'M FINE.
I UNDERSTAND YOU'RE A STRIKE TEAM. MY ADVICE IS TO GO AND STRIKE.
GO TO THAT ISLAND, FIND OUT WHO'S BREAKING INTO OUR COMPUTER, MAKE THEM KNOCK IT OFF, AND GET OUR MONEY BACK.
SHOULDN'T BE TOO HARD.
PIECE O' CAKE.
I'M SO SCREWED.

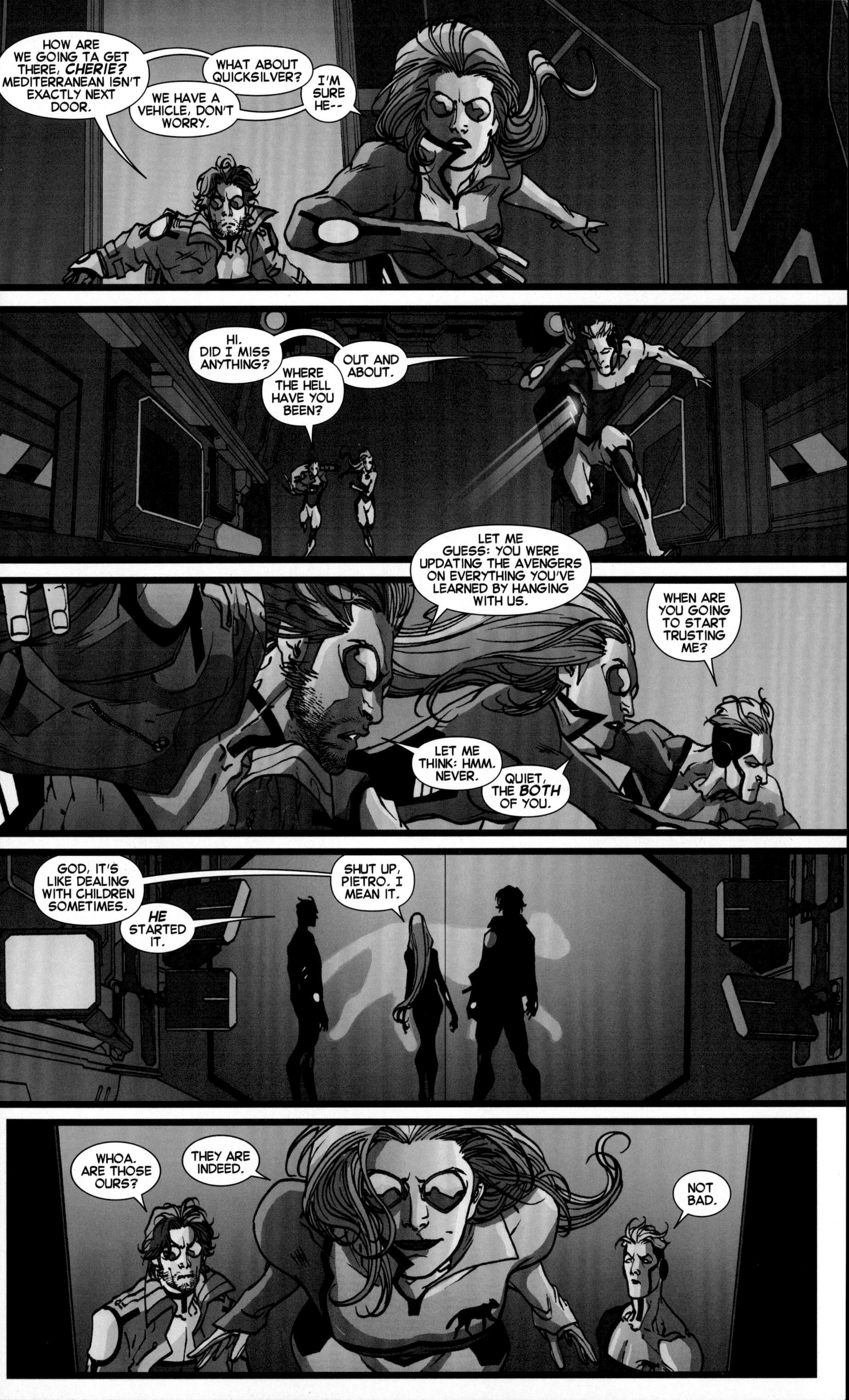
HOW ARE WE GOING TA GET THERE, CHERIE? MEDITERRANEAN ISN'T EXACTLY NEXT DOOR.
WHAT ABOUT QUICKSILVER?
WE HAVE A VEHICLE, DON'T WORRY.
I'M SURE HE--
HI. DID I MISS ANYTHING?
OUT AND ABOUT.
WHERE THE HELL HAVE YOU BEEN?
LET ME GUESS: YOU WERE UPDATING THE AVENGERS ON EVERYTHING YOU'VE LEARNED BY HANGING WITH US.
WHEN ARE YOU GOING TO START TRUSTING ME?
LET ME THINK: HMM. NEVER.
QUIET, THE BOTH OF YOU.
GOD, IT'S LIKE DEALING WITH CHILDREN SOMETIMES.
SHUT UP, PIETRO. I MEAN IT.
HE STARTED IT.
WHOA. ARE THOSE OURS?
THEY ARE INDEED.
NOT BAD.

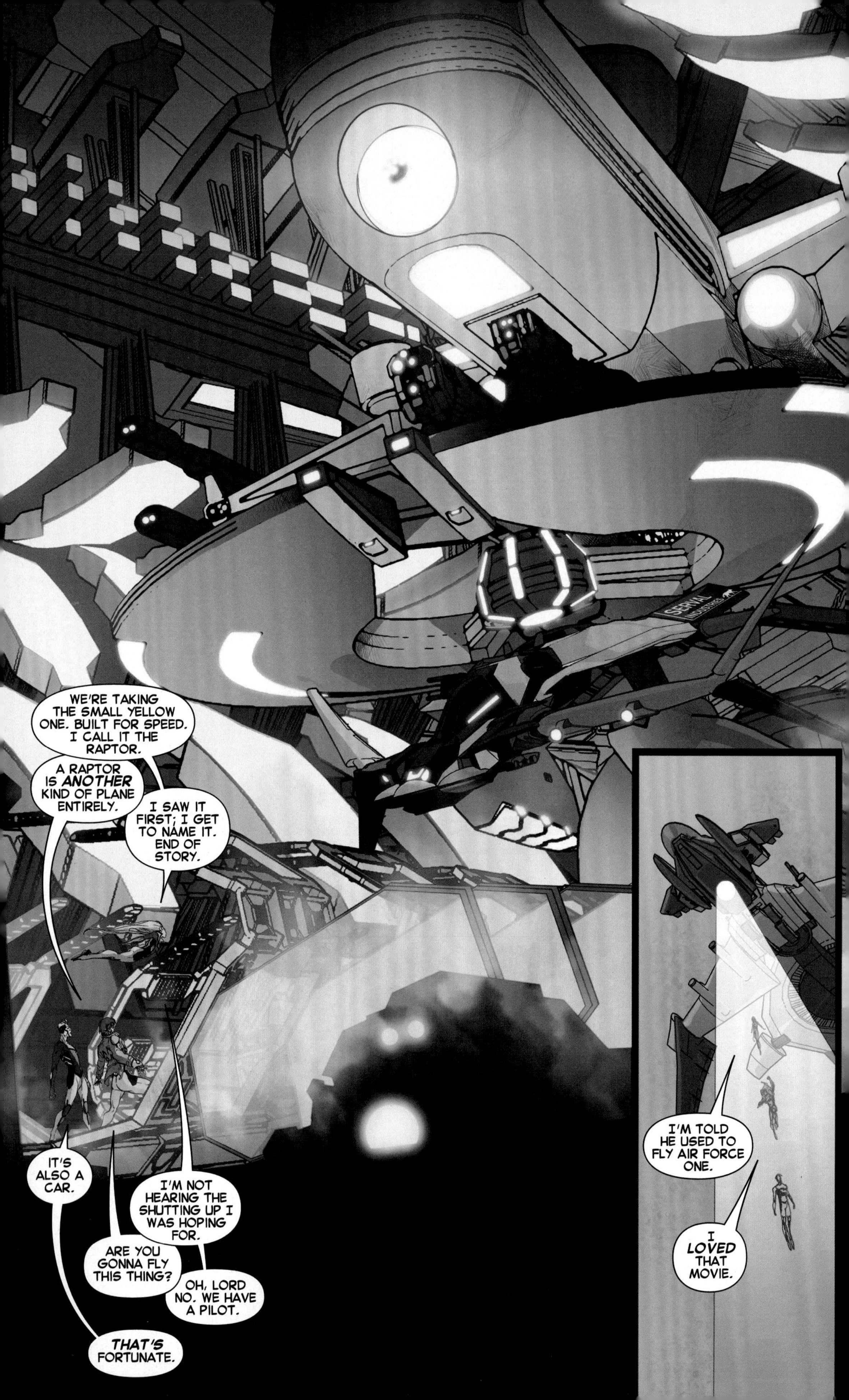

SERVAL INDUSTRIES
WE'RE TAKING THE SMALL YELLOW ONE. BUILT FOR SPEED. I CALL IT THE RAPTOR.
A RAPTOR IS *ANOTHER* KIND OF PLANE ENTIRELY.
I SAW IT FIRST; I GET TO NAME IT. END OF STORY.
IT'S ALSO A CAR.
I'M NOT HEARING THE SHUTTING UP I WAS HOPING FOR.
ARE YOU GONNA FLY THIS THING?
OH, LORD NO. WE HAVE A PILOT.
THAT'S FORTUNATE.
I'M TOLD HE USED TO FLY AIR FORCE ONE.
I *LOVED* THAT MOVIE.

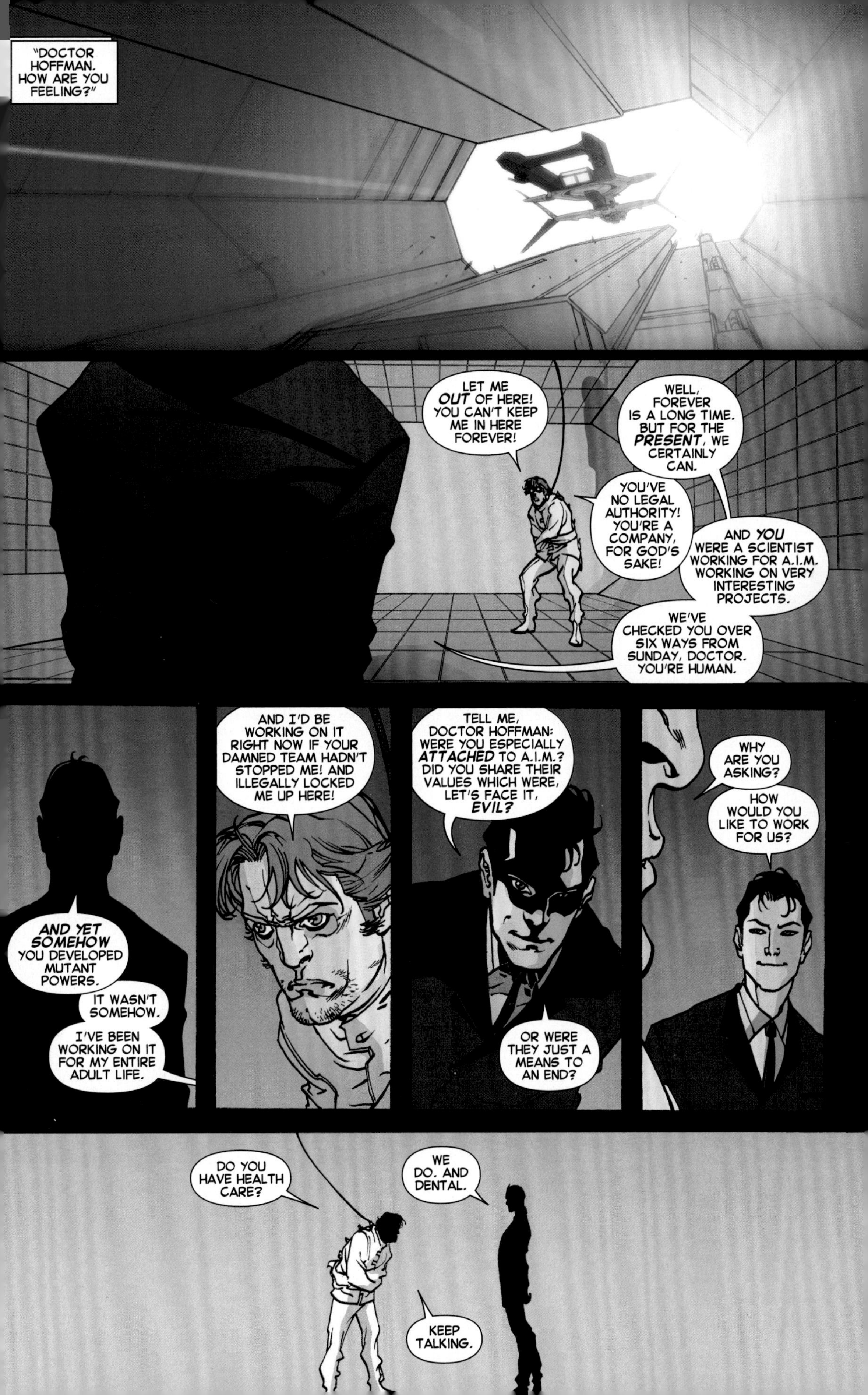
"DOCTOR HOFFMAN. HOW ARE YOU FEELING?"
LET ME OUT OF HERE! YOU CAN'T KEEP ME IN HERE FOREVER!
WELL, FOREVER IS A LONG TIME. BUT FOR THE PRESENT, WE CERTAINLY CAN.
YOU'VE NO LEGAL AUTHORITY! YOU'RE A COMPANY, FOR GOD'S SAKE!
AND YOU WERE A SCIENTIST WORKING FOR A.I.M. WORKING ON VERY INTERESTING PROJECTS.
WE'VE CHECKED YOU OVER SIX WAYS FROM SUNDAY, DOCTOR. YOU'RE HUMAN.
AND YET SOMEHOW YOU DEVELOPED MUTANT POWERS.
IT WASN'T SOMEHOW.
I'VE BEEN WORKING ON IT FOR MY ENTIRE ADULT LIFE.
AND I'D BE WORKING ON IT RIGHT NOW IF YOUR DAMNED TEAM HADN'T STOPPED ME! AND ILLEGALLY LOCKED ME UP HERE!
TELL ME, DOCTOR HOFFMAN: WERE YOU ESPECIALLY ATTACHED TO A.I.M.? DID YOU SHARE THEIR VALUES WHICH WERE, LET'S FACE IT, EVIL?
OR WERE THEY JUST A MEANS TO AN END?
WHY ARE YOU ASKING?
HOW WOULD YOU LIKE TO WORK FOR US?
DO YOU HAVE HEALTH CARE?
WE DO. AND DENTAL.
KEEP TALKING.

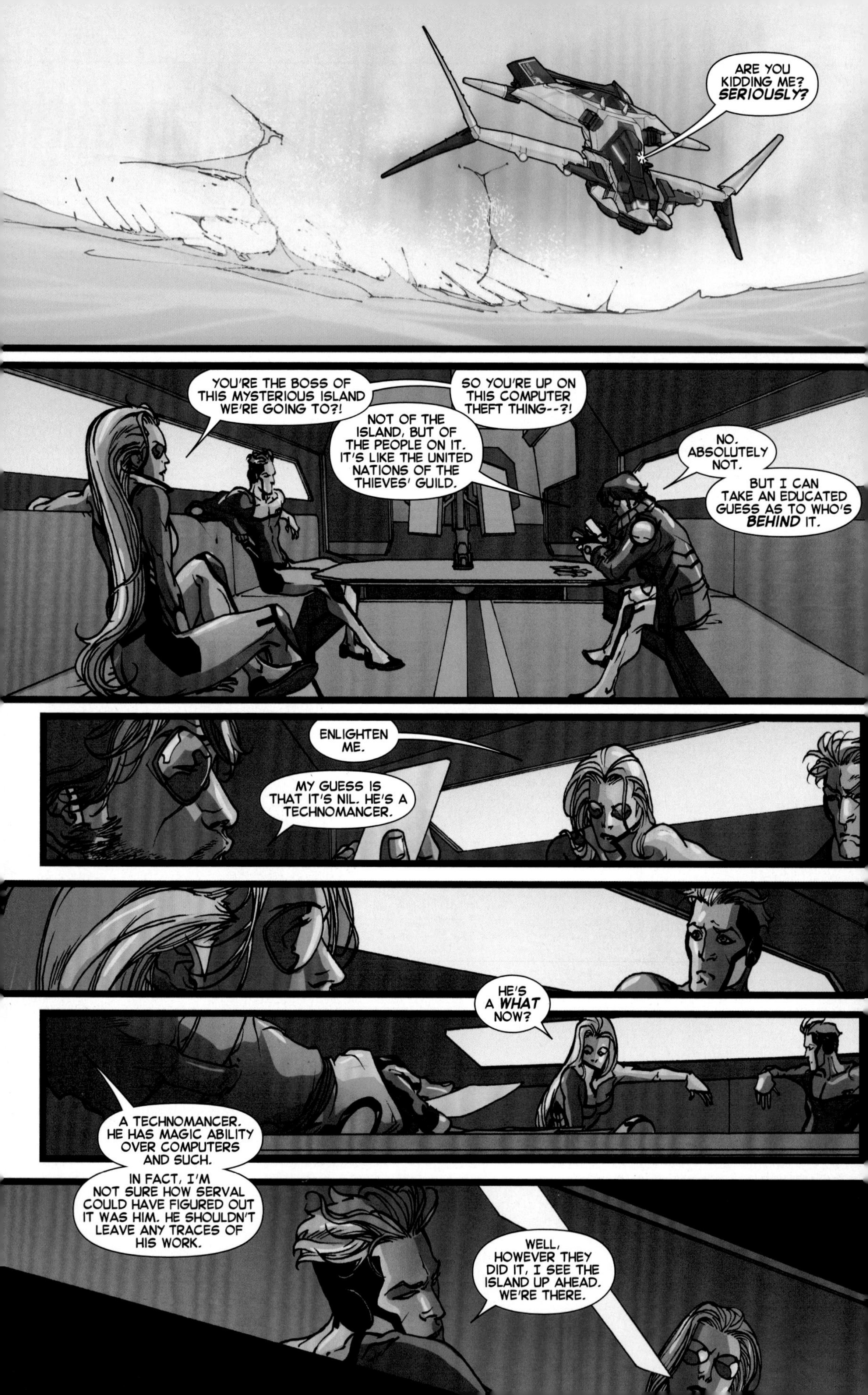
ARE YOU KIDDING ME? SERIOUSLY?
YOU'RE THE BOSS OF THIS MYSTERIOUS ISLAND WE'RE GOING TO?!
NOT OF THE ISLAND, BUT OF THE PEOPLE ON IT. IT'S LIKE THE UNITED NATIONS OF THE THIEVES' GUILD.
SO YOU'RE UP ON THIS COMPUTER THEFT THING--?!
NO. ABSOLUTELY NOT.
BUT I CAN TAKE AN EDUCATED GUESS AS TO WHO'S BEHIND IT.
ENLIGHTEN ME.
MY GUESS IS THAT IT'S NIL. HE'S A TECHNOMANCER.
HE'S A WHAT NOW?
A TECHNOMANCER. HE HAS MAGIC ABILITY OVER COMPUTERS AND SUCH.
IN FACT, I'M NOT SURE HOW SERVAL COULD HAVE FIGURED OUT IT WAS HIM. HE SHOULDN'T LEAVE ANY TRACES OF HIS WORK.
WELL, HOWEVER THEY DID IT, I SEE THE ISLAND UP AHEAD. WE'RE THERE.

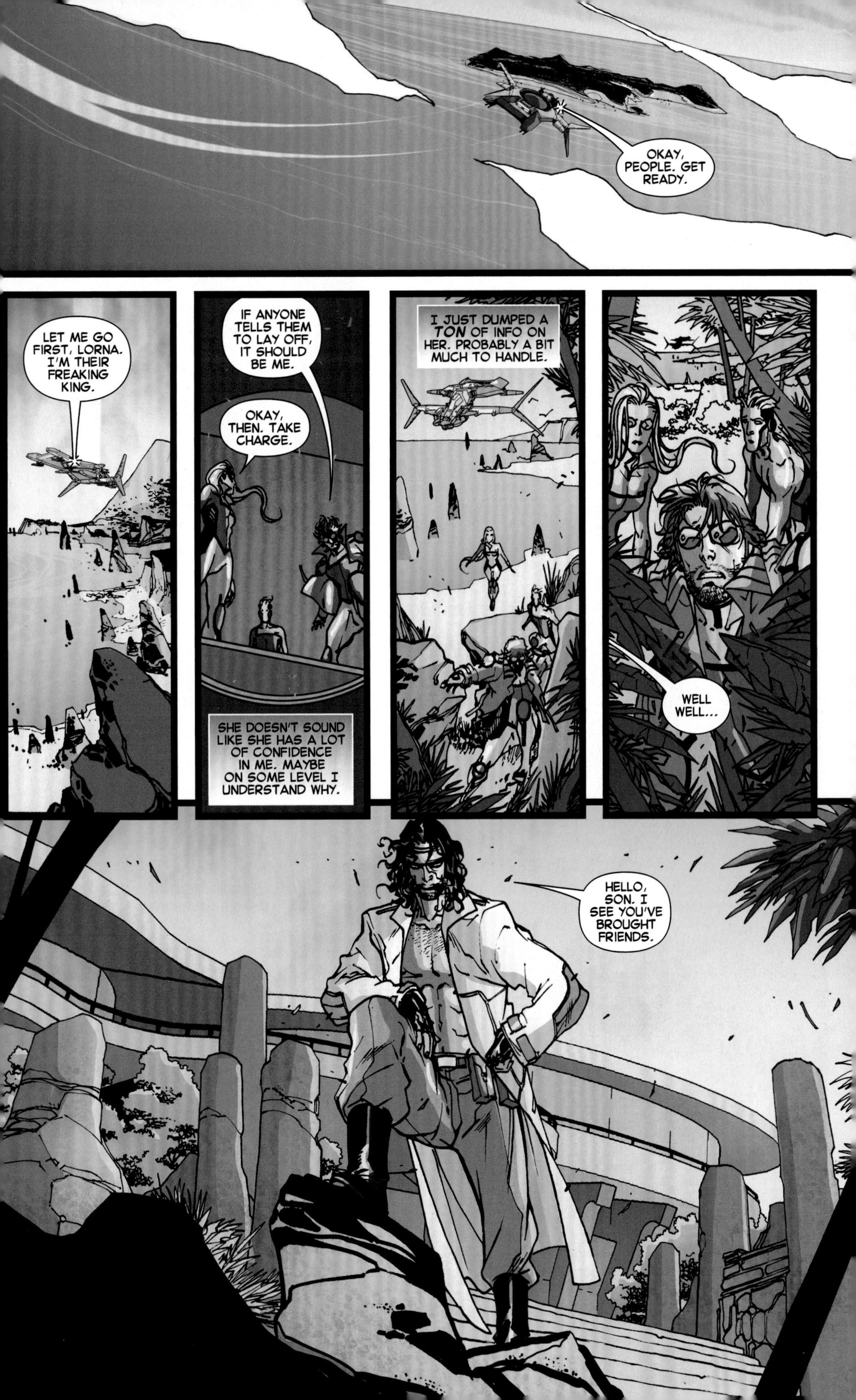
OKAY, PEOPLE. GET READY.
LET ME GO FIRST, LORNA. I'M THEIR FREAKING KING.
IF ANYONE TELLS THEM TO LAY OFF, IT SHOULD BE ME.
OKAY, THEN. TAKE CHARGE.
SHE DOESN'T SOUND LIKE SHE HAS A LOT OF CONFIDENCE IN ME. MAYBE ON SOME LEVEL I UNDERSTAND WHY.
I JUST DUMPED A TON OF INFO ON HER. PROBABLY A BIT MUCH TO HANDLE.
WELL WELL...
HELLO, SON. I SEE YOU'VE BROUGHT FRIENDS.

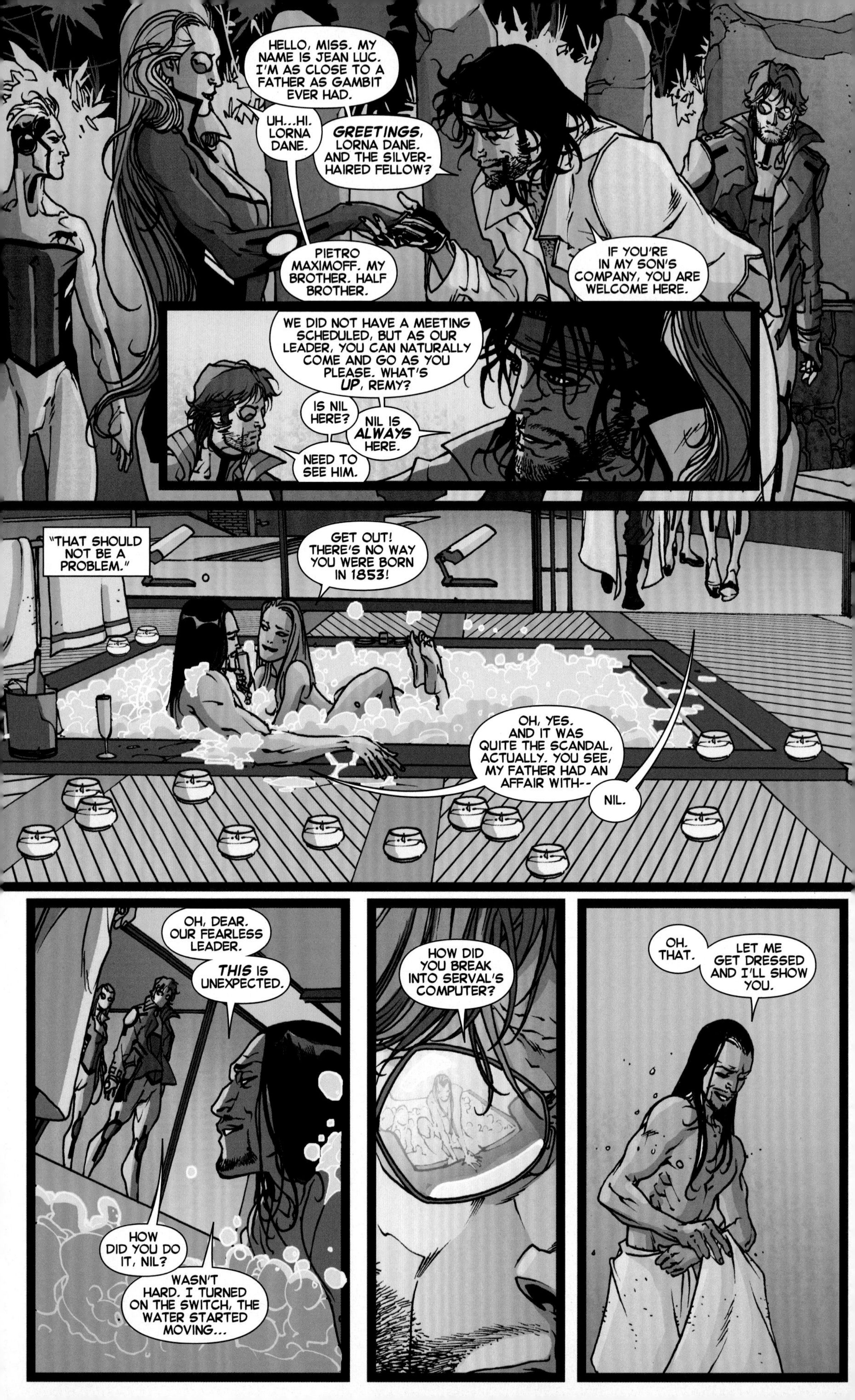
HELLO, MISS. MY NAME IS JEAN LUC. I'M AS CLOSE TO A FATHER AS GAMBIT EVER HAD.
UH...HI. LORNA DANE.
GREETINGS, LORNA DANE. AND THE SILVER-HAIRED FELLOW?
PIETRO MAXIMOFF. MY BROTHER. HALF BROTHER.
IF YOU'RE IN MY SON'S COMPANY, YOU ARE WELCOME HERE.
WE DID NOT HAVE A MEETING SCHEDULED, BUT AS OUR LEADER, YOU CAN NATURALLY COME AND GO AS YOU PLEASE. WHAT'S UP, REMY?
IS NIL HERE?
NIL IS ALWAYS HERE.
NEED TO SEE HIM.
"THAT SHOULD NOT BE A PROBLEM."
GET OUT! THERE'S NO WAY YOU WERE BORN IN 1853!
OH, YES. AND IT WAS QUITE THE SCANDAL, ACTUALLY. YOU SEE, MY FATHER HAD AN AFFAIR WITH--
NIL.
OH, DEAR. OUR FEARLESS LEADER.
THIS IS UNEXPECTED.
HOW DID YOU DO IT, NIL?
WASN'T HARD. I TURNED ON THE SWITCH, THE WATER STARTED MOVING...
HOW DID YOU BREAK INTO SERVAL'S COMPUTER?
OH. THAT.
LET ME GET DRESSED AND I'LL SHOW YOU.

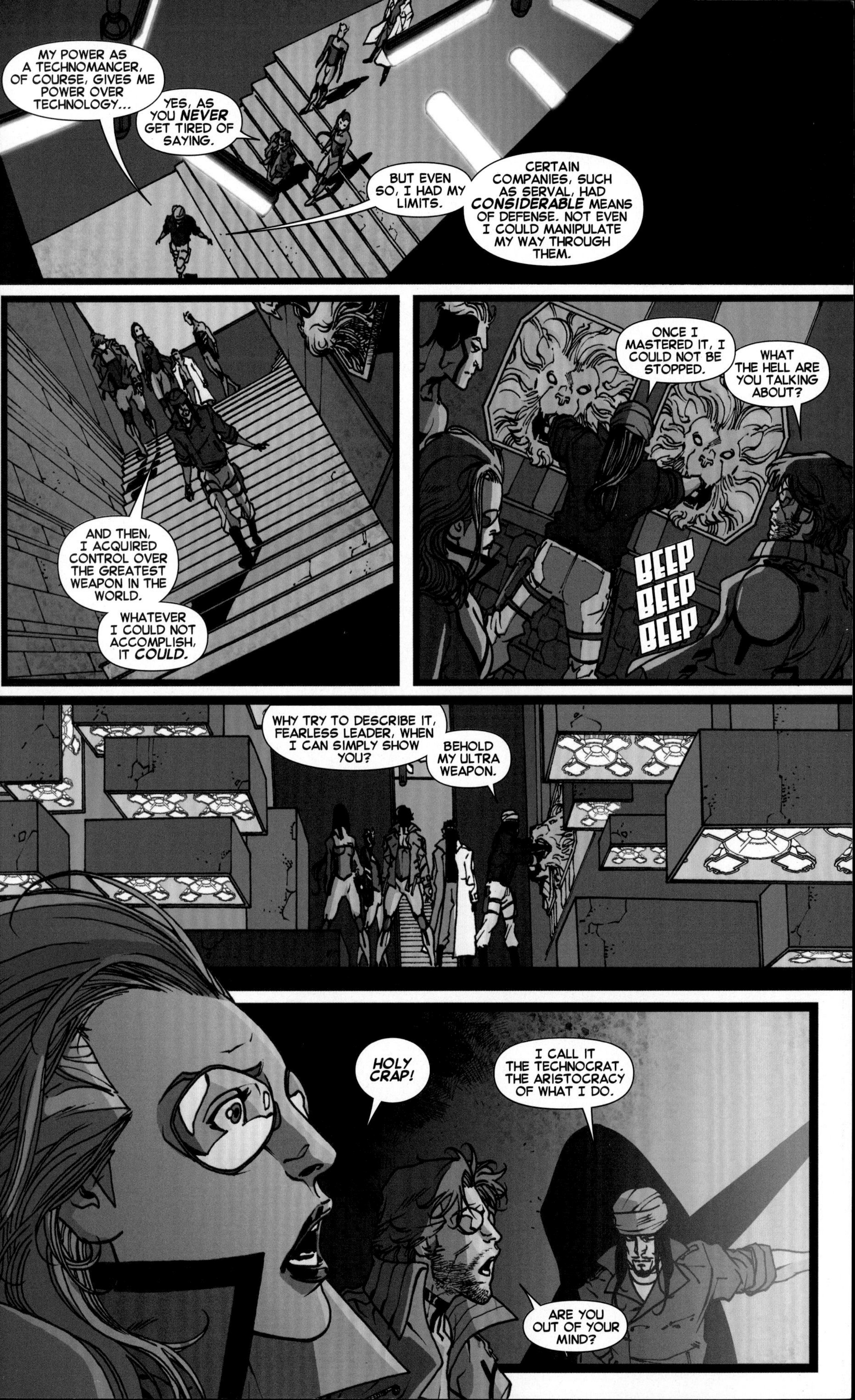
MY POWER AS A TECHNOMANCER, OF COURSE, GIVES ME POWER OVER TECHNOLOGY...
YES, AS YOU NEVER GET TIRED OF SAYING.
BUT EVEN SO, I HAD MY LIMITS.
CERTAIN COMPANIES, SUCH AS SERVAL, HAD CONSIDERABLE MEANS OF DEFENSE. NOT EVEN I COULD MANIPULATE MY WAY THROUGH THEM.
AND THEN, I ACQUIRED CONTROL OVER THE GREATEST WEAPON IN THE WORLD.
WHATEVER I COULD NOT ACCOMPLISH, IT COULD.
ONCE I MASTERED IT, I COULD NOT BE STOPPED.
WHAT THE HELL ARE YOU TALKING ABOUT?
BEEP BEEP BEEP
WHY TRY TO DESCRIBE IT, FEARLESS LEADER, WHEN I CAN SIMPLY SHOW YOU?
BEHOLD MY ULTRA WEAPON.
HOLY CRAP!
I CALL IT THE TECHNOCRAT. THE ARISTOCRACY OF WHAT I DO.
ARE YOU OUT OF YOUR MIND?

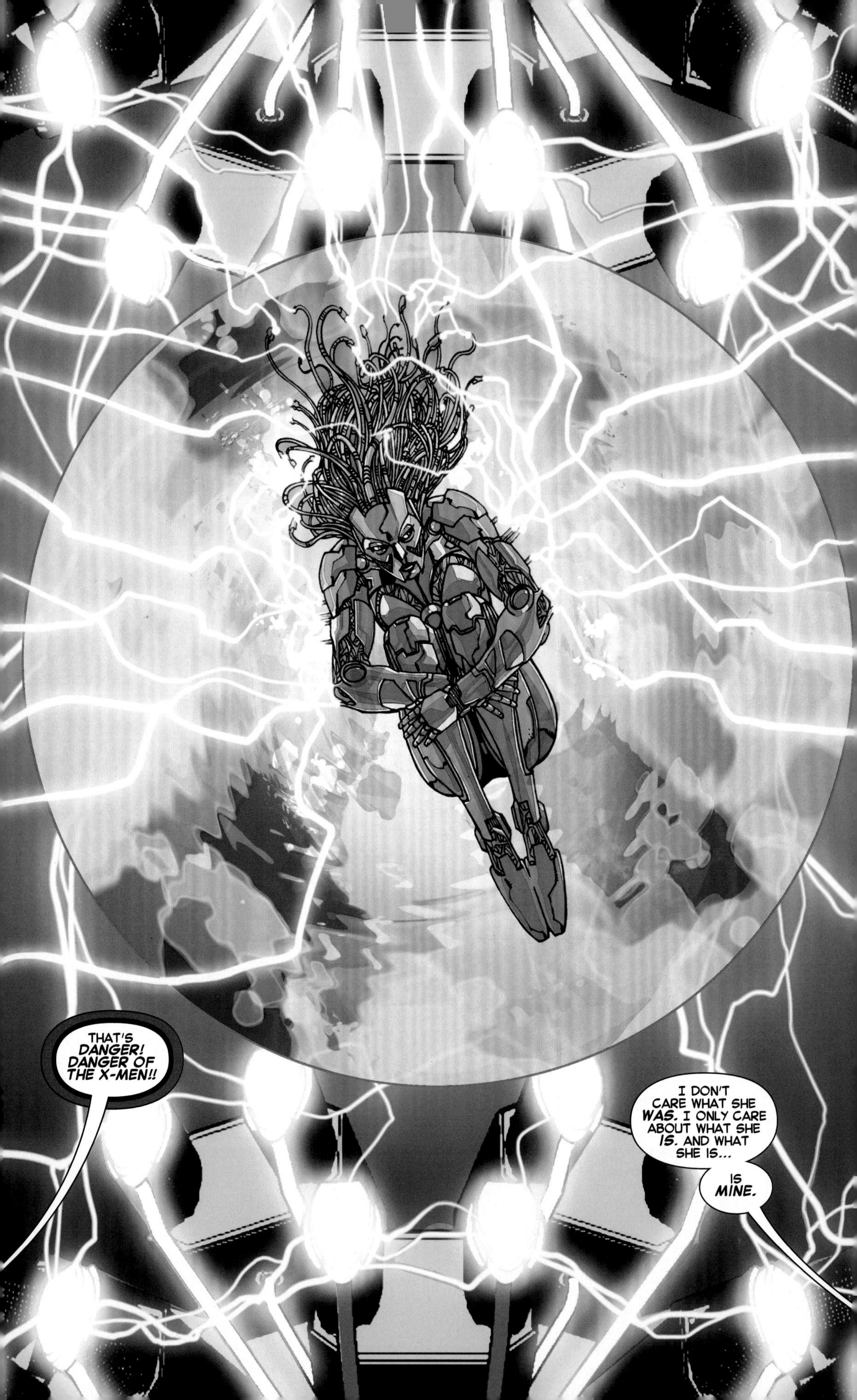
THAT'S *DANGER!* DANGER OF THE X-MEN!!
I DON'T CARE WHAT SHE *WAS.* I ONLY CARE ABOUT WHAT SHE *IS.* AND WHAT SHE IS...
IS *MINE.*

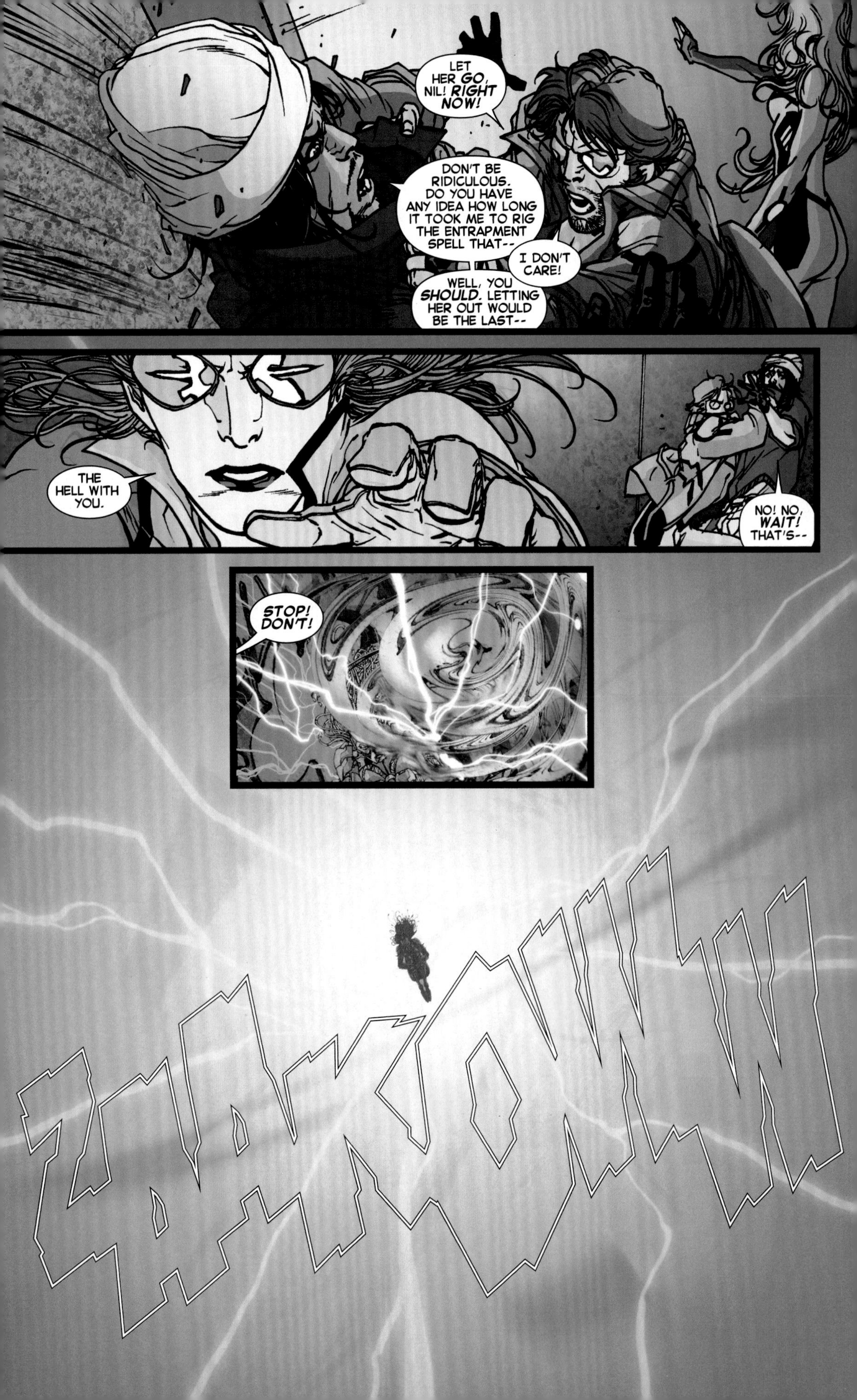
LET HER GO, NIL! RIGHT NOW!
DON'T BE RIDICULOUS. DO YOU HAVE ANY IDEA HOW LONG IT TOOK ME TO RIG THE ENTRAPMENT SPELL THAT--
I DON'T CARE!
WELL, YOU SHOULD. LETTING HER OUT WOULD BE THE LAST--
THE HELL WITH YOU.
NO! NO, WAIT! THAT'S--
STOP! DON'T!

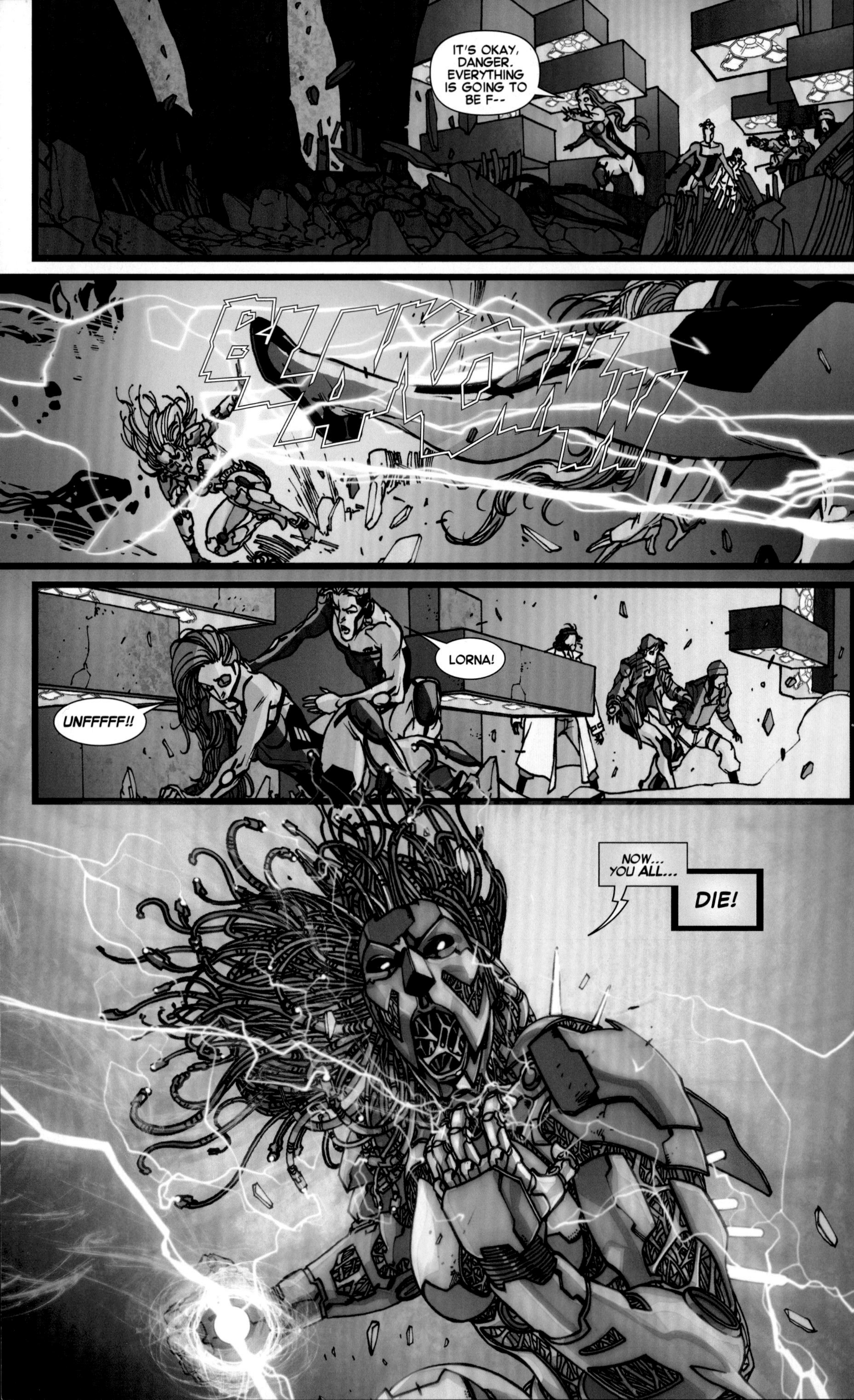
IT'S OKAY, DANGER. EVERYTHING IS GOING TO BE F--
LORNA!
UNFFFFF!!
NOW... YOU ALL... DIE!

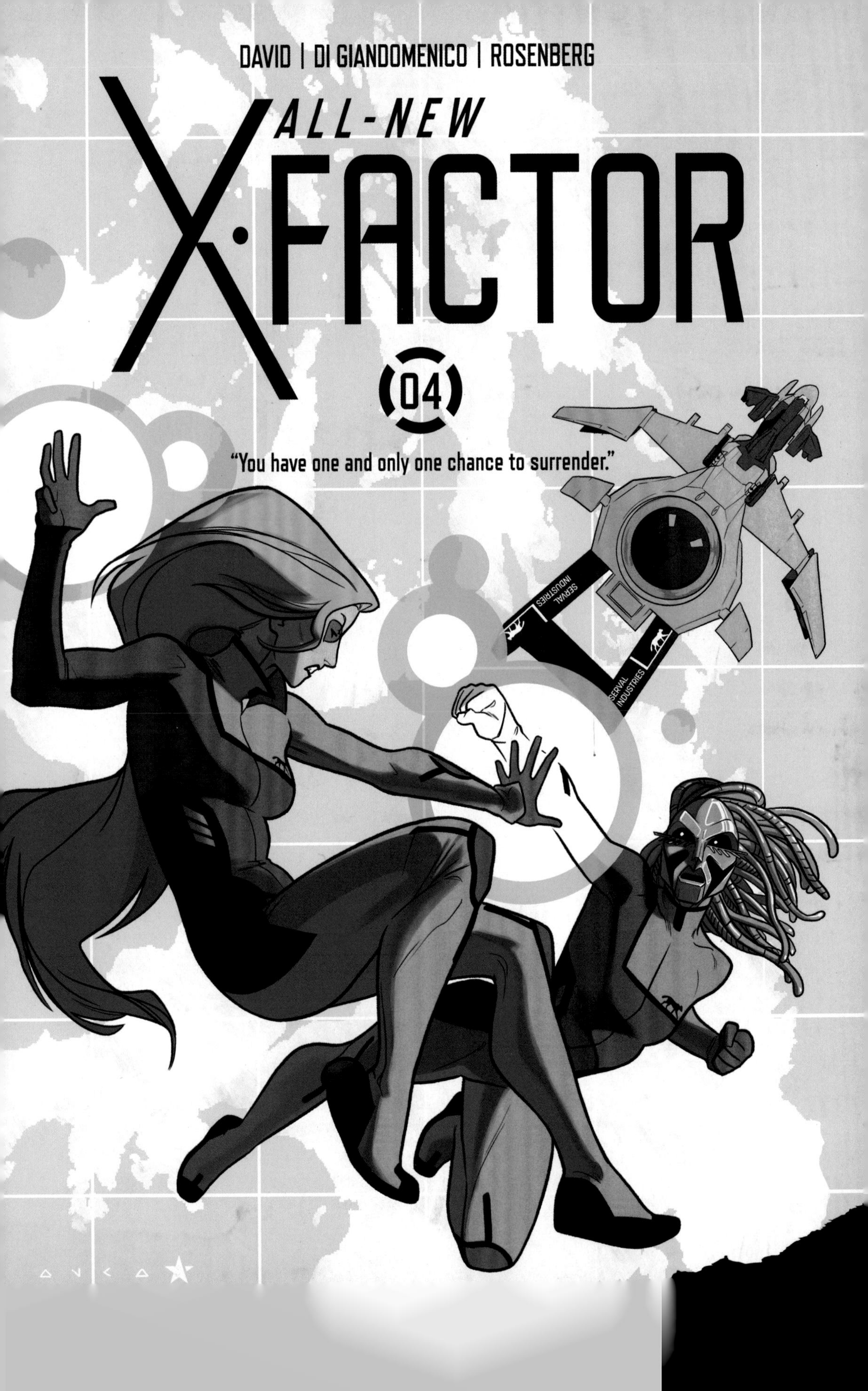
DAVID | DI GIANDOMENICO | ROSENBERG
ALL-NEW
X-FACTOR
04
"You have one and only one chance to surrender."
SERVAL INDUSTRIES
SERVAL INDUSTRIES

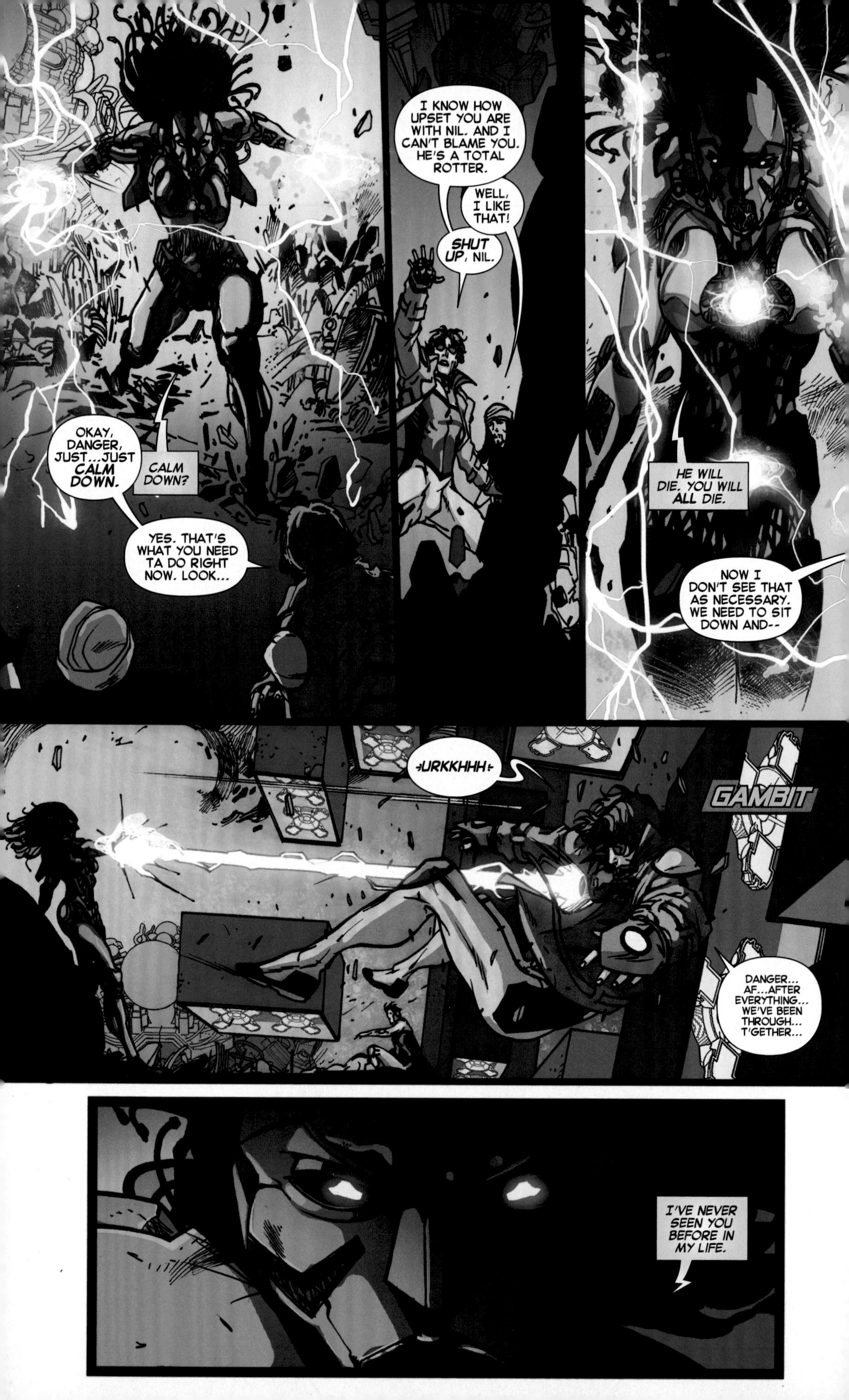
OKAY, DANGER, JUST...JUST CALM DOWN.
CALM DOWN?
YES. THAT'S WHAT YOU NEED TA DO RIGHT NOW. LOOK...
I KNOW HOW UPSET YOU ARE WITH NIL. AND I CAN'T BLAME YOU. HE'S A TOTAL ROTTER.
WELL, I LIKE THAT!
SHUT UP, NIL.
HE WILL DIE. YOU WILL ALL DIE.
NOW I DON'T SEE THAT AS NECESSARY. WE NEED TO SIT DOWN AND--
URKKHHH
GAMBIT
DANGER... AF...AFTER EVERYTHING... WE'VE BEEN THROUGH... T'GETHER...
I'VE NEVER SEEN YOU BEFORE IN MY LIFE.

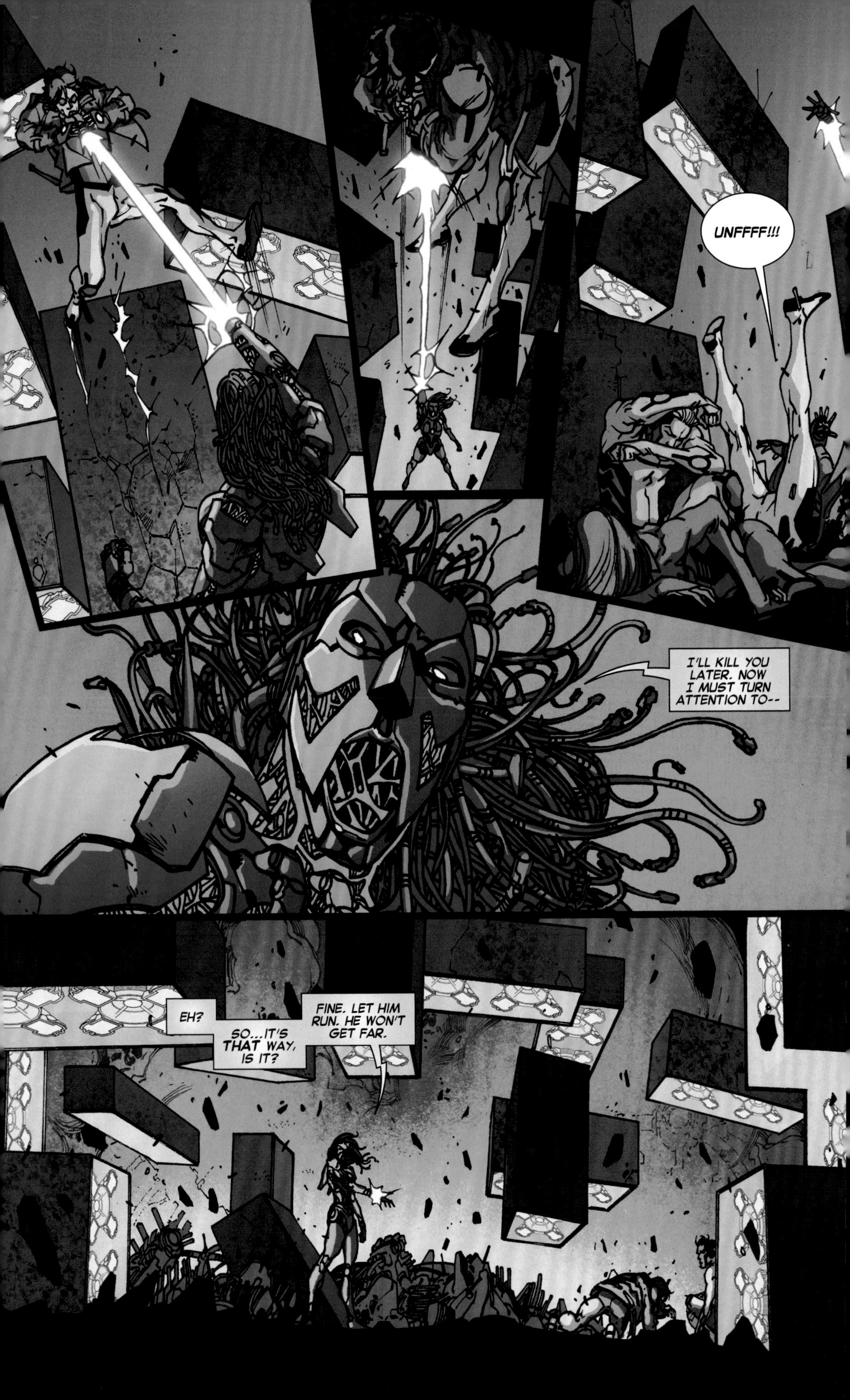
UNFFFF!!!
I'LL KILL YOU LATER. NOW I MUST TURN ATTENTION TO--
EH?
SO...IT'S THAT WAY, IS IT?
FINE. LET HIM RUN. HE WON'T GET FAR.

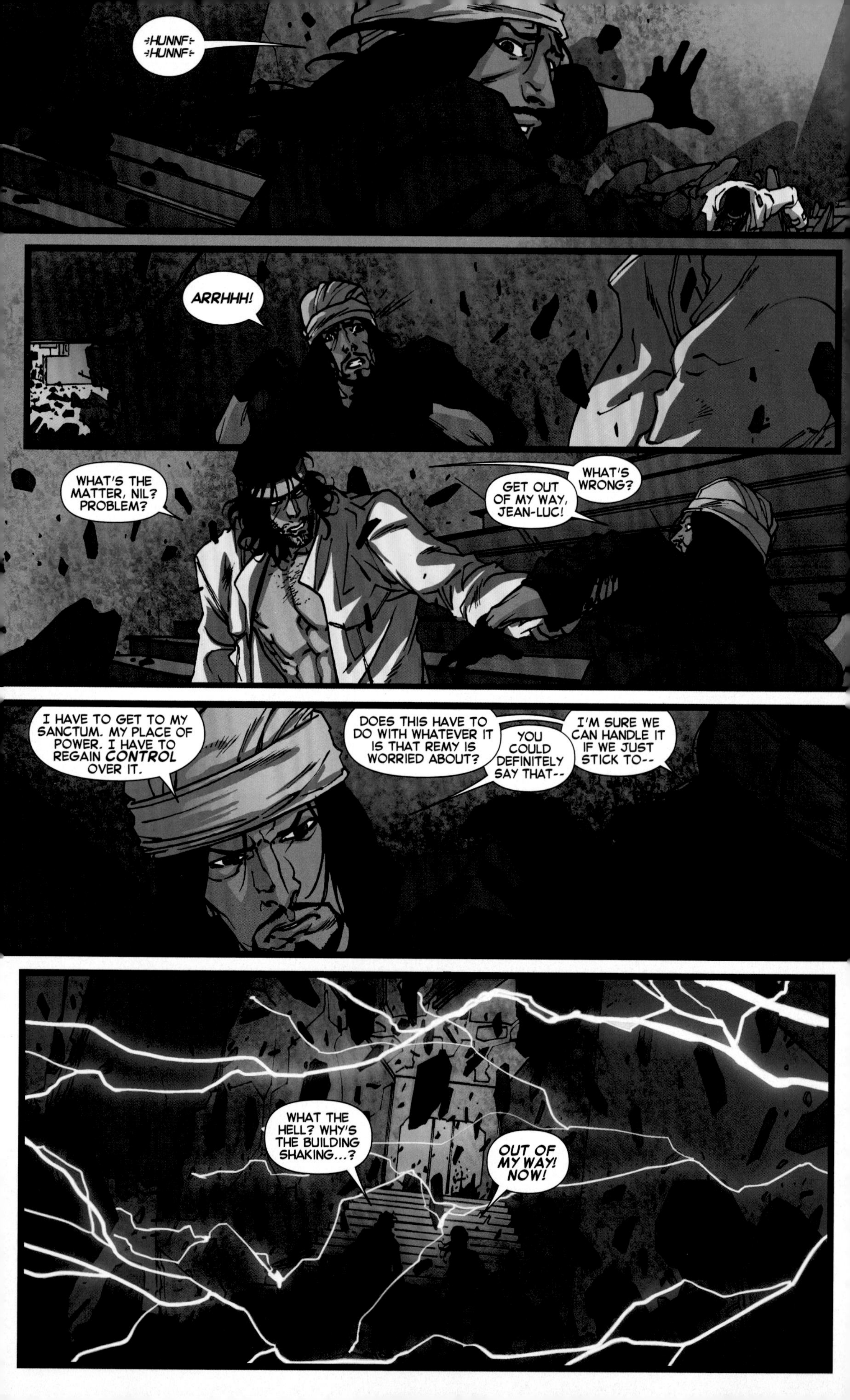

=HUNNF= =HUNNF=
ARRHHH!
WHAT'S THE MATTER, NIL? PROBLEM?
GET OUT OF MY WAY, JEAN-LUC!
WHAT'S WRONG?
I HAVE TO GET TO MY SANCTUM. MY PLACE OF POWER. I HAVE TO REGAIN CONTROL OVER IT.
DOES THIS HAVE TO DO WITH WHATEVER IT IS THAT REMY IS WORRIED ABOUT?
YOU COULD DEFINITELY SAY THAT--
I'M SURE WE CAN HANDLE IT IF WE JUST STICK TO--
WHAT THE HELL? WHY'S THE BUILDING SHAKING...?
OUT OF MY WAY! NOW!

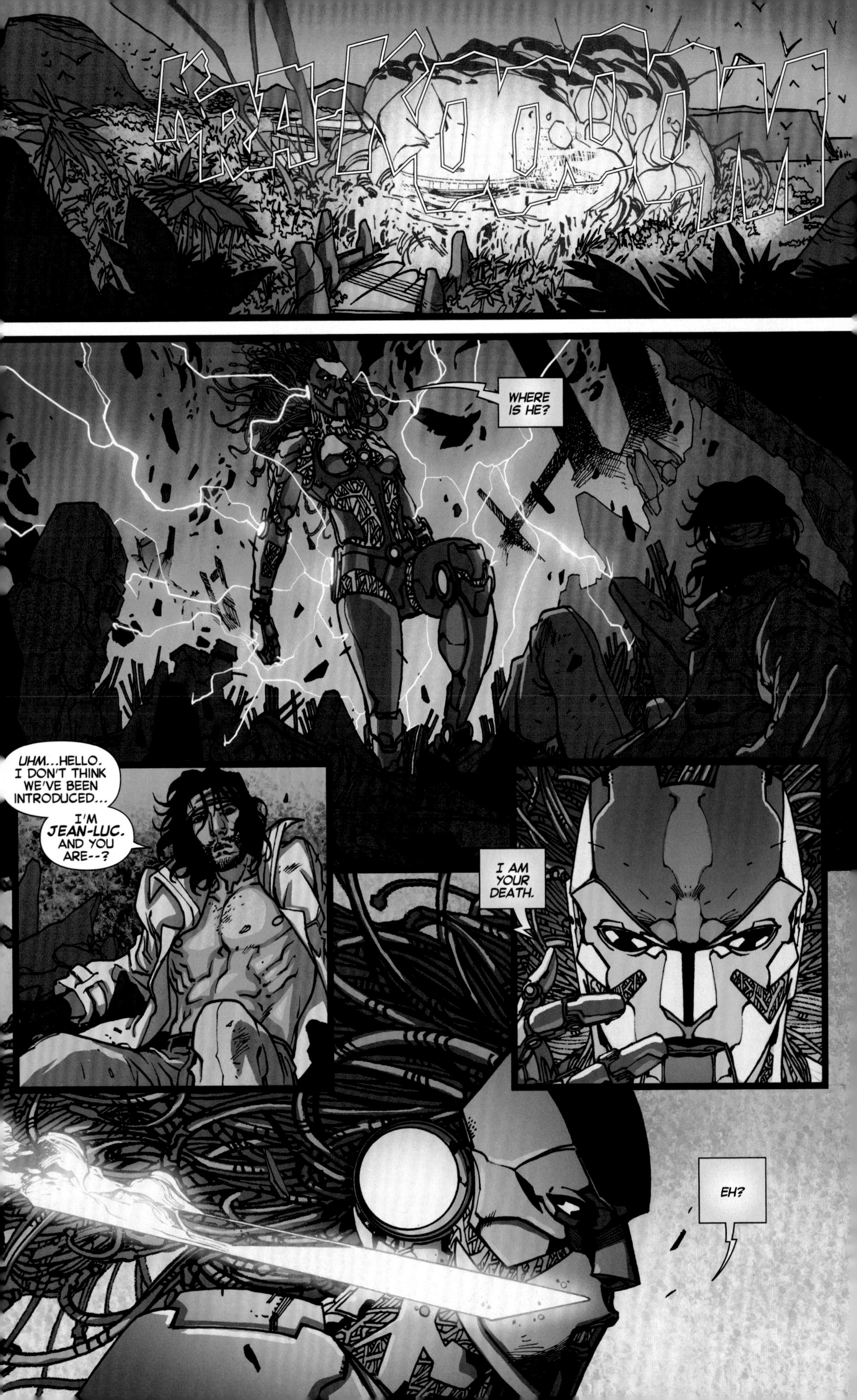
KRAKOOOOOM
WHERE IS HE?
UHM...HELLO. I DON'T THINK WE'VE BEEN INTRODUCED...
I'M JEAN-LUC. AND YOU ARE--?
I AM YOUR DEATH.
EH?

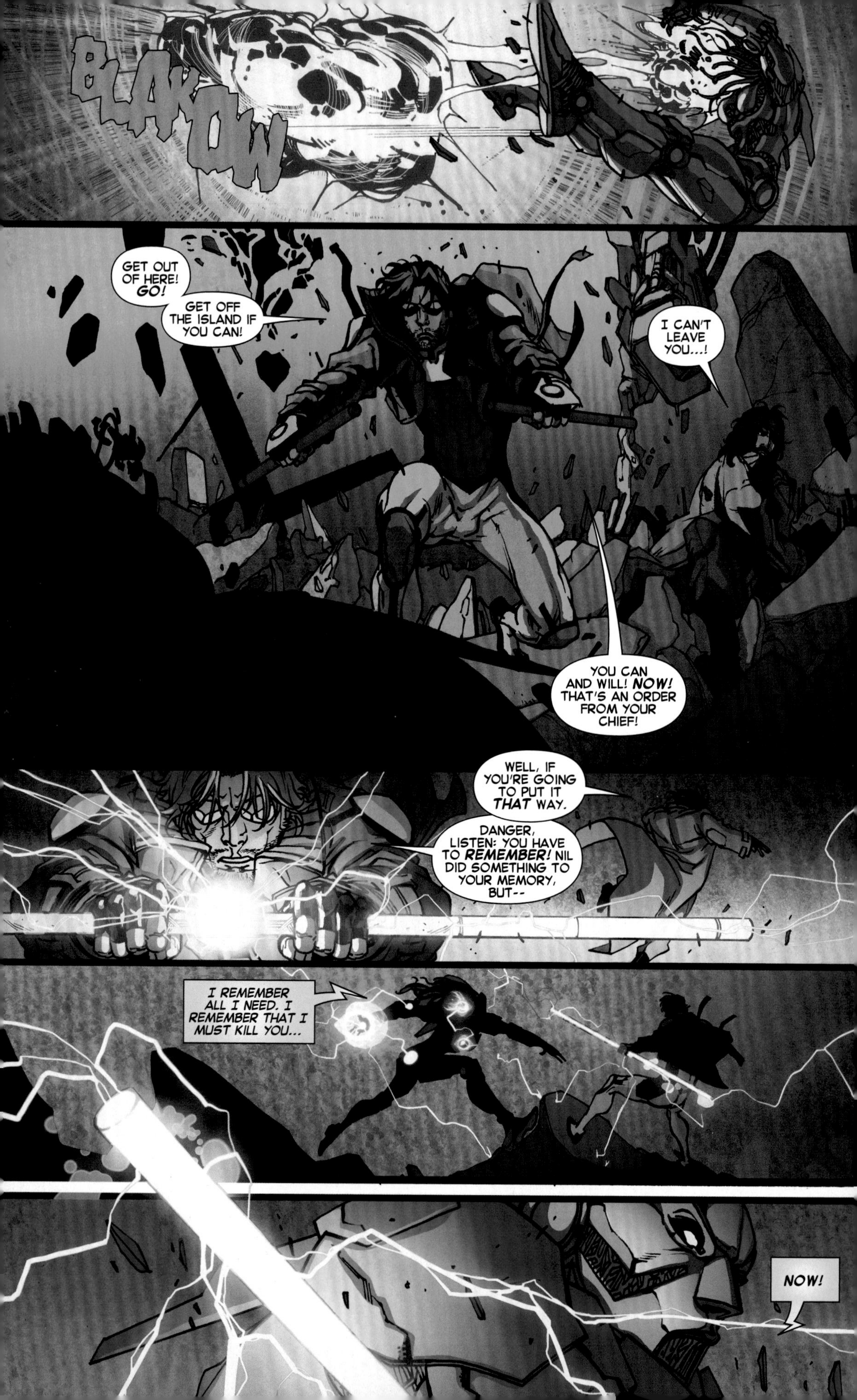
BLAKOW
GET OUT OF HERE! GO!
GET OFF THE ISLAND IF YOU CAN!
I CAN'T LEAVE YOU...!
YOU CAN AND WILL! NOW! THAT'S AN ORDER FROM YOUR CHIEF!
WELL, IF YOU'RE GOING TO PUT IT THAT WAY.
DANGER, LISTEN: YOU HAVE TO REMEMBER! NIL DID SOMETHING TO YOUR MEMORY, BUT--
I REMEMBER ALL I NEED. I REMEMBER THAT I MUST KILL YOU...
NOW!

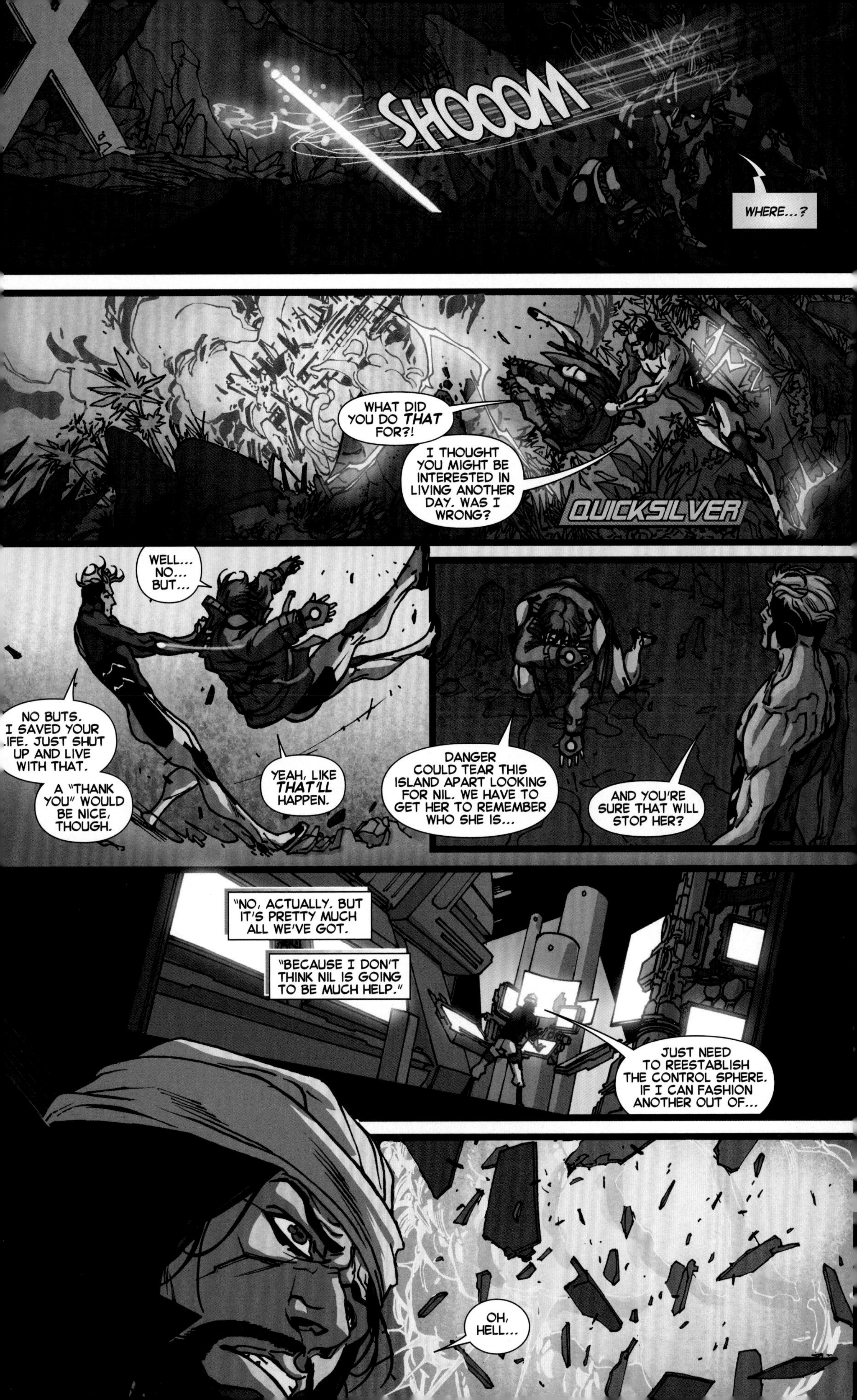
SHOOOM
WHERE...?
WHAT DID YOU DO *THAT* FOR?!
I THOUGHT YOU MIGHT BE INTERESTED IN LIVING ANOTHER DAY. WAS I WRONG?
QUICKSILVER
WELL... NO... BUT...
NO BUTS. I SAVED YOUR .IFE. JUST SHUT UP AND LIVE WITH THAT.
A "THANK YOU" WOULD BE NICE, THOUGH.
YEAH, LIKE *THAT'LL* HAPPEN.
DANGER COULD TEAR THIS ISLAND APART LOOKING FOR NIL. WE HAVE TO GET HER TO REMEMBER WHO SHE IS...
AND YOU'RE SURE THAT WILL STOP HER?
"NO, ACTUALLY. BUT IT'S PRETTY MUCH ALL WE'VE GOT.
"BECAUSE I DON'T THINK NIL IS GOING TO BE MUCH HELP."
JUST NEED TO REESTABLISH THE CONTROL SPHERE. IF I CAN FASHION ANOTHER OUT OF...
OH, HELL...

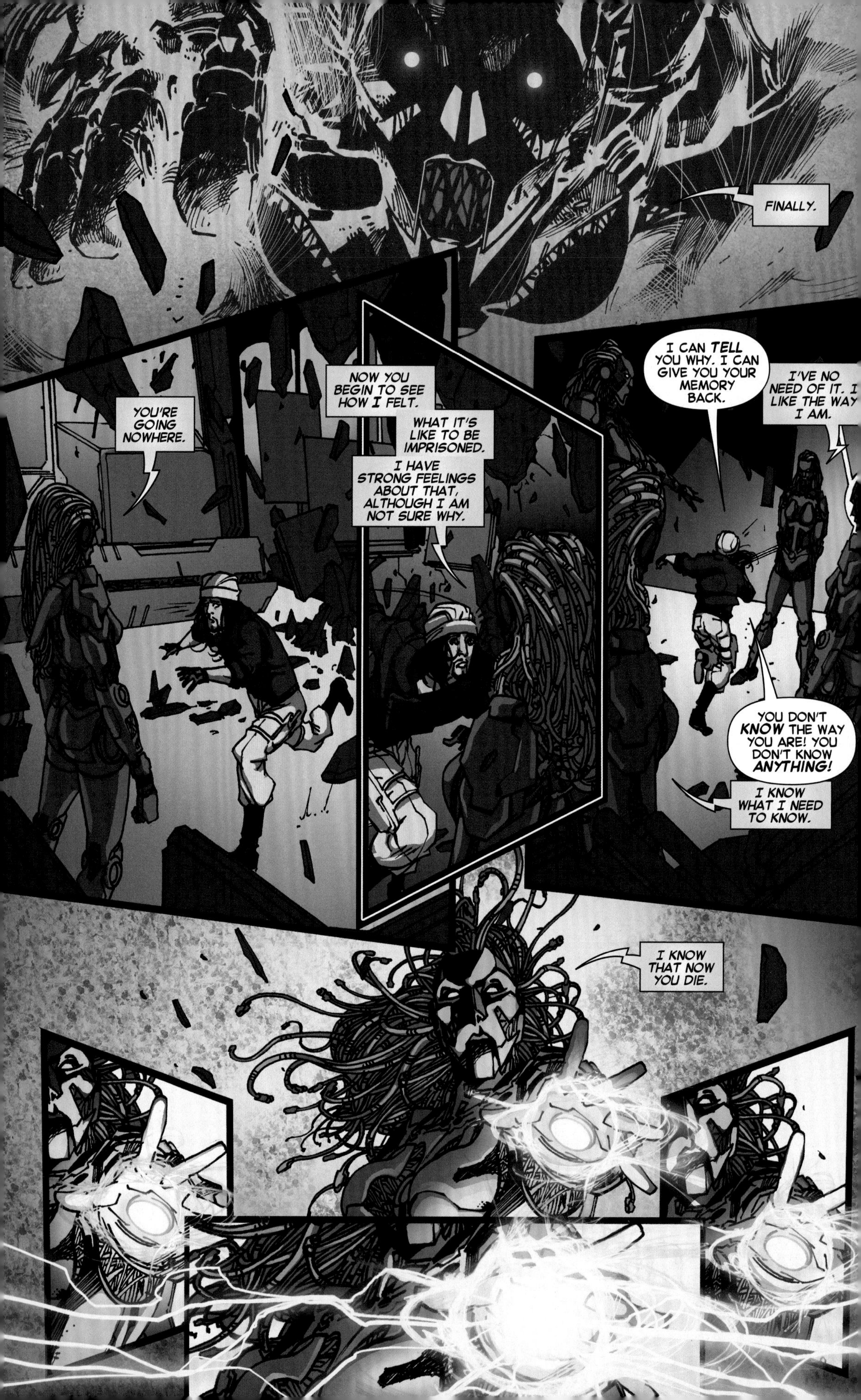
FINALLY.
YOU'RE GOING NOWHERE.
NOW YOU BEGIN TO SEE HOW I FELT.
WHAT IT'S LIKE TO BE IMPRISONED.
I HAVE STRONG FEELINGS ABOUT THAT, ALTHOUGH I AM NOT SURE WHY.
I CAN TELL YOU WHY. I CAN GIVE YOU YOUR MEMORY BACK.
I'VE NO NEED OF IT. I LIKE THE WAY I AM.
YOU DON'T KNOW THE WAY YOU ARE! YOU DON'T KNOW ANYTHING!
I KNOW WHAT I NEED TO KNOW.
I KNOW THAT NOW YOU DIE.

ZWAKOWWW

SHOOOM

ALL RIGHT! THAT'S ENOUGH OF THAT!

STOP MOVING AROUND! YOU'RE MAKING IT HARD TO *HOLD ON.*

SORRY! I'M SOR--

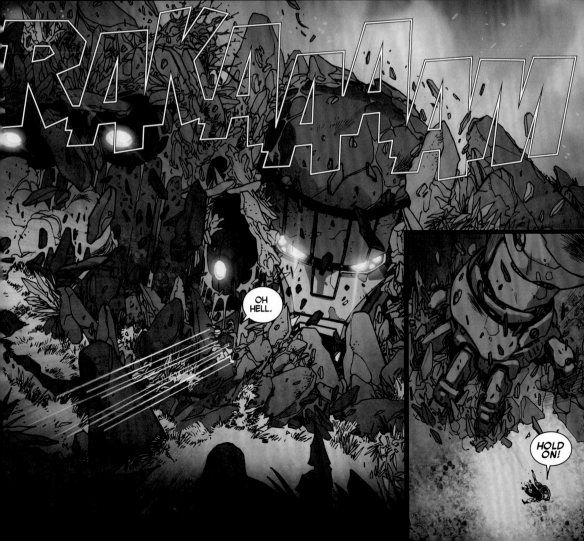

RAKAAAAAM

OH HELL.

HOLD ON!

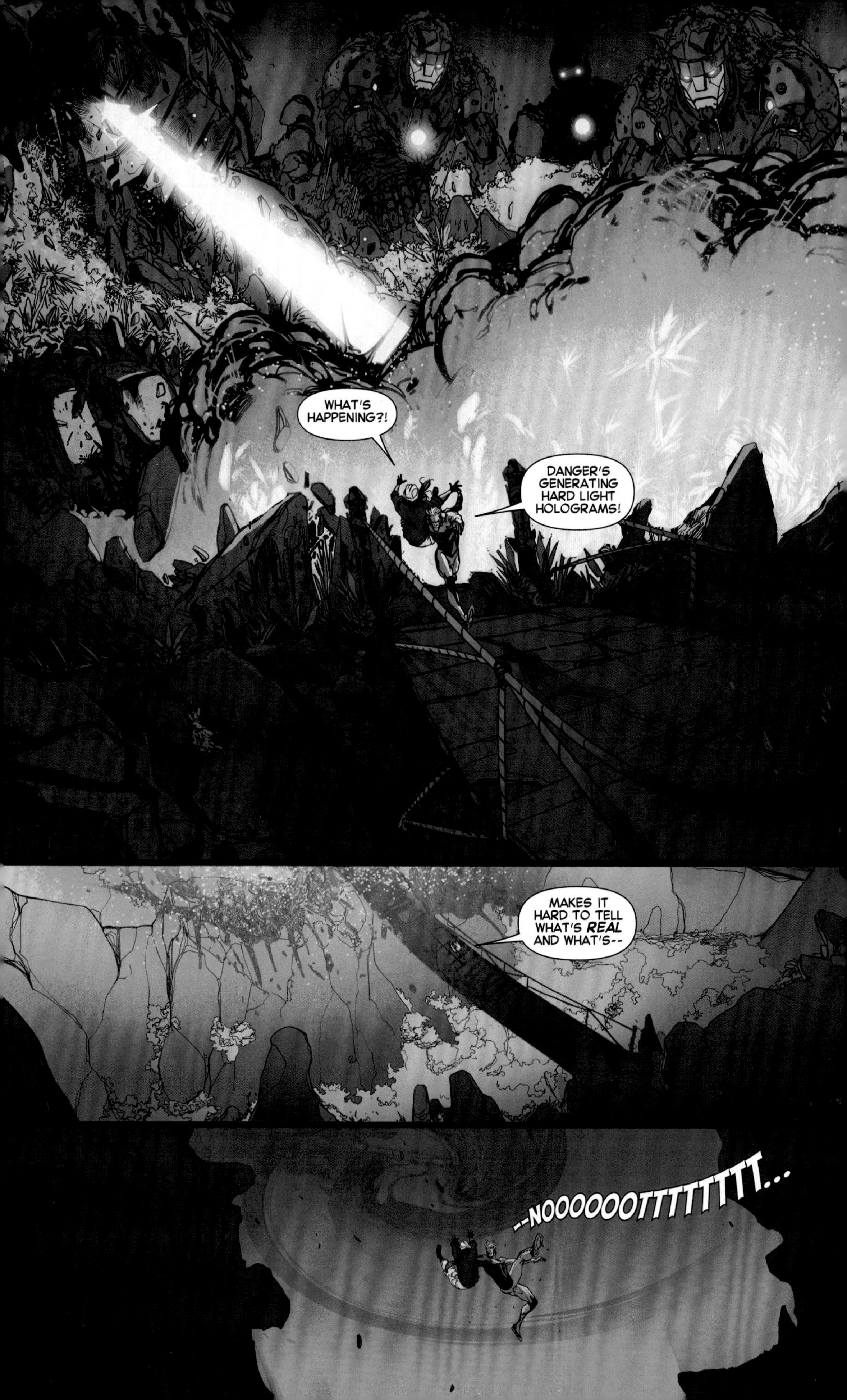
WHAT'S HAPPENING?!
DANGER'S GENERATING HARD LIGHT HOLOGRAMS!
MAKES IT HARD TO TELL WHAT'S *REAL* AND WHAT'S--
--NOOOOOOTTTTTTTT...

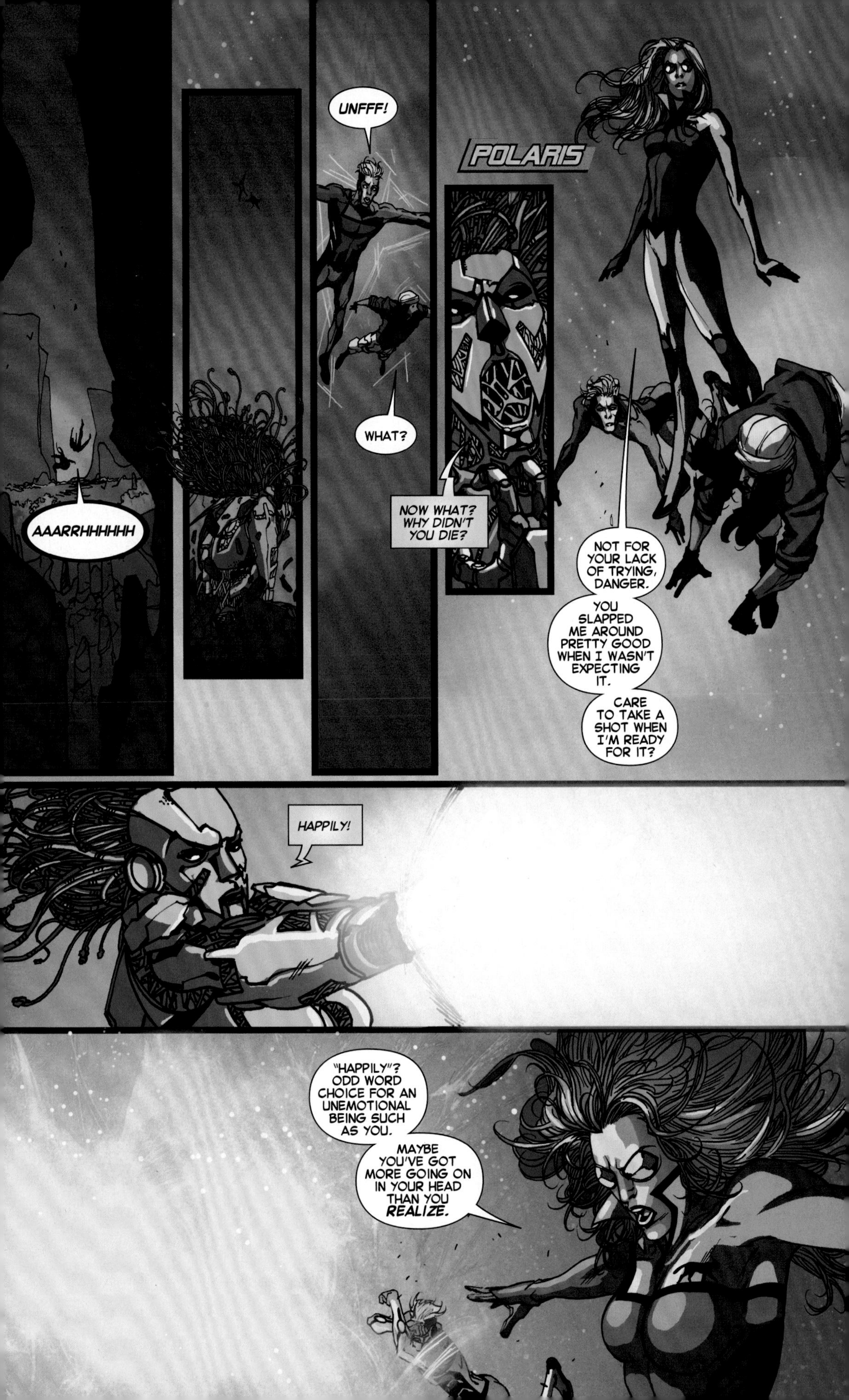
AAARRHHHHHH
UNFFF!
WHAT?
POLARIS
NOW WHAT? WHY DIDN'T YOU DIE?
NOT FOR YOUR LACK OF TRYING, DANGER.
YOU SLAPPED ME AROUND PRETTY GOOD WHEN I WASN'T EXPECTING IT.
CARE TO TAKE A SHOT WHEN I'M READY FOR IT?
HAPPILY!
"HAPPILY"? ODD WORD CHOICE FOR AN UNEMOTIONAL BEING SUCH AS YOU.
MAYBE YOU'VE GOT MORE GOING ON IN YOUR HEAD THAN YOU *REALIZE.*

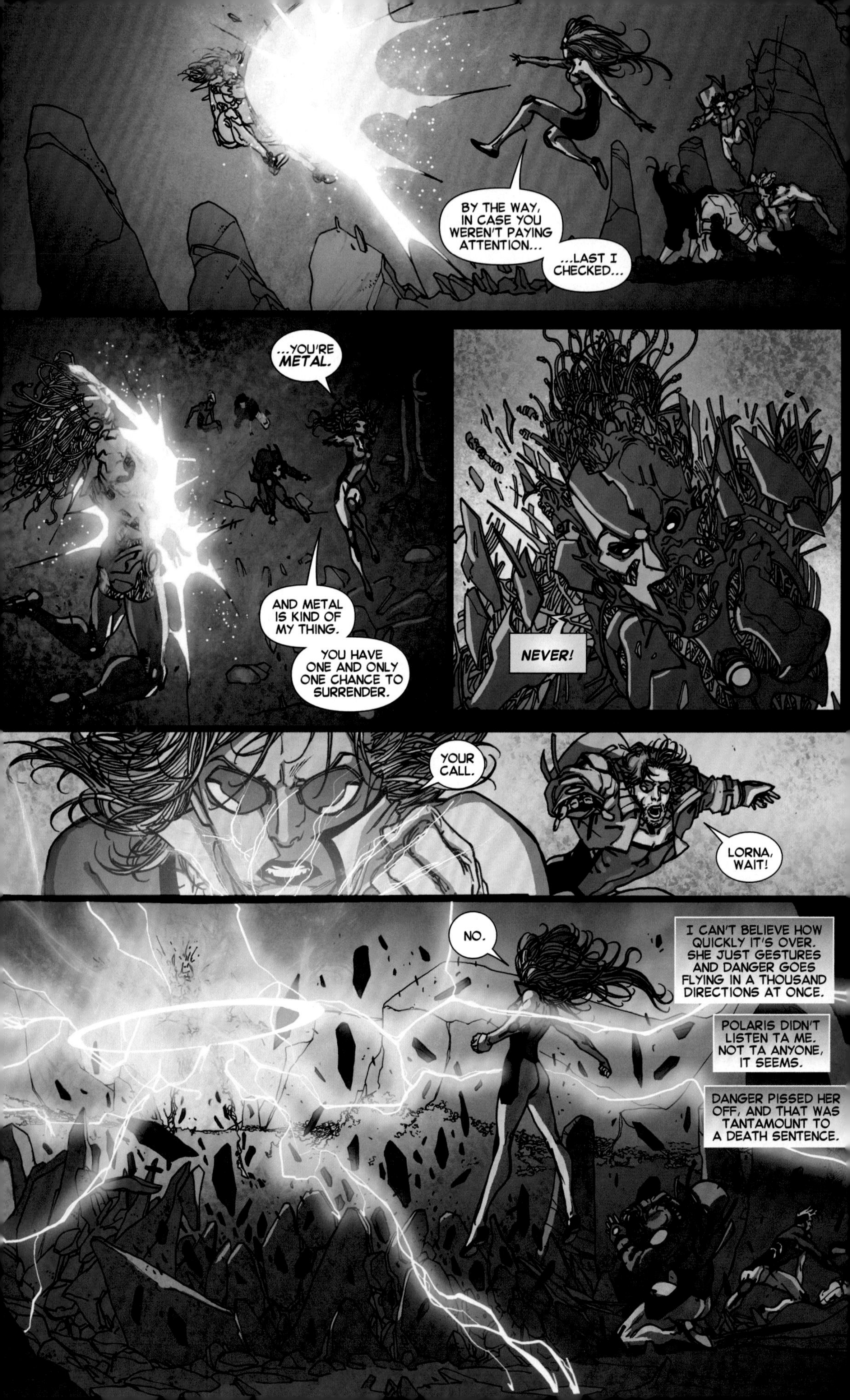

BY THE WAY, IN CASE YOU WEREN'T PAYING ATTENTION...
...LAST I CHECKED...
...YOU'RE METAL.
AND METAL IS KIND OF MY THING.
YOU HAVE ONE AND ONLY ONE CHANCE TO SURRENDER.
NEVER!
YOUR CALL.
LORNA, WAIT!
NO.
I CAN'T BELIEVE HOW QUICKLY IT'S OVER. SHE JUST GESTURES AND DANGER GOES FLYING IN A THOUSAND DIRECTIONS AT ONCE.
POLARIS DIDN'T LISTEN TA ME. NOT TA ANYONE, IT SEEMS.
DANGER PISSED HER OFF, AND THAT WAS TANTAMOUNT TO A DEATH SENTENCE.

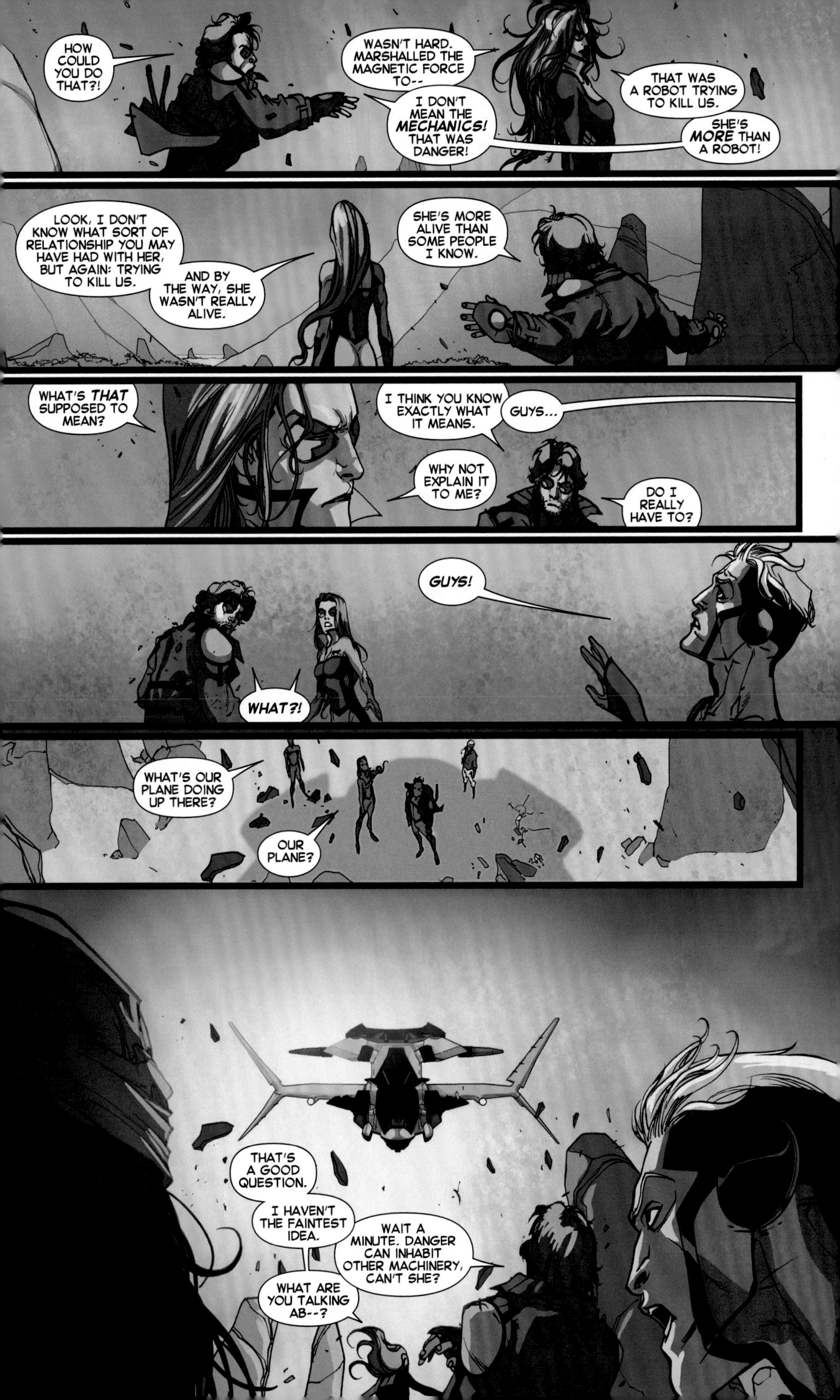

HOW COULD YOU DO THAT?!
WASN'T HARD. MARSHALLED THE MAGNETIC FORCE TO--
I DON'T MEAN THE MECHANICS! THAT WAS DANGER!
THAT WAS A ROBOT TRYING TO KILL US.
SHE'S MORE THAN A ROBOT!
SHE'S MORE ALIVE THAN SOME PEOPLE I KNOW.
LOOK, I DON'T KNOW WHAT SORT OF RELATIONSHIP YOU MAY HAVE HAD WITH HER, BUT AGAIN: TRYING TO KILL US.
AND BY THE WAY, SHE WASN'T REALLY ALIVE.
WHAT'S THAT SUPPOSED TO MEAN?
I THINK YOU KNOW EXACTLY WHAT IT MEANS.
GUYS...
WHY NOT EXPLAIN IT TO ME?
DO I REALLY HAVE TO?
GUYS!
WHAT?!
WHAT'S OUR PLANE DOING UP THERE?
OUR PLANE?
THAT'S A GOOD QUESTION.
I HAVEN'T THE FAINTEST IDEA.
WAIT A MINUTE. DANGER CAN INHABIT OTHER MACHINERY, CAN'T SHE?
WHAT ARE YOU TALKING AB--?

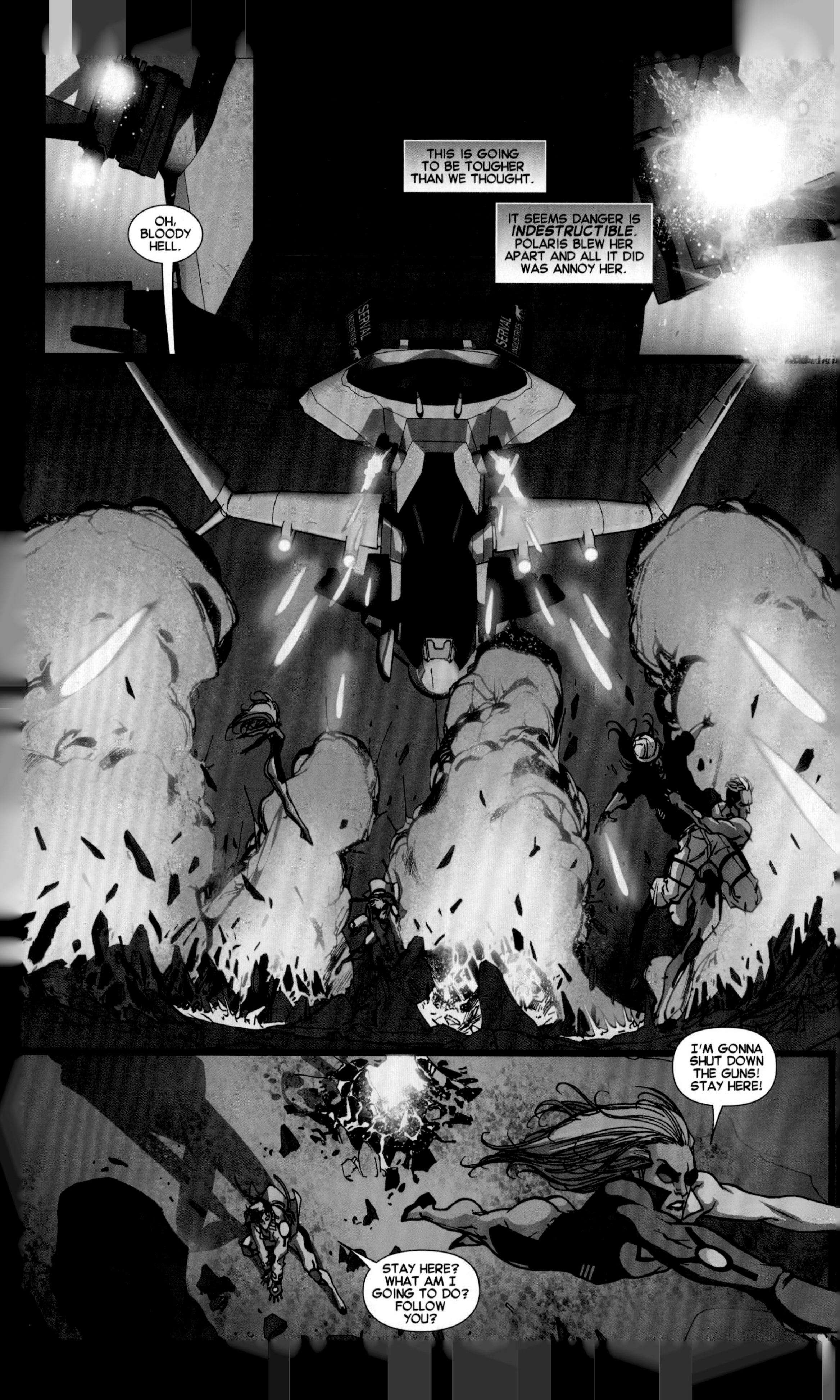
OH, BLOODY HELL.
THIS IS GOING TO BE TOUGHER THAN WE THOUGHT.
IT SEEMS DANGER IS *INDESTRUCTIBLE.* POLARIS BLEW HER APART AND ALL IT DID WAS ANNOY HER.
SERIVAL INDUSTRIES
SERIVAL INDUSTRIES
I'M GONNA SHUT DOWN THE GUNS! STAY HERE!
STAY HERE? WHAT AM I GOING TO DO? FOLLOW YOU?

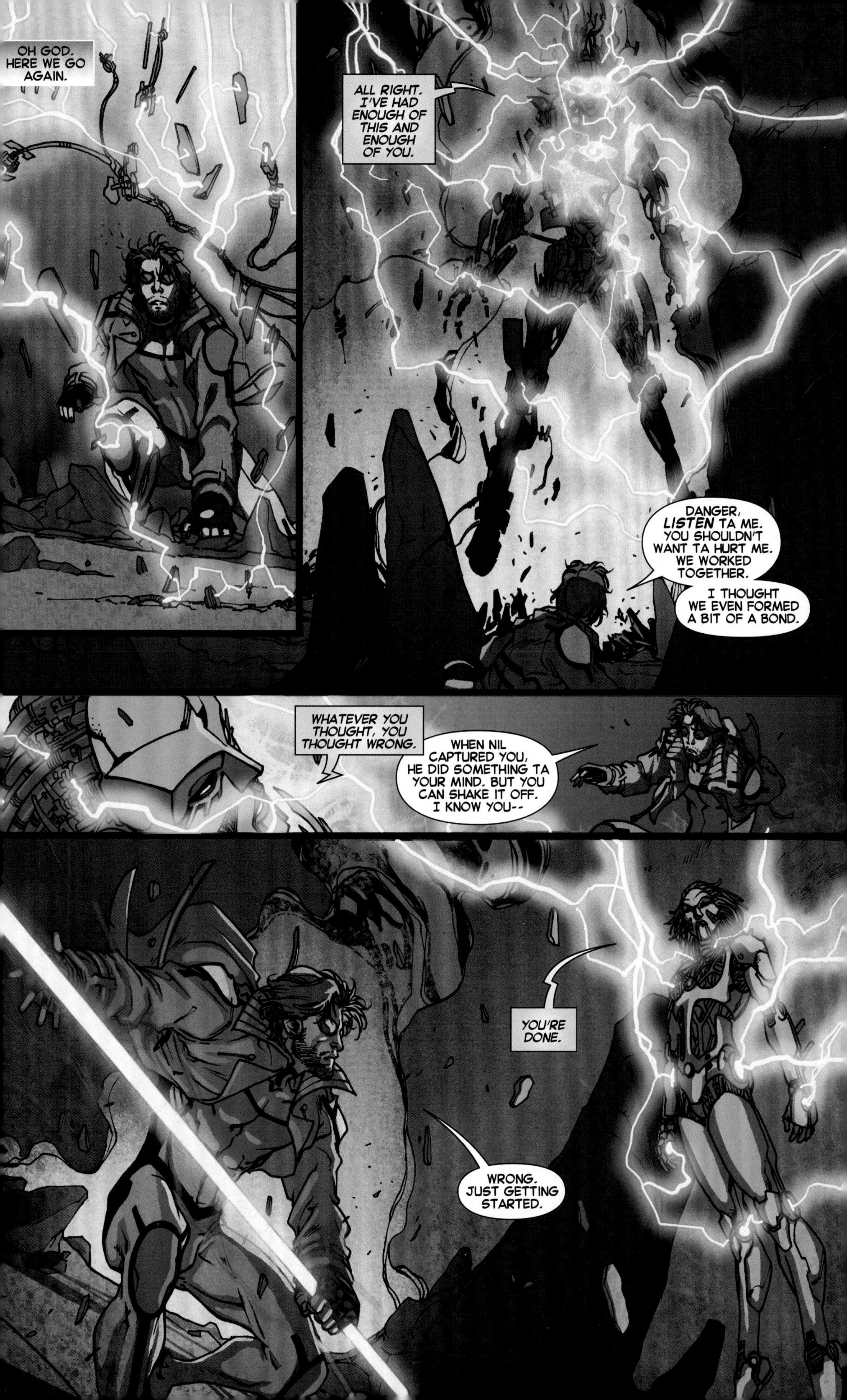
OH GOD. HERE WE GO AGAIN.
ALL RIGHT. I'VE HAD ENOUGH OF THIS AND ENOUGH OF YOU.
DANGER, LISTEN TA ME. YOU SHOULDN'T WANT TA HURT ME. WE WORKED TOGETHER.
I THOUGHT WE EVEN FORMED A BIT OF A BOND.
WHATEVER YOU THOUGHT, YOU THOUGHT WRONG.
WHEN NIL CAPTURED YOU, HE DID SOMETHING TA YOUR MIND. BUT YOU CAN SHAKE IT OFF. I KNOW YOU--
YOU'RE DONE.
WRONG. JUST GETTING STARTED.

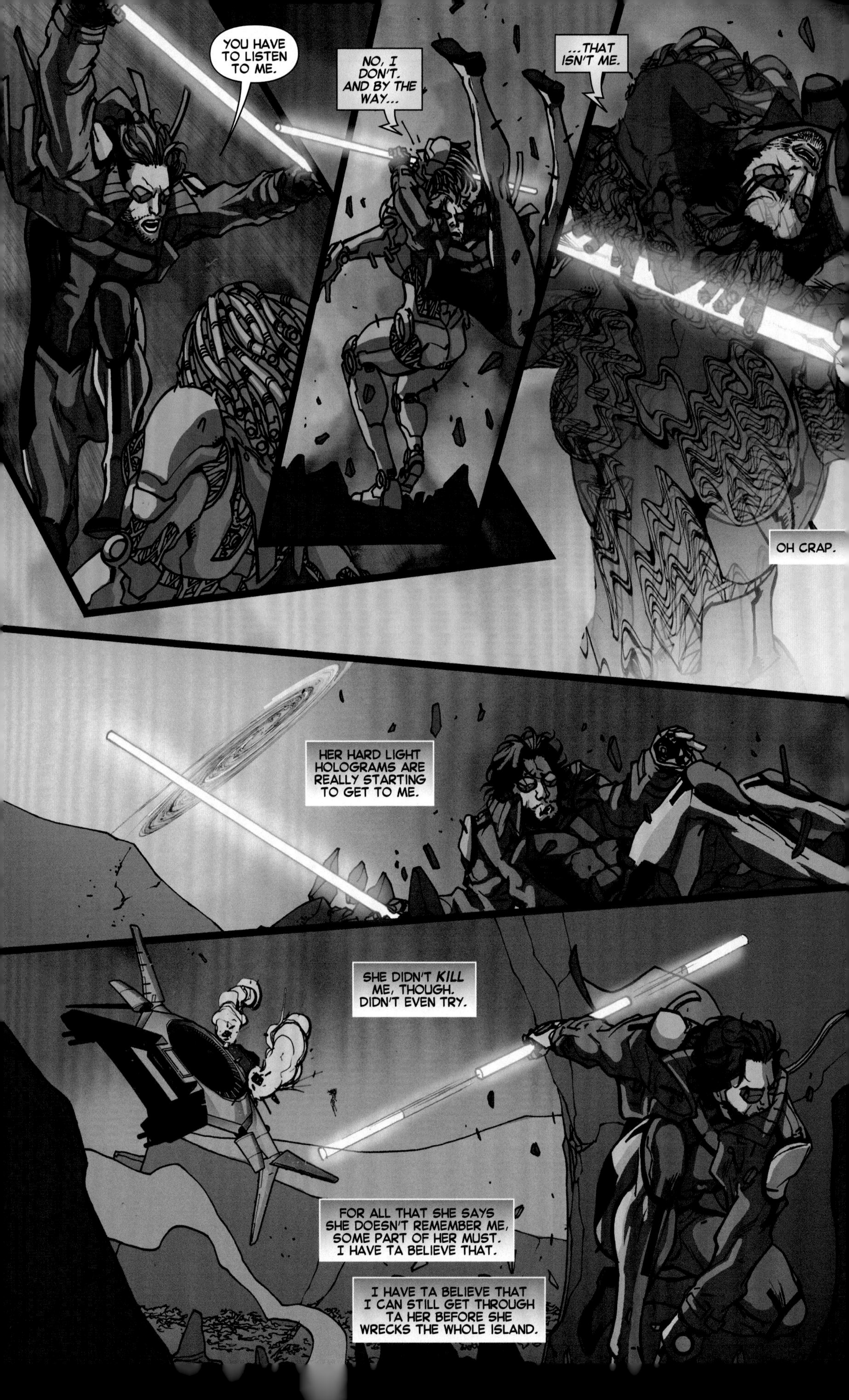

YOU HAVE TO LISTEN TO ME.
NO, I DON'T. AND BY THE WAY...
...THAT ISN'T ME.
OH CRAP.
HER HARD LIGHT HOLOGRAMS ARE REALLY STARTING TO GET TO ME.
SHE DIDN'T KILL ME, THOUGH. DIDN'T EVEN TRY.
FOR ALL THAT SHE SAYS SHE DOESN'T REMEMBER ME, SOME PART OF HER MUST. I HAVE TA BELIEVE THAT.
I HAVE TA BELIEVE THAT I CAN STILL GET THROUGH TA HER BEFORE SHE WRECKS THE WHOLE ISLAND.

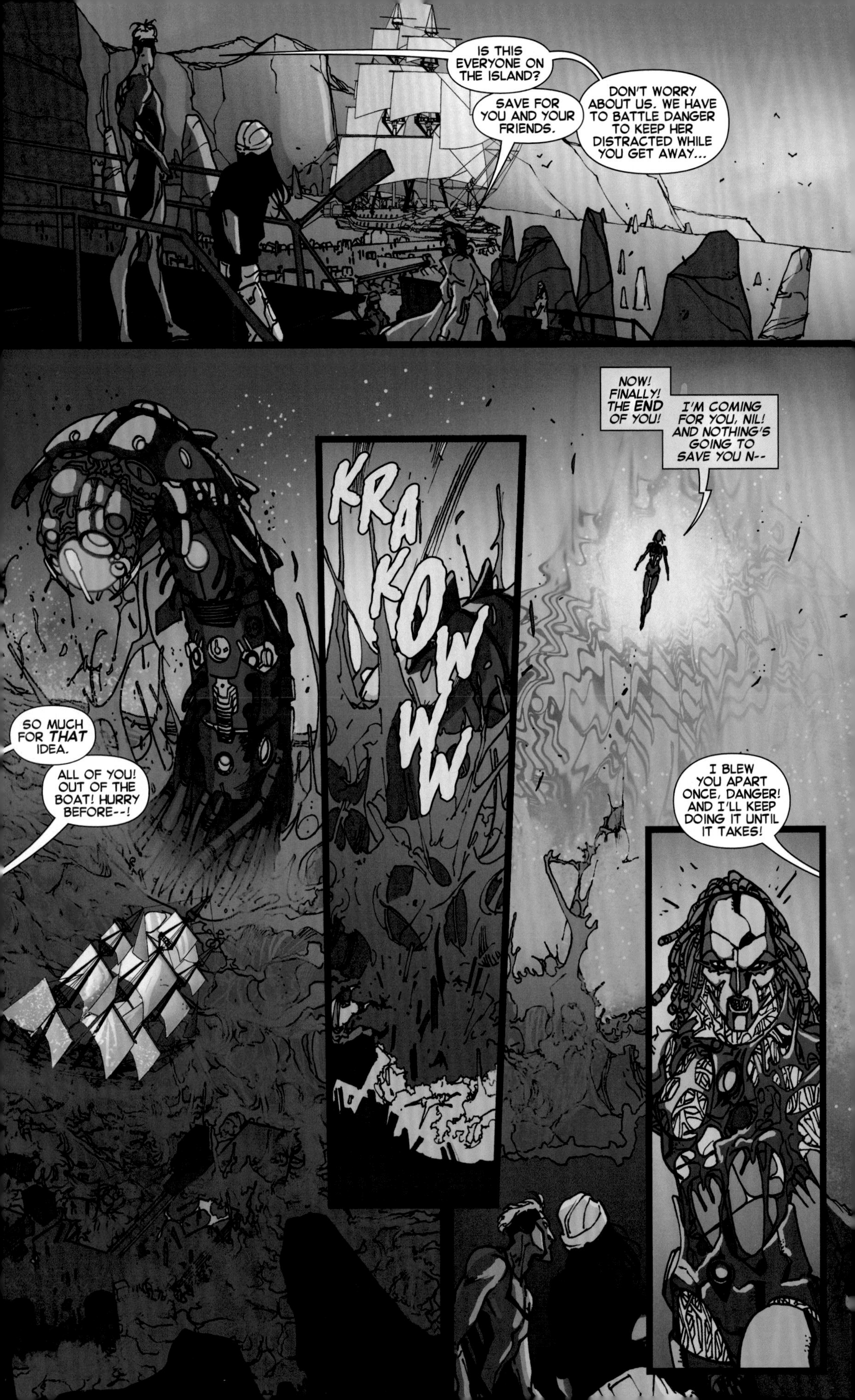
IS THIS EVERYONE ON THE ISLAND?
SAVE FOR YOU AND YOUR FRIENDS.
DON'T WORRY ABOUT US. WE HAVE TO BATTLE DANGER TO KEEP HER DISTRACTED WHILE YOU GET AWAY...
NOW! FINALLY! THE END OF YOU!
I'M COMING FOR YOU, NIL! AND NOTHING'S GOING TO SAVE YOU N--
KRAKOWWW
SO MUCH FOR THAT IDEA.
ALL OF YOU! OUT OF THE BOAT! HURRY BEFORE--!
I BLEW YOU APART ONCE, DANGER! AND I'LL KEEP DOING IT UNTIL IT TAKES!

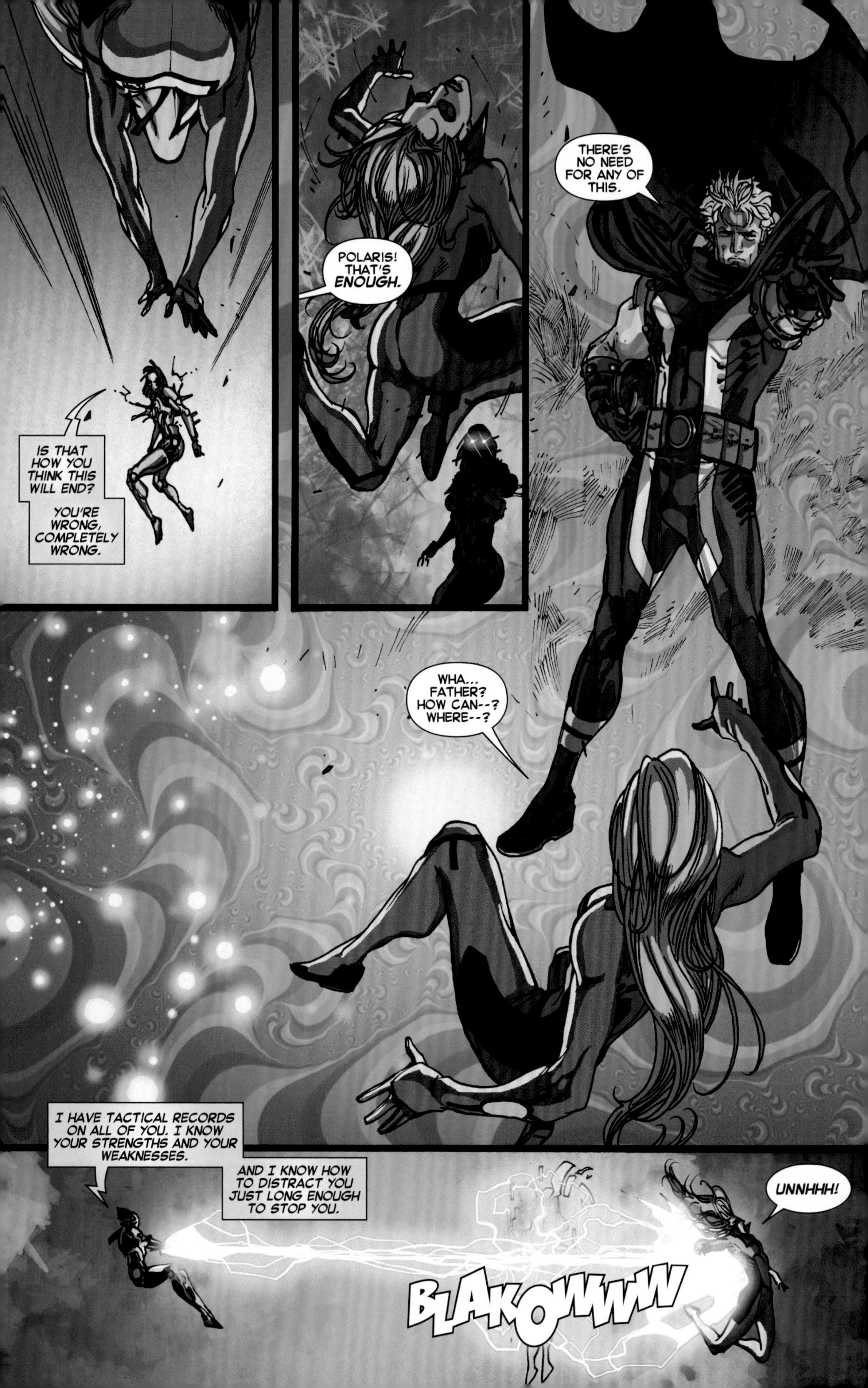

IS THAT HOW YOU THINK THIS WILL END?
YOU'RE WRONG, COMPLETELY WRONG.
POLARIS! THAT'S ENOUGH.
THERE'S NO NEED FOR ANY OF THIS.
WHA... FATHER? HOW CAN--? WHERE--?
I HAVE TACTICAL RECORDS ON ALL OF YOU. I KNOW YOUR STRENGTHS AND YOUR WEAKNESSES.
AND I KNOW HOW TO DISTRACT YOU JUST LONG ENOUGH TO STOP YOU.
UNNHHH!
BLAKOWWWW

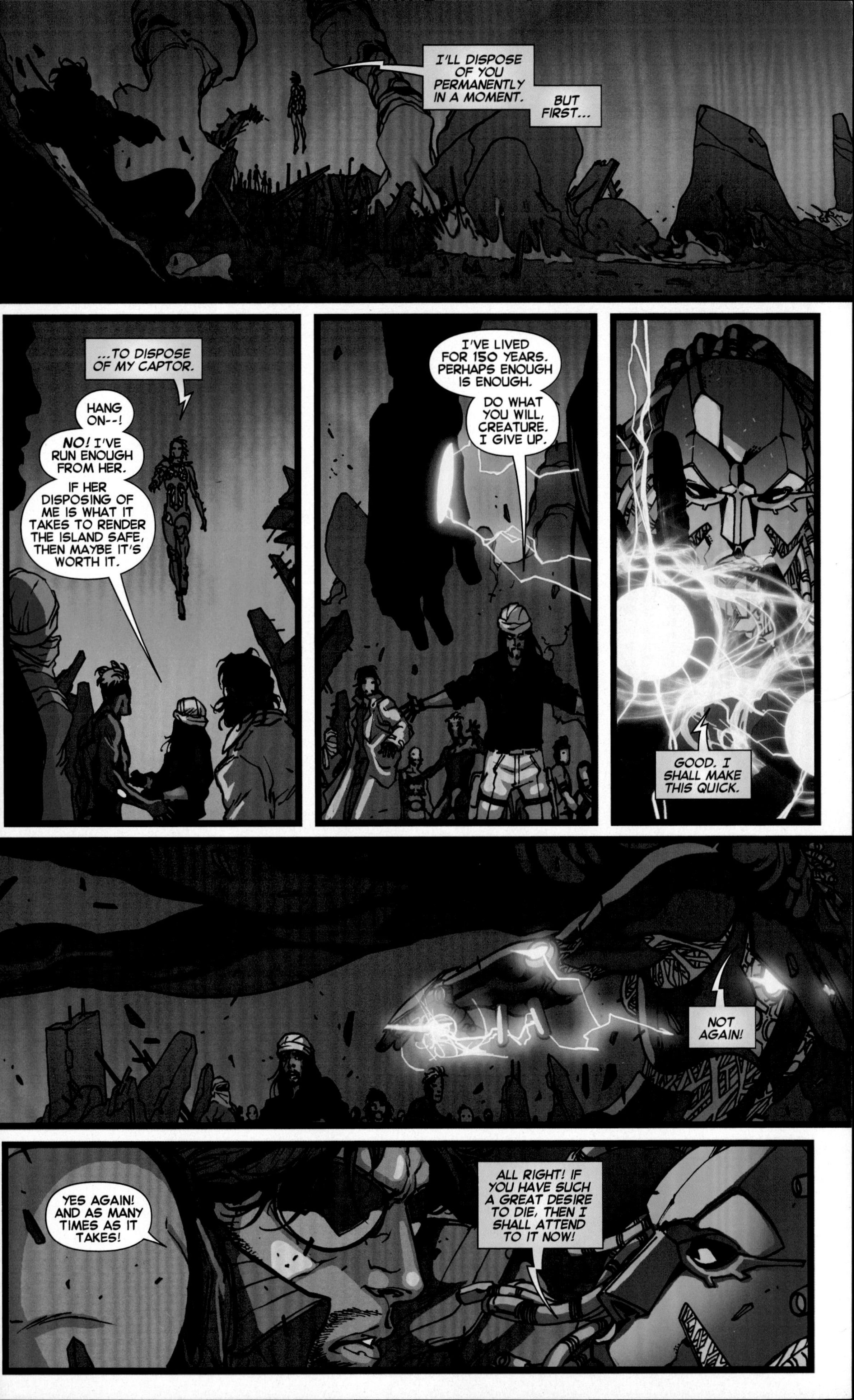
I'LL DISPOSE OF YOU PERMANENTLY IN A MOMENT.
BUT FIRST...
...TO DISPOSE OF MY CAPTOR.
HANG ON--!
NO! I'VE RUN ENOUGH FROM HER.
IF HER DISPOSING OF ME IS WHAT IT TAKES TO RENDER THE ISLAND SAFE, THEN MAYBE IT'S WORTH IT.
I'VE LIVED FOR 150 YEARS. PERHAPS ENOUGH IS ENOUGH.
DO WHAT YOU WILL, CREATURE. I GIVE UP.
GOOD. I SHALL MAKE THIS QUICK.
NOT AGAIN!
YES AGAIN! AND AS MANY TIMES AS IT TAKES!
ALL RIGHT! IF YOU HAVE SUCH A GREAT DESIRE TO DIE, THEN I SHALL ATTEND TO IT NOW!

AND I DO THE ONLY THING I CAN THINK OF.

WE'VE NEVER HAD ANY SORT OF ROMANTIC CONNECTION. HELL, SHE'S THE LIVING INCARNATION OF THE DANGER ROOM: I DOUBT SHE COULD.

BUT STILL, IT JUST SEEMS THE THING TA DO.

WHAT THE--?

HUNH.

OKAY. WASN'T EXPECTING THAT.

G-GAMBIT?

YEAH.

GAMBIT?

STILL YEAH.

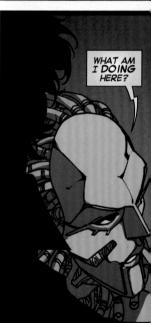

WHAT AM I DOING HERE?

WELL, YOU WERE--

OH. RIGHT.

SHUT UP.

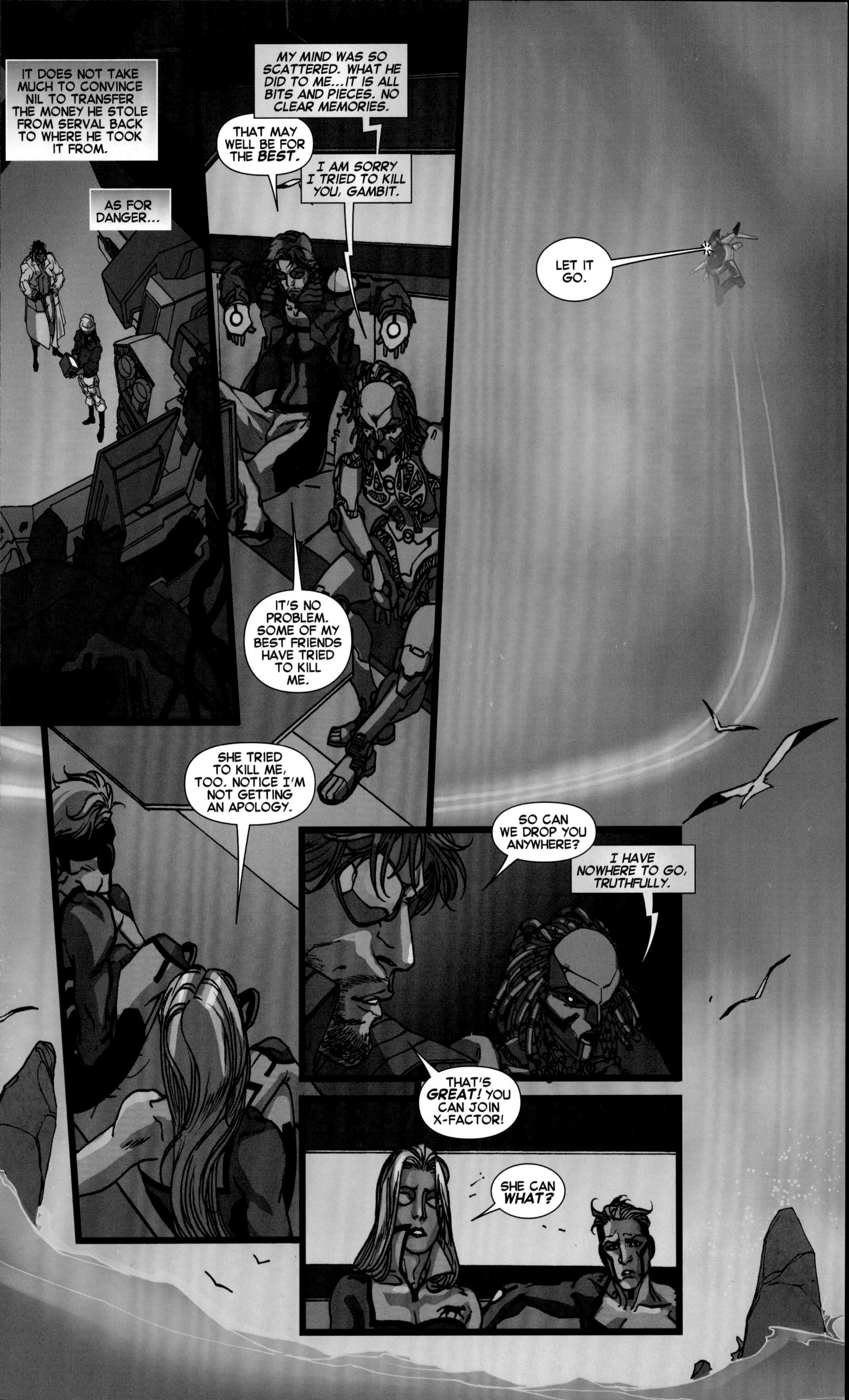
IT DOES NOT TAKE MUCH TO CONVINCE NIL TO TRANSFER THE MONEY HE STOLE FROM SERVAL BACK TO WHERE HE TOOK IT FROM.
AS FOR DANGER...
MY MIND WAS SO SCATTERED. WHAT HE DID TO ME...IT IS ALL BITS AND PIECES. NO CLEAR MEMORIES.
THAT MAY WELL BE FOR THE BEST.
I AM SORRY I TRIED TO KILL YOU, GAMBIT.
IT'S NO PROBLEM. SOME OF MY BEST FRIENDS HAVE TRIED TO KILL ME.
LET IT GO.
SHE TRIED TO KILL ME, TOO. NOTICE I'M NOT GETTING AN APOLOGY.
SO CAN WE DROP YOU ANYWHERE?
I HAVE NOWHERE TO GO, TRUTHFULLY.
THAT'S GREAT! YOU CAN JOIN X-FACTOR!
SHE CAN WHAT?

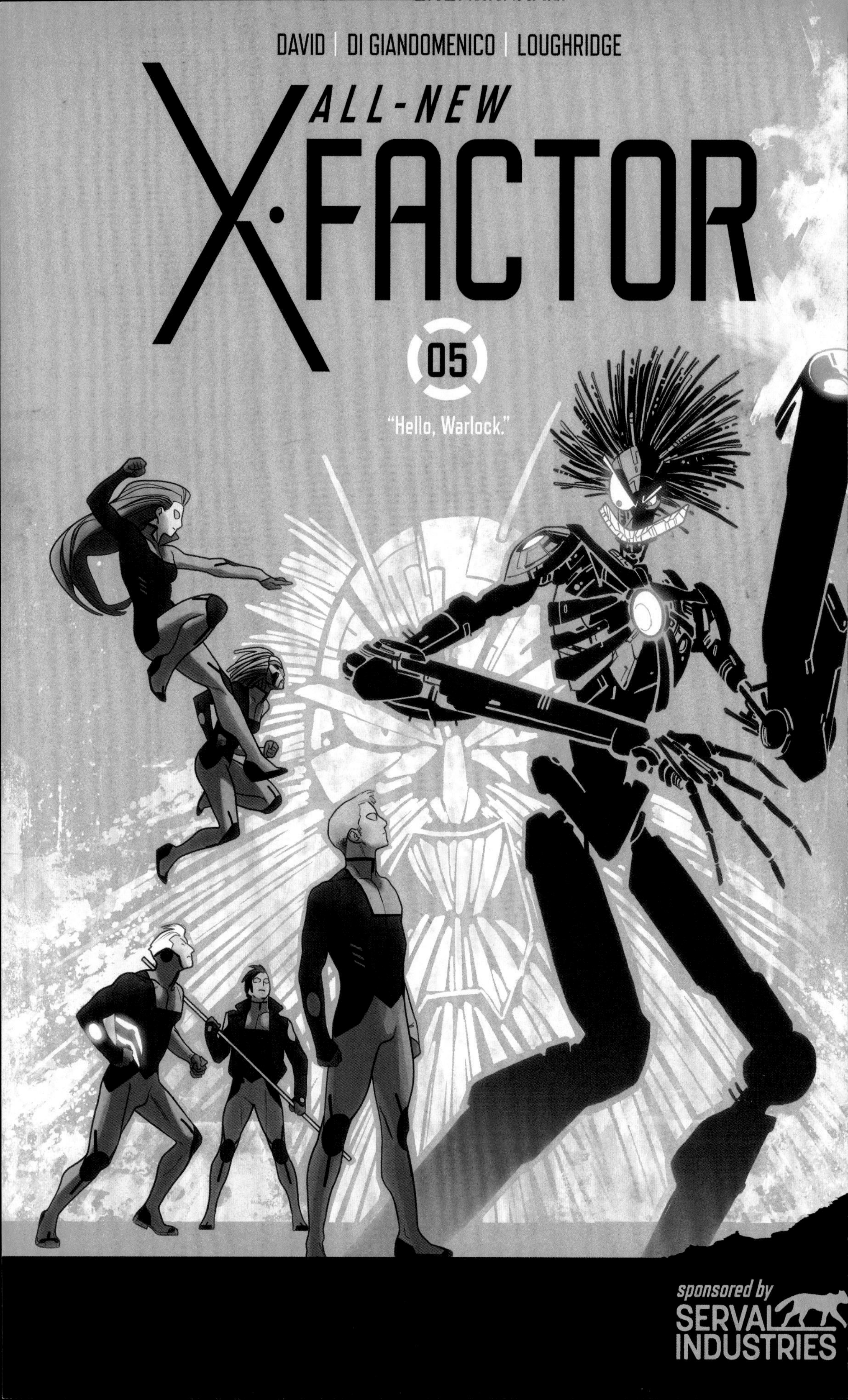
DAVID | DI GIANDOMENICO | LOUGHRIDGE
ALL-NEW
X-FACTOR
05
"Hello, Warlock."
sponsored by
SERVAL
INDUSTRIES

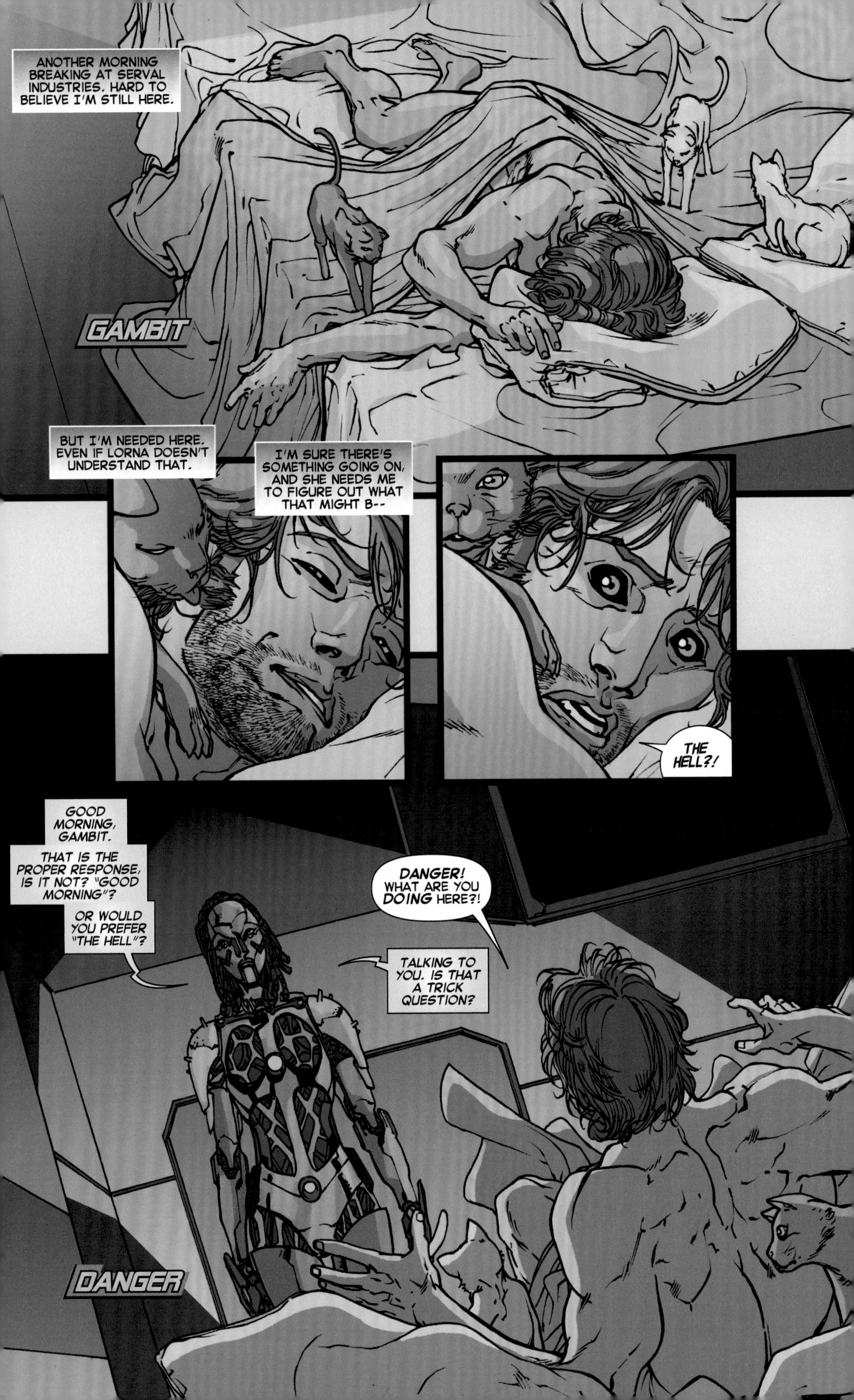
ANOTHER MORNING BREAKING AT SERVAL INDUSTRIES. HARD TO BELIEVE I'M STILL HERE.
GAMBIT
BUT I'M NEEDED HERE. EVEN IF LORNA DOESN'T UNDERSTAND THAT.
I'M SURE THERE'S SOMETHING GOING ON, AND SHE NEEDS ME TO FIGURE OUT WHAT THAT MIGHT B--
THE HELL?!
GOOD MORNING, GAMBIT.
THAT IS THE PROPER RESPONSE, IS IT NOT? "GOOD MORNING"?
OR WOULD YOU PREFER "THE HELL"?
DANGER! WHAT ARE YOU DOING HERE?!
TALKING TO YOU. IS THAT A TRICK QUESTION?
DANGER

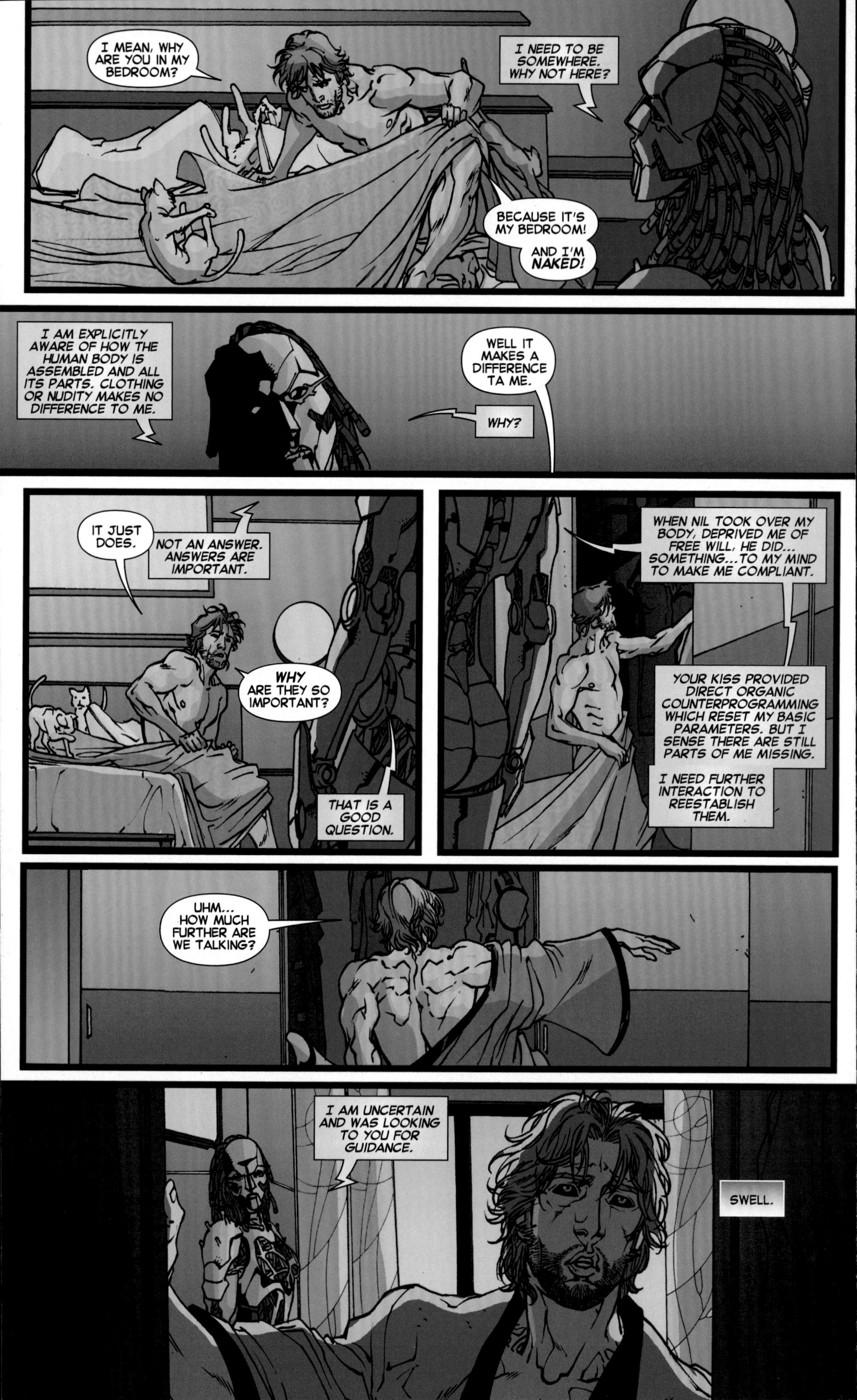
I MEAN, WHY ARE YOU IN MY BEDROOM?
I NEED TO BE SOMEWHERE. WHY NOT HERE?
BECAUSE IT'S MY BEDROOM!
AND I'M NAKED!
I AM EXPLICITLY AWARE OF HOW THE HUMAN BODY IS ASSEMBLED AND ALL ITS PARTS. CLOTHING OR NUDITY MAKES NO DIFFERENCE TO ME.
WELL IT MAKES A DIFFERENCE TA ME.
WHY?
IT JUST DOES.
NOT AN ANSWER. ANSWERS ARE IMPORTANT.
WHY ARE THEY SO IMPORTANT?
THAT IS A GOOD QUESTION.
WHEN NIL TOOK OVER MY BODY, DEPRIVED ME OF FREE WILL, HE DID... SOMETHING...TO MY MIND TO MAKE ME COMPLIANT.
YOUR KISS PROVIDED DIRECT ORGANIC COUNTERPROGRAMMING WHICH RESET MY BASIC PARAMETERS. BUT I SENSE THERE ARE STILL PARTS OF ME MISSING.
I NEED FURTHER INTERACTION TO REESTABLISH THEM.
UHM... HOW MUCH FURTHER ARE WE TALKING?
I AM UNCERTAIN AND WAS LOOKING TO YOU FOR GUIDANCE.
SWELL.

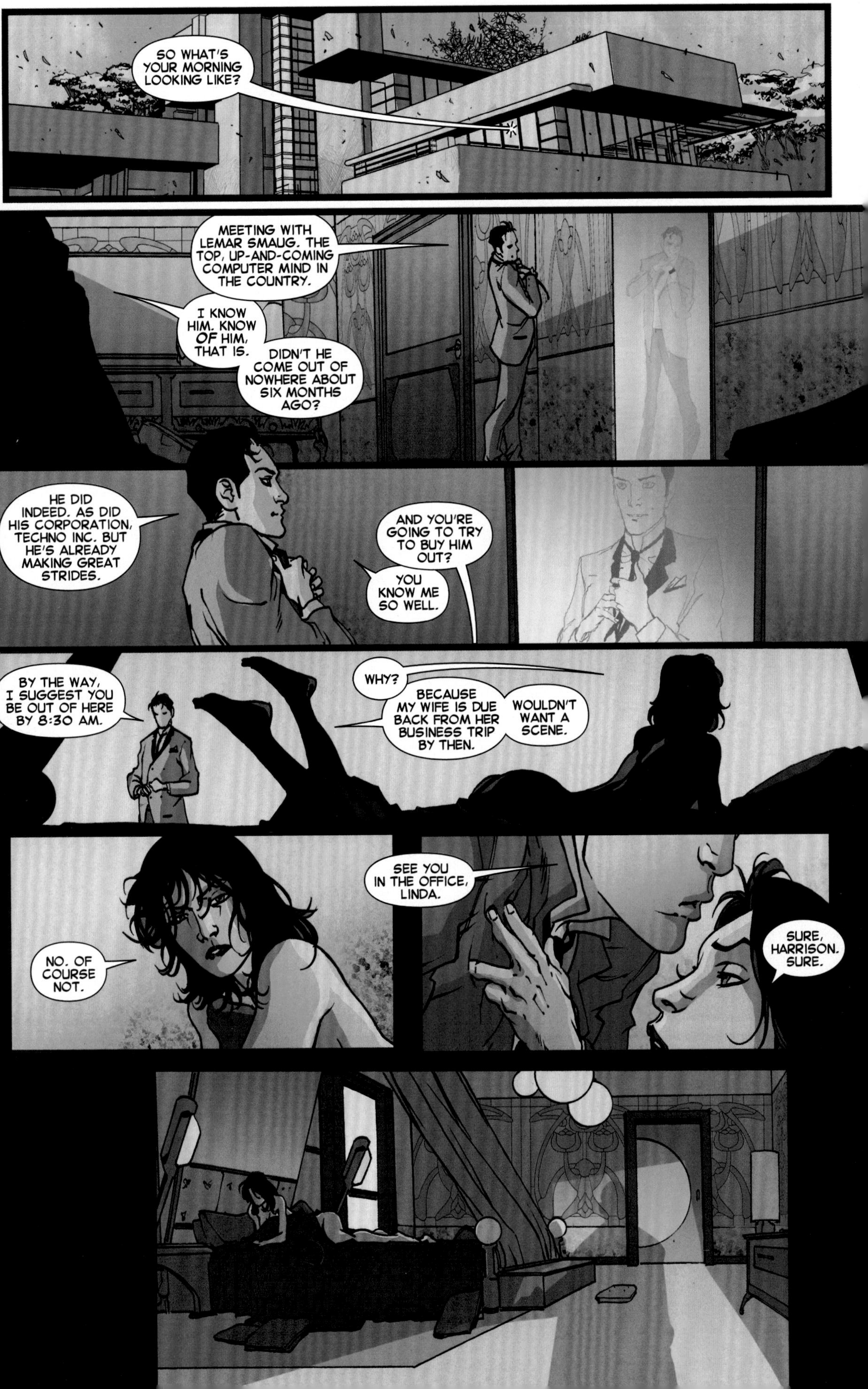
SO WHAT'S YOUR MORNING LOOKING LIKE?
MEETING WITH LEMAR SMAUG. THE TOP, UP-AND-COMING COMPUTER MIND IN THE COUNTRY.
I KNOW HIM. KNOW OF HIM, THAT IS.
DIDN'T HE COME OUT OF NOWHERE ABOUT SIX MONTHS AGO?
HE DID INDEED. AS DID HIS CORPORATION, TECHNO INC. BUT HE'S ALREADY MAKING GREAT STRIDES.
AND YOU'RE GOING TO TRY TO BUY HIM OUT?
YOU KNOW ME SO WELL.
BY THE WAY, I SUGGEST YOU BE OUT OF HERE BY 8:30 AM.
WHY?
BECAUSE MY WIFE IS DUE BACK FROM HER BUSINESS TRIP BY THEN.
WOULDN'T WANT A SCENE.
NO. OF COURSE NOT.
SEE YOU IN THE OFFICE, LINDA.
SURE, HARRISON. SURE.

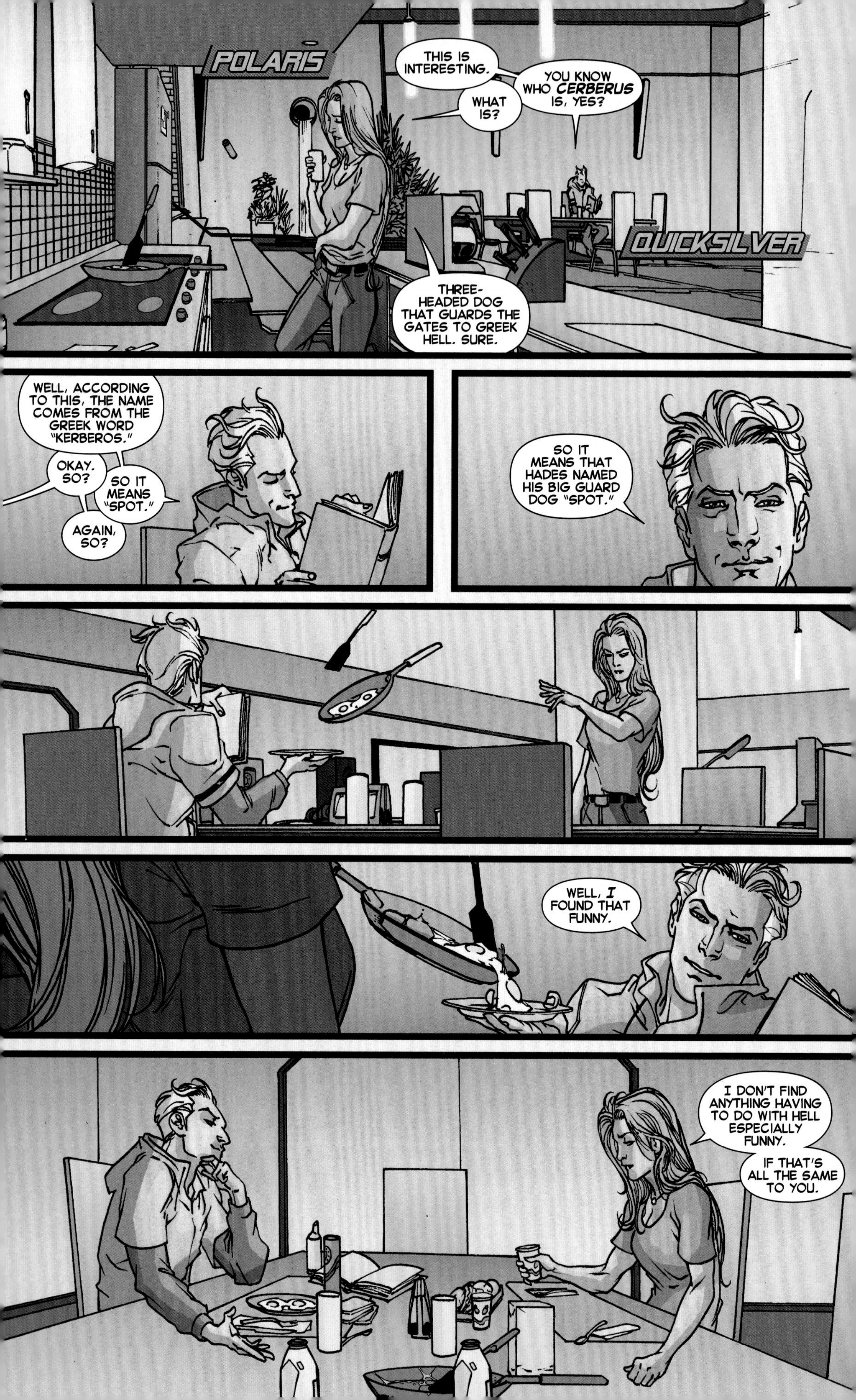
POLARIS
THIS IS INTERESTING.
WHAT IS?
YOU KNOW WHO CERBERUS IS, YES?
QUICKSILVER
THREE-HEADED DOG THAT GUARDS THE GATES TO GREEK HELL. SURE.
WELL, ACCORDING TO THIS, THE NAME COMES FROM THE GREEK WORD "KERBEROS."
OKAY. SO?
SO IT MEANS "SPOT."
AGAIN, SO?
SO IT MEANS THAT HADES NAMED HIS BIG GUARD DOG "SPOT."
WELL, I FOUND THAT FUNNY.
I DON'T FIND ANYTHING HAVING TO DO WITH HELL ESPECIALLY FUNNY.
IF THAT'S ALL THE SAME TO YOU.

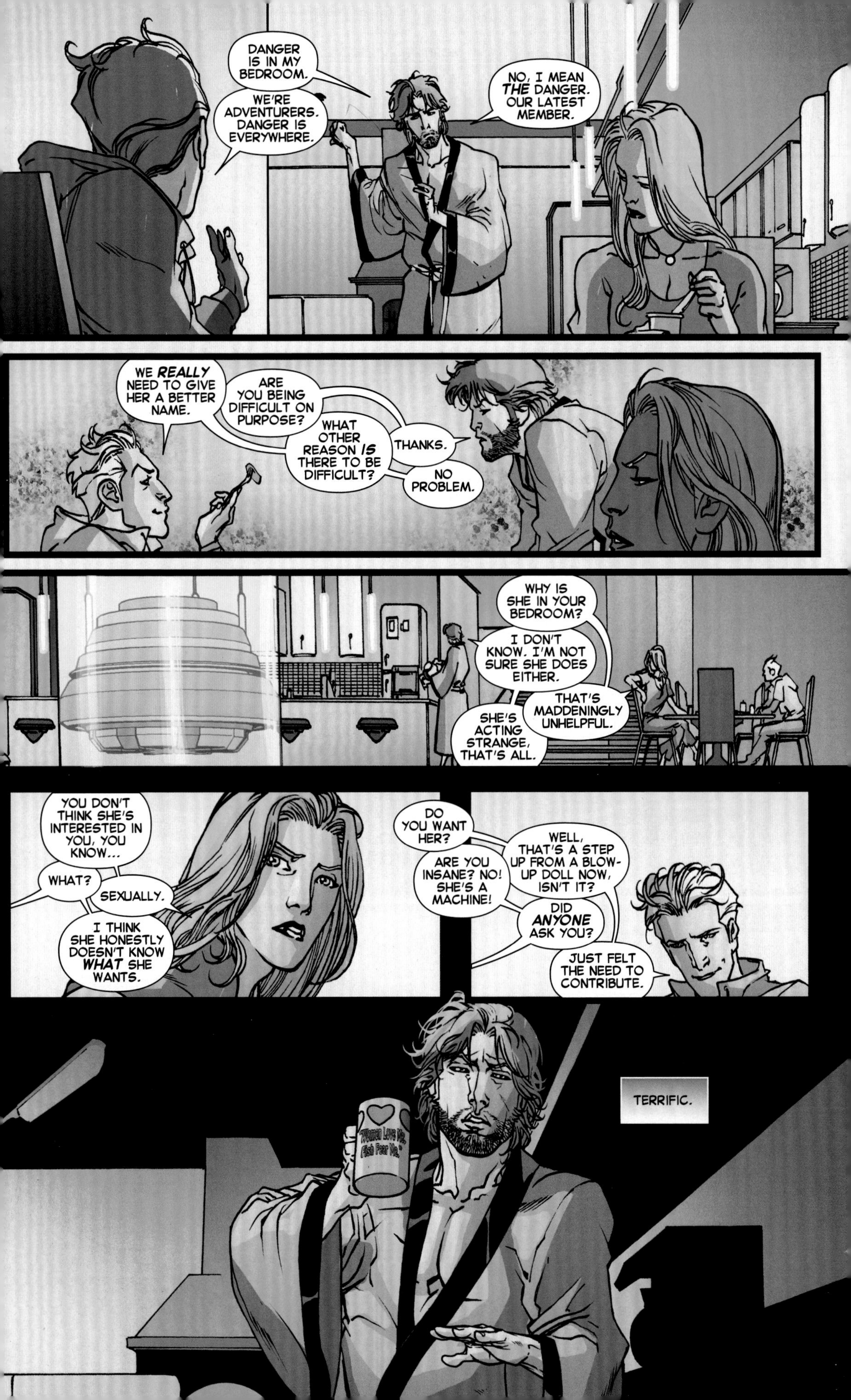
DANGER IS IN MY BEDROOM.
WE'RE ADVENTURERS. DANGER IS EVERYWHERE.
NO, I MEAN THE DANGER. OUR LATEST MEMBER.
WE REALLY NEED TO GIVE HER A BETTER NAME.
ARE YOU BEING DIFFICULT ON PURPOSE?
WHAT OTHER REASON IS THERE TO BE DIFFICULT?
THANKS.
NO PROBLEM.
WHY IS SHE IN YOUR BEDROOM?
I DON'T KNOW. I'M NOT SURE SHE DOES EITHER.
THAT'S MADDENINGLY UNHELPFUL.
SHE'S ACTING STRANGE, THAT'S ALL.
YOU DON'T THINK SHE'S INTERESTED IN YOU, YOU KNOW...
WHAT?
SEXUALLY.
I THINK SHE HONESTLY DOESN'T KNOW WHAT SHE WANTS.
DO YOU WANT HER?
ARE YOU INSANE? NO! SHE'S A MACHINE!
WELL, THAT'S A STEP UP FROM A BLOW-UP DOLL NOW, ISN'T IT?
DID ANYONE ASK YOU?
JUST FELT THE NEED TO CONTRIBUTE.
"Women Love Me, Fish Fear Me."
TERRIFIC.

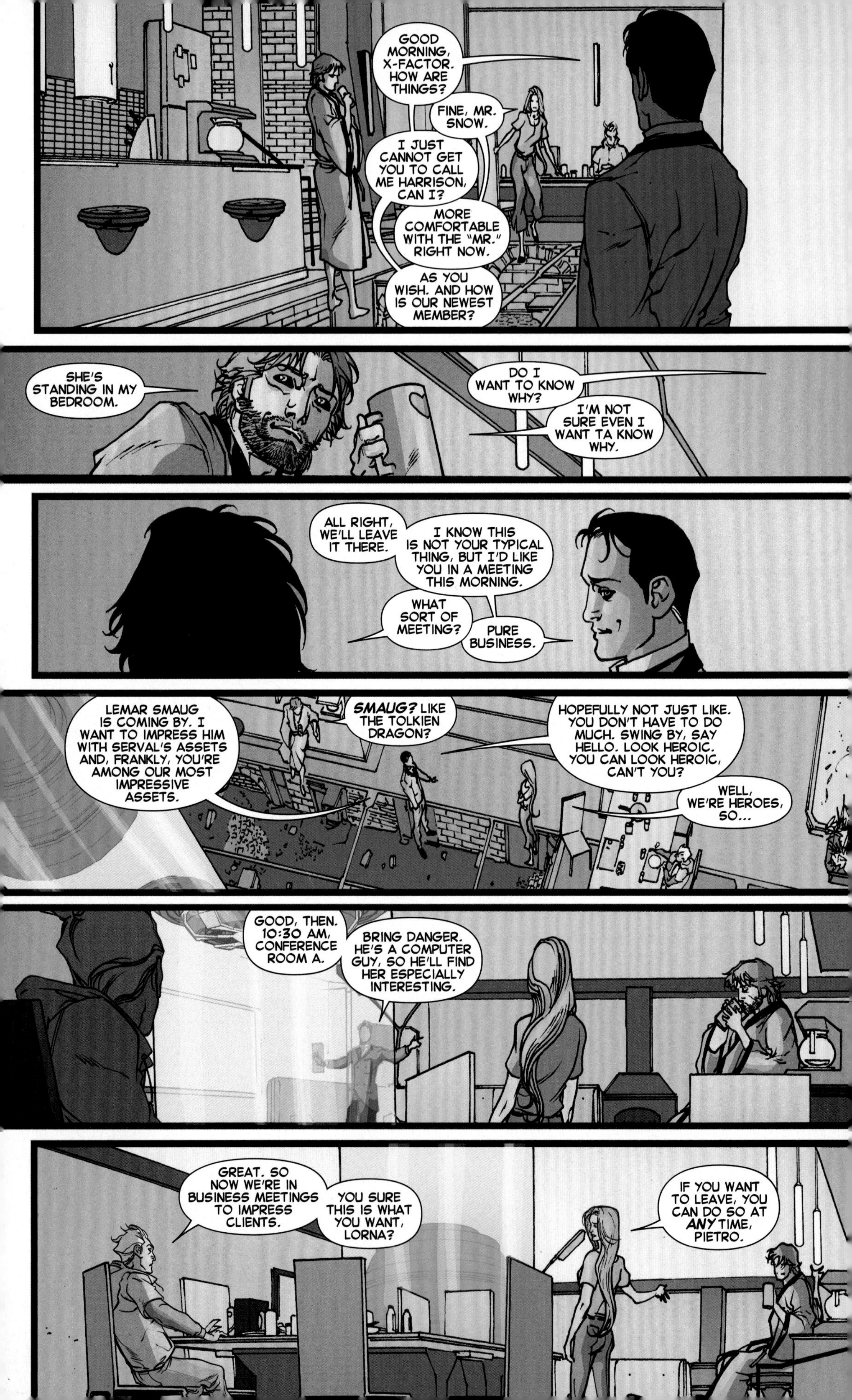
GOOD MORNING, X-FACTOR. HOW ARE THINGS?
FINE, MR. SNOW.
I JUST CANNOT GET YOU TO CALL ME HARRISON, CAN I?
MORE COMFORTABLE WITH THE "MR." RIGHT NOW.
AS YOU WISH. AND HOW IS OUR NEWEST MEMBER?
SHE'S STANDING IN MY BEDROOM.
DO I WANT TO KNOW WHY?
I'M NOT SURE EVEN I WANT TA KNOW WHY.
ALL RIGHT, WE'LL LEAVE IT THERE.
I KNOW THIS IS NOT YOUR TYPICAL THING, BUT I'D LIKE YOU IN A MEETING THIS MORNING.
WHAT SORT OF MEETING?
PURE BUSINESS.
LEMAR SMAUG IS COMING BY. I WANT TO IMPRESS HIM WITH SERVAL'S ASSETS AND, FRANKLY, YOU'RE AMONG OUR MOST IMPRESSIVE ASSETS.
SMAUG? LIKE THE TOLKIEN DRAGON?
HOPEFULLY NOT JUST LIKE. YOU DON'T HAVE TO DO MUCH. SWING BY, SAY HELLO. LOOK HEROIC. YOU CAN LOOK HEROIC, CAN'T YOU?
WELL, WE'RE HEROES, SO...
GOOD, THEN. 10:30 AM, CONFERENCE ROOM A.
BRING DANGER. HE'S A COMPUTER GUY, SO HE'LL FIND HER ESPECIALLY INTERESTING.
GREAT. SO NOW WE'RE IN BUSINESS MEETINGS TO IMPRESS CLIENTS.
YOU SURE THIS IS WHAT YOU WANT, LORNA?
IF YOU WANT TO LEAVE, YOU CAN DO SO AT ANY TIME, PIETRO.

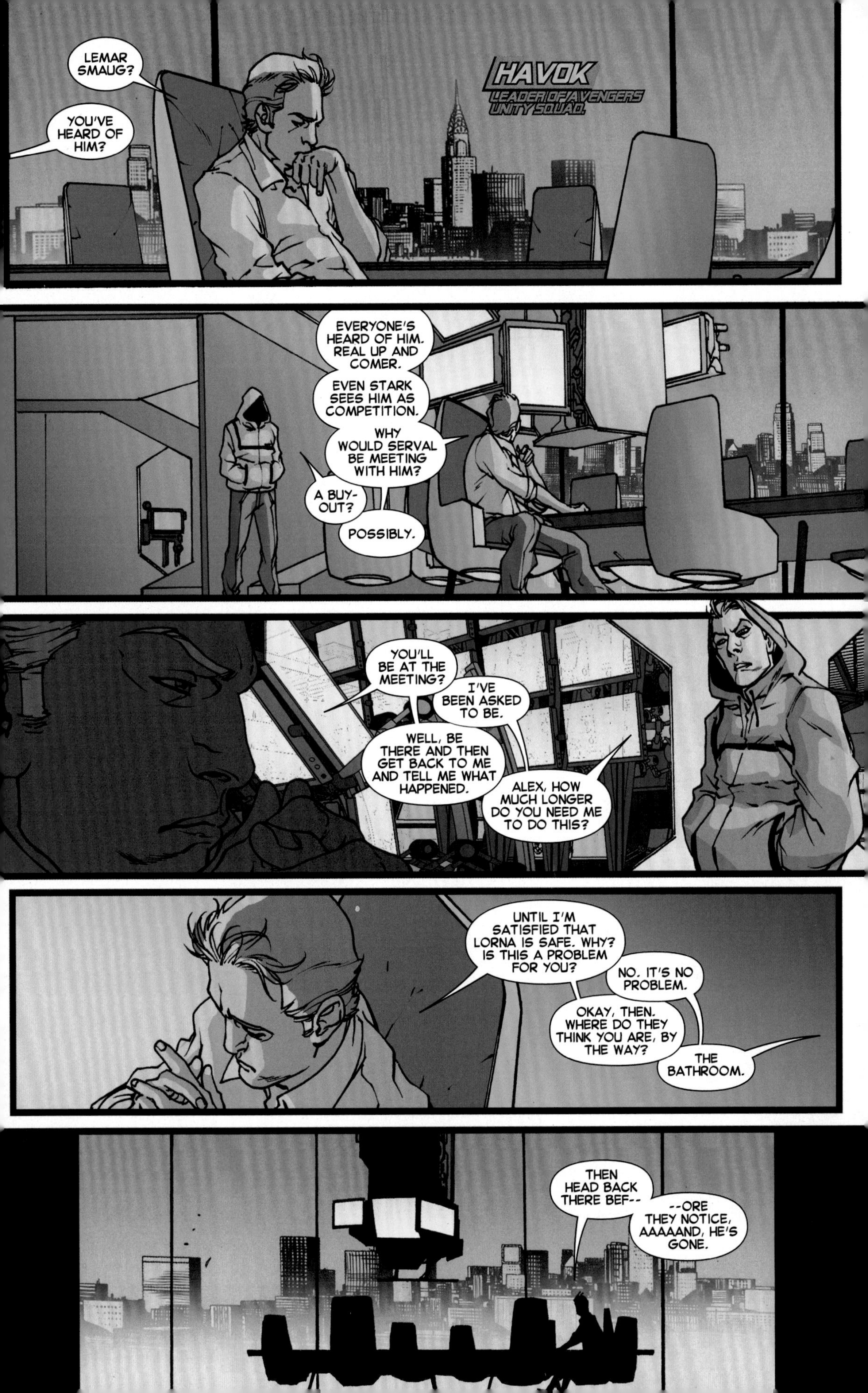
LEMAR SMAUG?
YOU'VE HEARD OF HIM?
HAVOK
LEADER OF AVENGERS UNITY SQUAD.
EVERYONE'S HEARD OF HIM. REAL UP AND COMER.
EVEN STARK SEES HIM AS COMPETITION.
WHY WOULD SERVAL BE MEETING WITH HIM?
A BUY-OUT?
POSSIBLY.
YOU'LL BE AT THE MEETING?
I'VE BEEN ASKED TO BE.
WELL, BE THERE AND THEN GET BACK TO ME AND TELL ME WHAT HAPPENED.
ALEX, HOW MUCH LONGER DO YOU NEED ME TO DO THIS?
UNTIL I'M SATISFIED THAT LORNA IS SAFE. WHY? IS THIS A PROBLEM FOR YOU?
NO. IT'S NO PROBLEM.
OKAY, THEN. WHERE DO THEY THINK YOU ARE, BY THE WAY?
THE BATHROOM.
THEN HEAD BACK THERE BEF--
--ORE THEY NOTICE, AAAAAND, HE'S GONE.

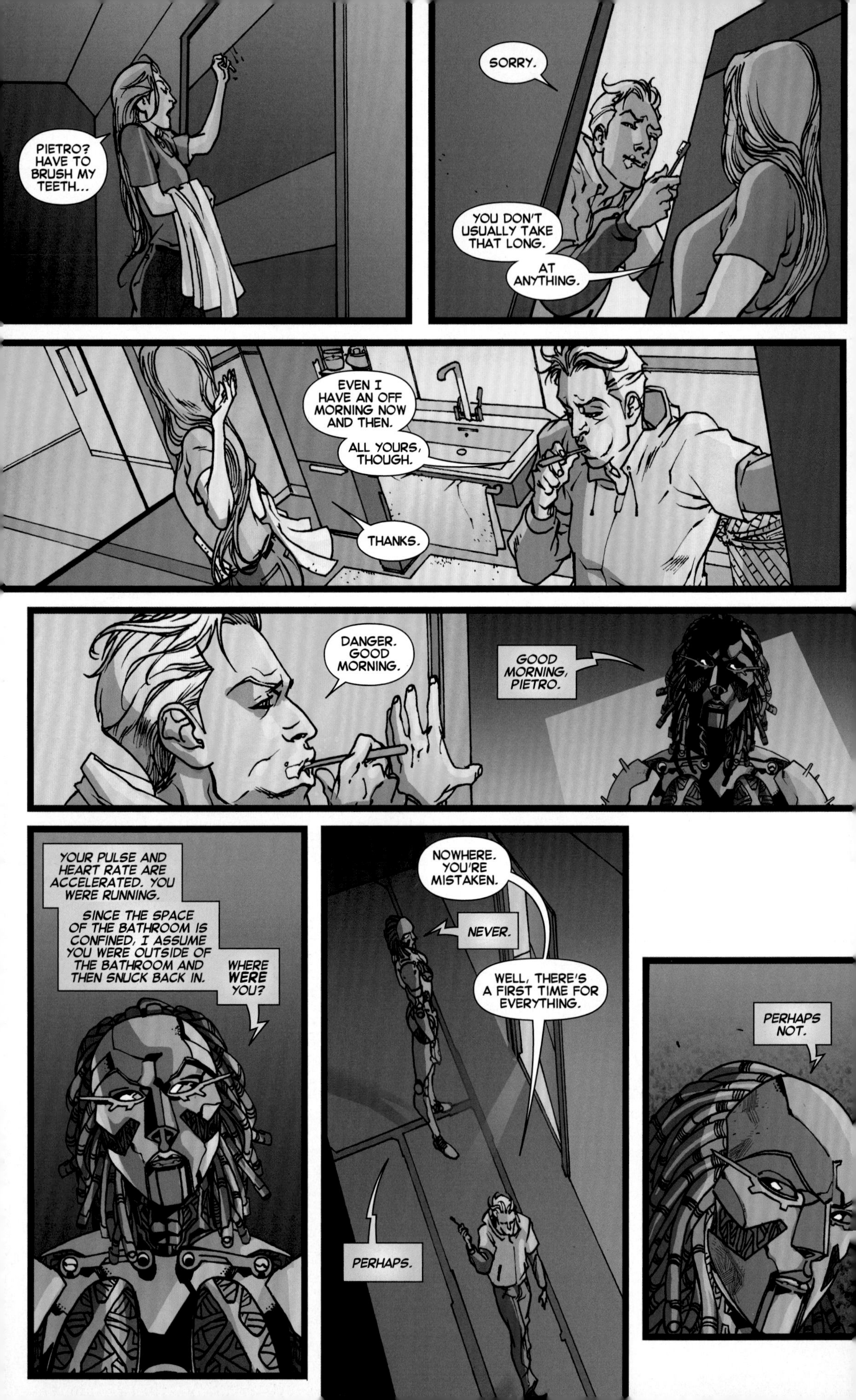

PIETRO? HAVE TO BRUSH MY TEETH...
SORRY.
YOU DON'T USUALLY TAKE THAT LONG.
AT ANYTHING.
EVEN I HAVE AN OFF MORNING NOW AND THEN.
ALL YOURS, THOUGH.
THANKS.
DANGER. GOOD MORNING.
GOOD MORNING, PIETRO.
YOUR PULSE AND HEART RATE ARE ACCELERATED. YOU WERE RUNNING.
SINCE THE SPACE OF THE BATHROOM IS CONFINED, I ASSUME YOU WERE OUTSIDE OF THE BATHROOM AND THEN SNUCK BACK IN.
WHERE WERE YOU?
NOWHERE. YOU'RE MISTAKEN.
NEVER.
WELL, THERE'S A FIRST TIME FOR EVERYTHING.
PERHAPS.
PERHAPS NOT.

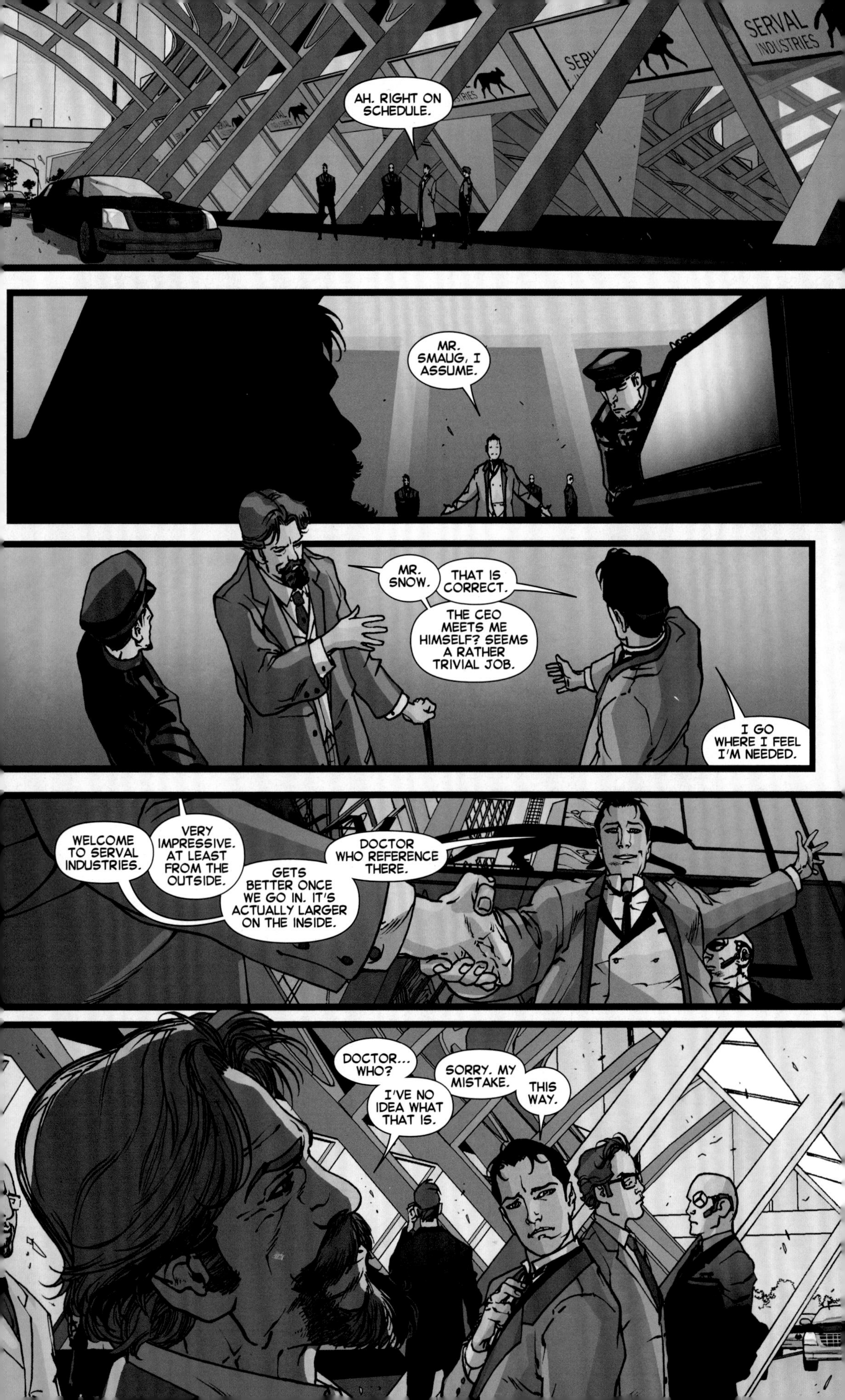
SERVAL INDUSTRIES
AH. RIGHT ON SCHEDULE.
MR. SMAUG, I ASSUME.
MR. SNOW.
THAT IS CORRECT.
THE CEO MEETS ME HIMSELF? SEEMS A RATHER TRIVIAL JOB.
I GO WHERE I FEEL I'M NEEDED.
WELCOME TO SERVAL INDUSTRIES.
VERY IMPRESSIVE. AT LEAST FROM THE OUTSIDE.
GETS BETTER ONCE WE GO IN. IT'S ACTUALLY LARGER ON THE INSIDE.
DOCTOR WHO REFERENCE THERE.
DOCTOR... WHO?
I'VE NO IDEA WHAT THAT IS.
SORRY. MY MISTAKE.
THIS WAY.

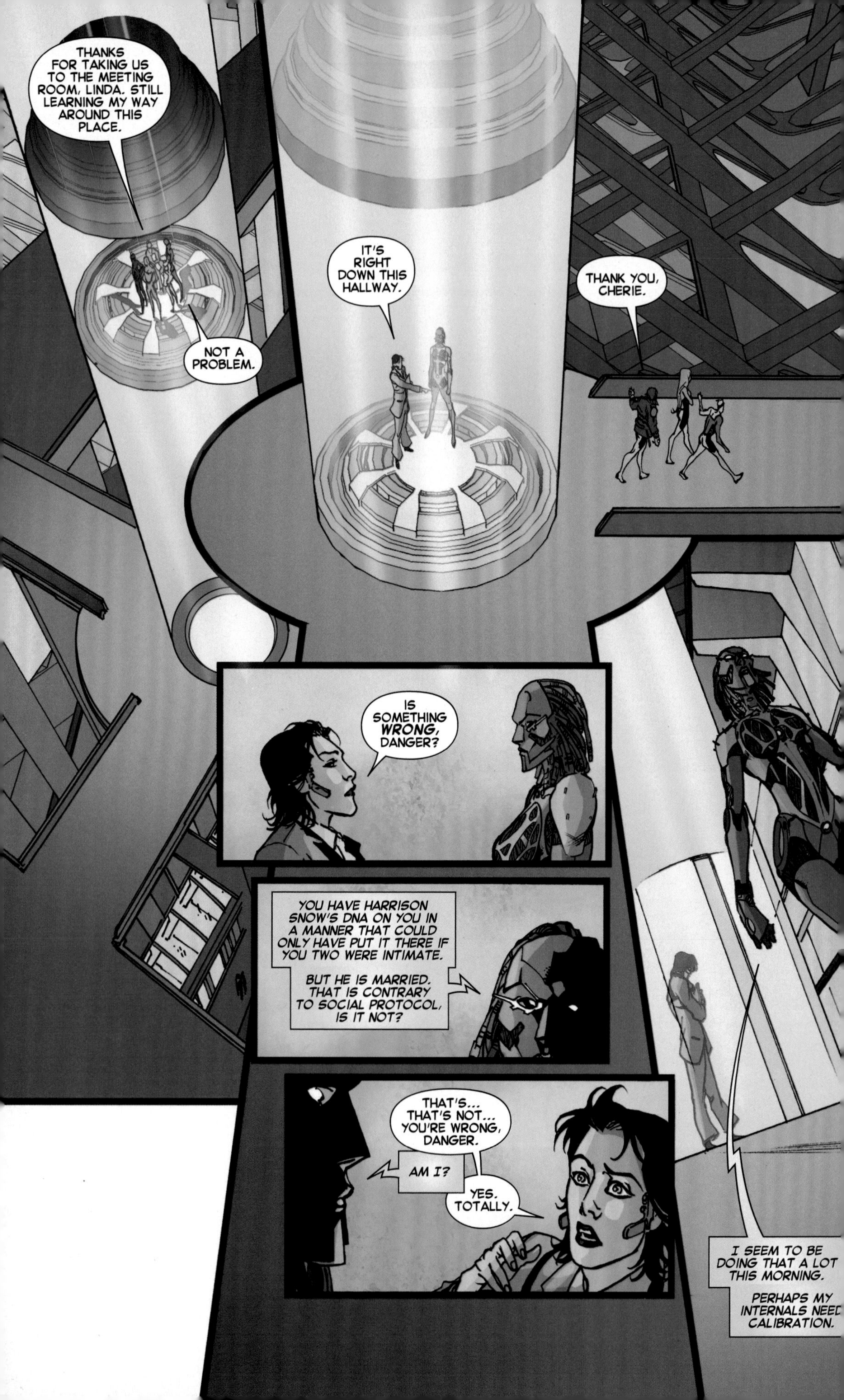
THANKS FOR TAKING US TO THE MEETING ROOM, LINDA. STILL LEARNING MY WAY AROUND THIS PLACE.
NOT A PROBLEM.
IT'S RIGHT DOWN THIS HALLWAY.
THANK YOU, CHERIE.
IS SOMETHING WRONG, DANGER?
YOU HAVE HARRISON SNOW'S DNA ON YOU IN A MANNER THAT COULD ONLY HAVE PUT IT THERE IF YOU TWO WERE INTIMATE.
BUT HE IS MARRIED. THAT IS CONTRARY TO SOCIAL PROTOCOL, IS IT NOT?
THAT'S... THAT'S NOT... YOU'RE WRONG, DANGER.
AM I?
YES. TOTALLY.
I SEEM TO BE DOING THAT A LOT THIS MORNING.
PERHAPS MY INTERNALS NEED CALIBRATION.

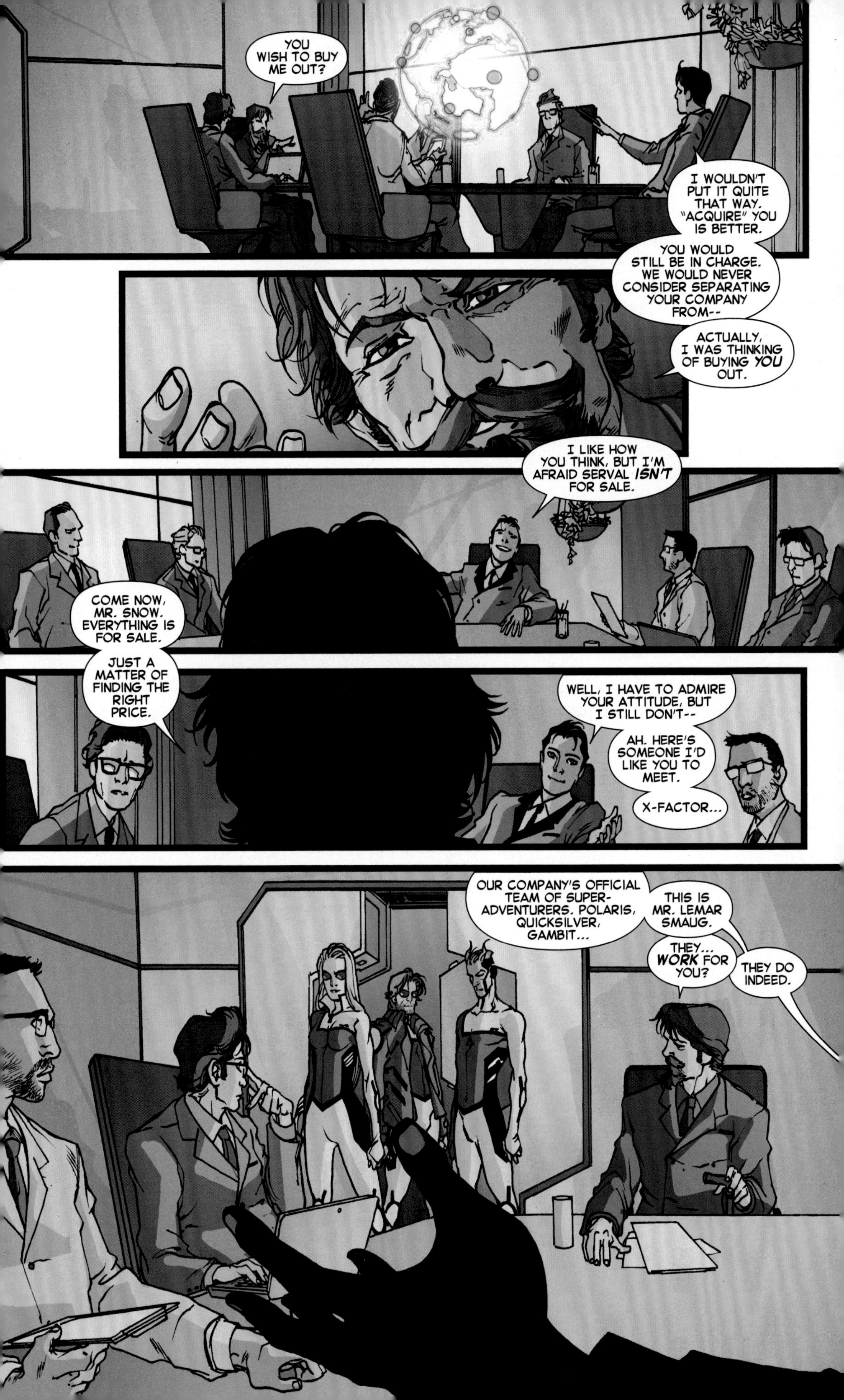
YOU WISH TO BUY ME OUT?
I WOULDN'T PUT IT QUITE THAT WAY. "ACQUIRE" YOU IS BETTER.
YOU WOULD STILL BE IN CHARGE. WE WOULD NEVER CONSIDER SEPARATING YOUR COMPANY FROM--
ACTUALLY, I WAS THINKING OF BUYING YOU OUT.
I LIKE HOW YOU THINK, BUT I'M AFRAID SERVAL ISN'T FOR SALE.
COME NOW, MR. SNOW. EVERYTHING IS FOR SALE.
JUST A MATTER OF FINDING THE RIGHT PRICE.
WELL, I HAVE TO ADMIRE YOUR ATTITUDE, BUT I STILL DON'T--
AH. HERE'S SOMEONE I'D LIKE YOU TO MEET.
X-FACTOR...
OUR COMPANY'S OFFICIAL TEAM OF SUPER-ADVENTURERS. POLARIS, QUICKSILVER, GAMBIT...
THIS IS MR. LEMAR SMAUG.
THEY... WORK FOR YOU?
THEY DO INDEED.

IT'S A PLEASURE, MR. SMAUG.

LEMAR, PLEASE.

I WAS NOT EXPECTING TO SEE ANY MUTANT SUPER HEROES HERE.

WELL, WE TEND TO POP UP WHEN LEAST EXPECTED.

OH, AND THIS IS OUR FOURTH MEMBER. DANGER.

STRICTLY SPEAKING, SHE'S NOT HUMAN, BUT THAT DOESN'T MEAN--

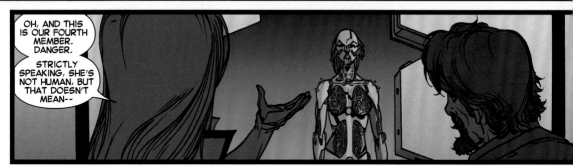

NEITHER IS HE.

WHAT? LOOK, DANGER, HE--

I'M AFRAID YOU'RE MISTAKEN.

YOUR BIOMETRIC READINGS ARE COMPLETELY WRONG.

YOU ARE NOT HUMAN. NOT REMOTELY.

THIS IS ABSURD!

I DO NOT HAVE TO STAND HERE AND ENDURE THIS SORT OF--

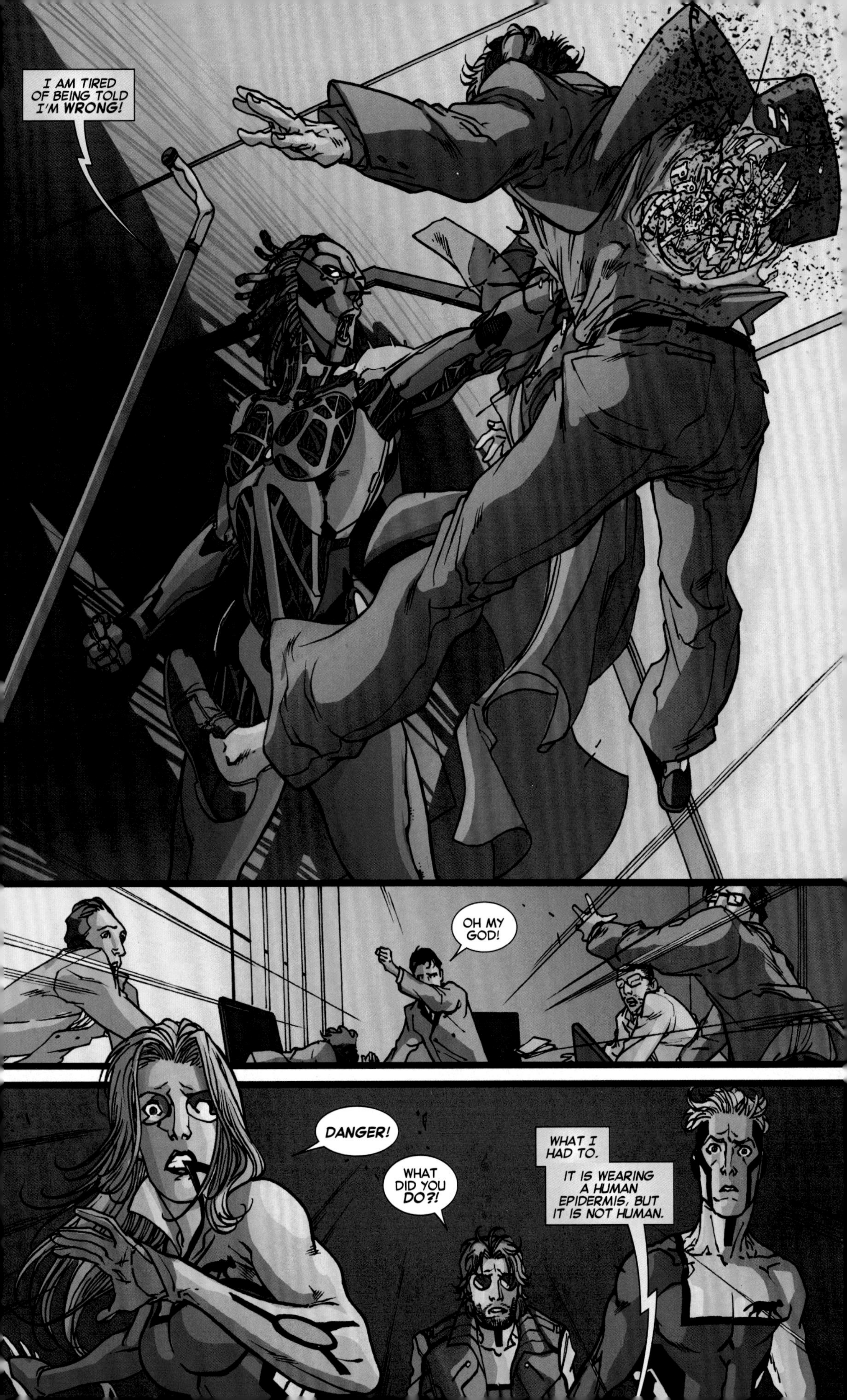
I AM TIRED OF BEING TOLD I'M WRONG!
OH MY GOD!
DANGER!
WHAT DID YOU DO?!
WHAT I HAD TO.
IT IS WEARING A HUMAN EPIDERMIS, BUT IT IS NOT HUMAN.

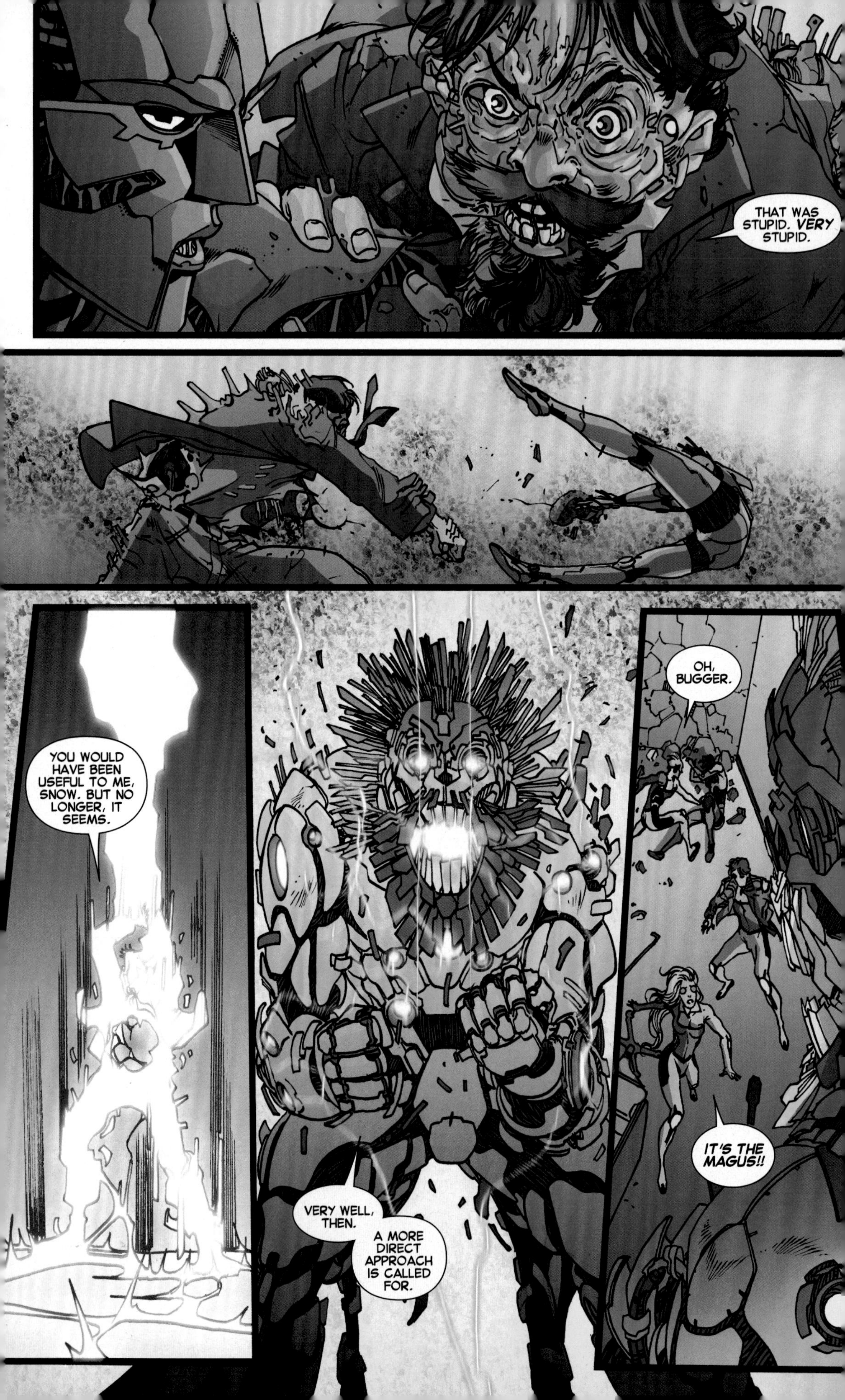
THAT WAS STUPID. VERY STUPID.
YOU WOULD HAVE BEEN USEFUL TO ME, SNOW. BUT NO LONGER, IT SEEMS.
VERY WELL, THEN.
A MORE DIRECT APPROACH IS CALLED FOR.
OH, BUGGER.
IT'S THE MAGUS!!

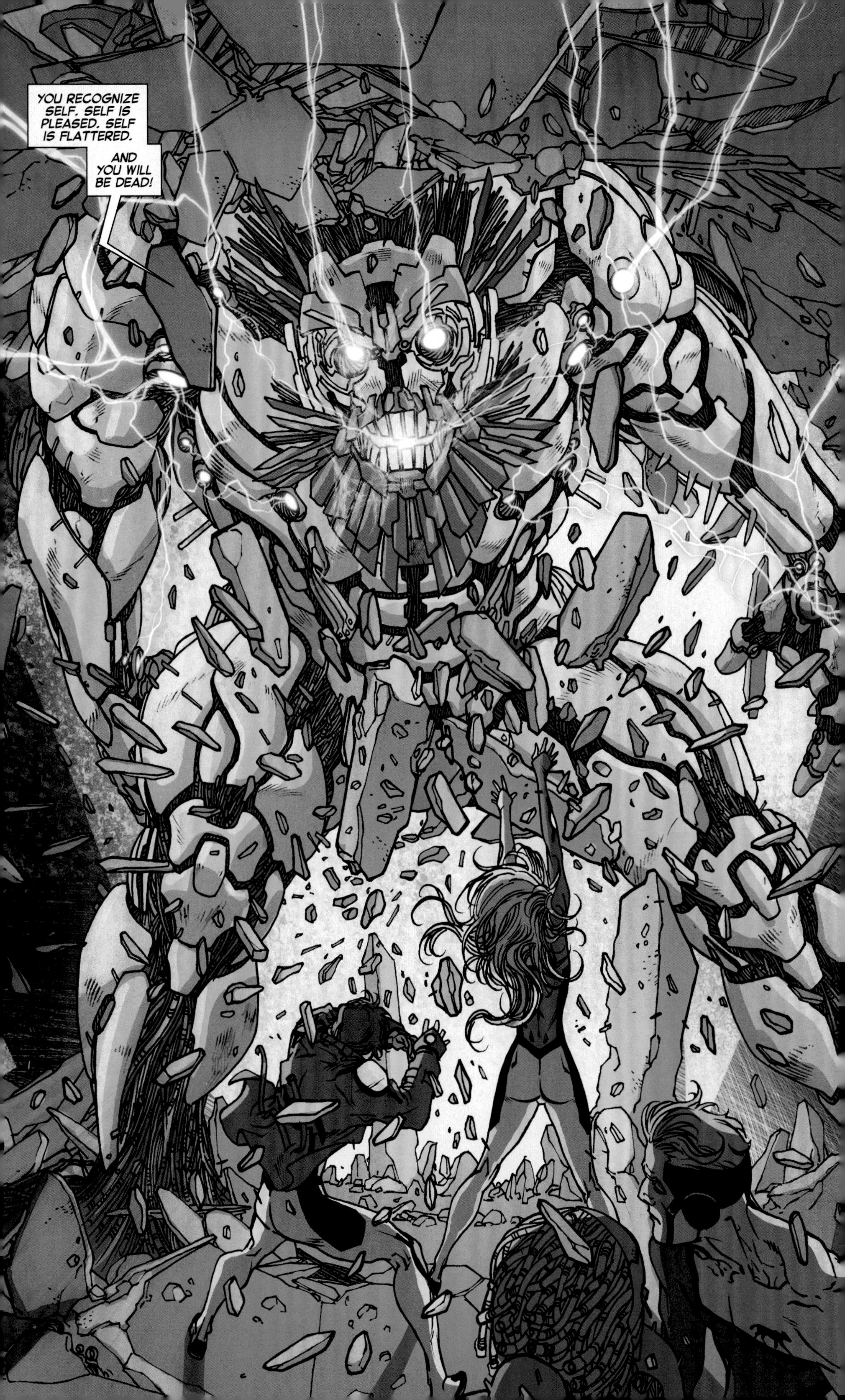
YOU RECOGNIZE SELF. SELF IS PLEASED. SELF IS FLATTERED.
AND YOU WILL BE DEAD!

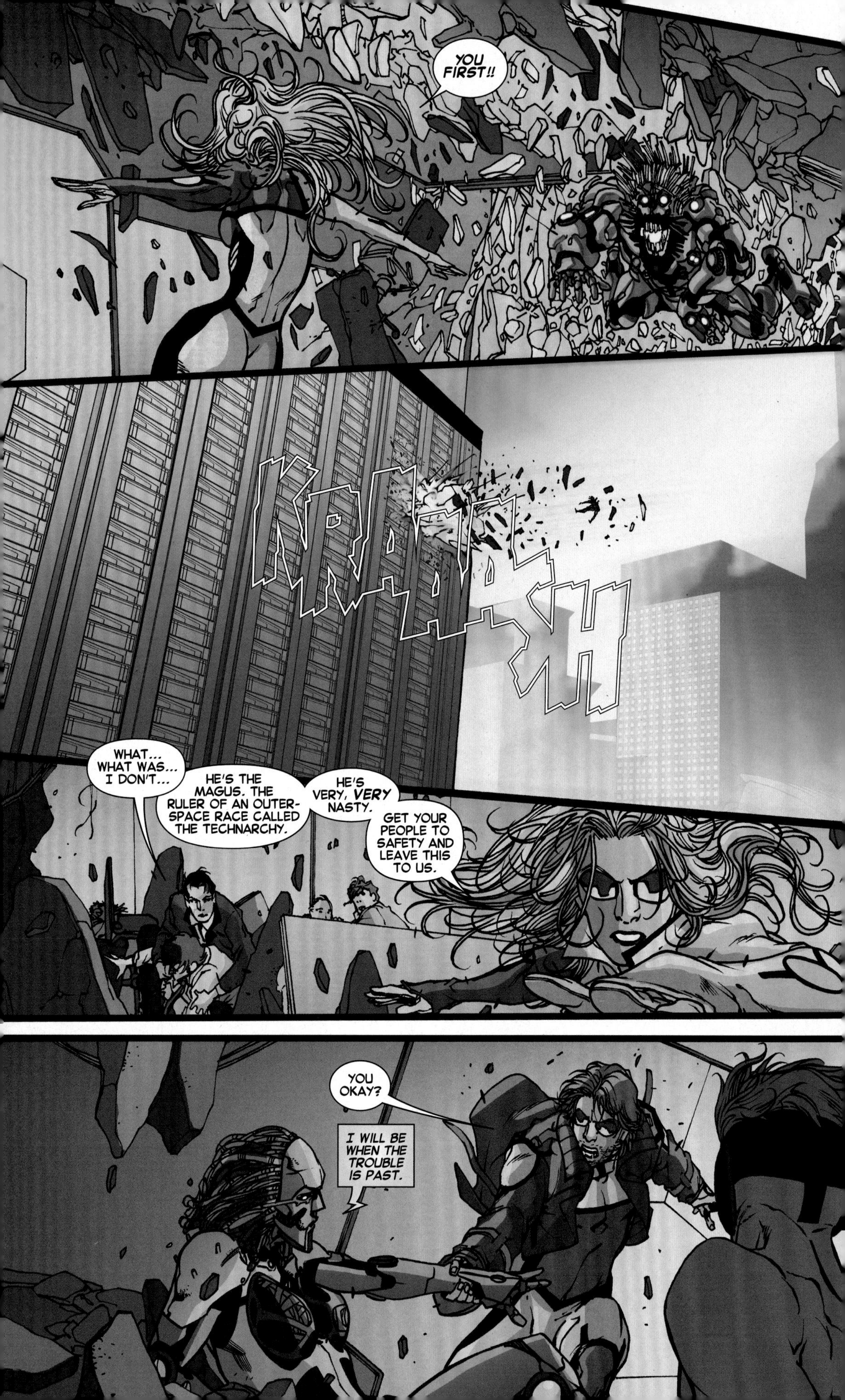
YOU FIRST!!
KRAAASH
WHAT... WHAT WAS... I DON'T...
HE'S THE MAGUS. THE RULER OF AN OUTER-SPACE RACE CALLED THE TECHNARCHY.
HE'S VERY, VERY NASTY.
GET YOUR PEOPLE TO SAFETY AND LEAVE THIS TO US.
YOU OKAY?
I WILL BE WHEN THE TROUBLE IS PAST.

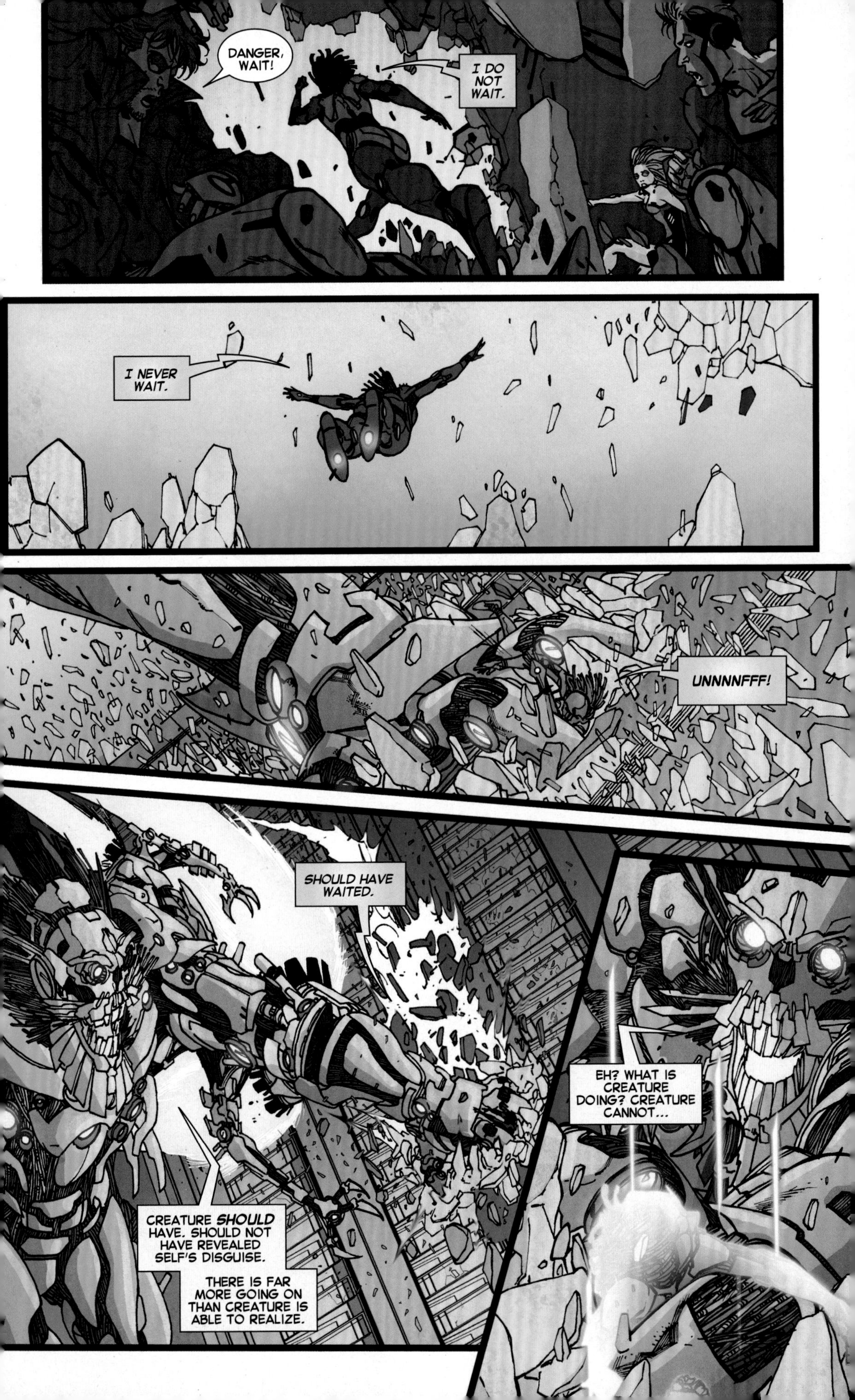
DANGER, WAIT!
I DO NOT WAIT.
I NEVER WAIT.
UNNNNFFF!
SHOULD HAVE WAITED.
CREATURE SHOULD HAVE. SHOULD NOT HAVE REVEALED SELF'S DISGUISE.
THERE IS FAR MORE GOING ON THAN CREATURE IS ABLE TO REALIZE.
EH? WHAT IS CREATURE DOING? CREATURE CANNOT...

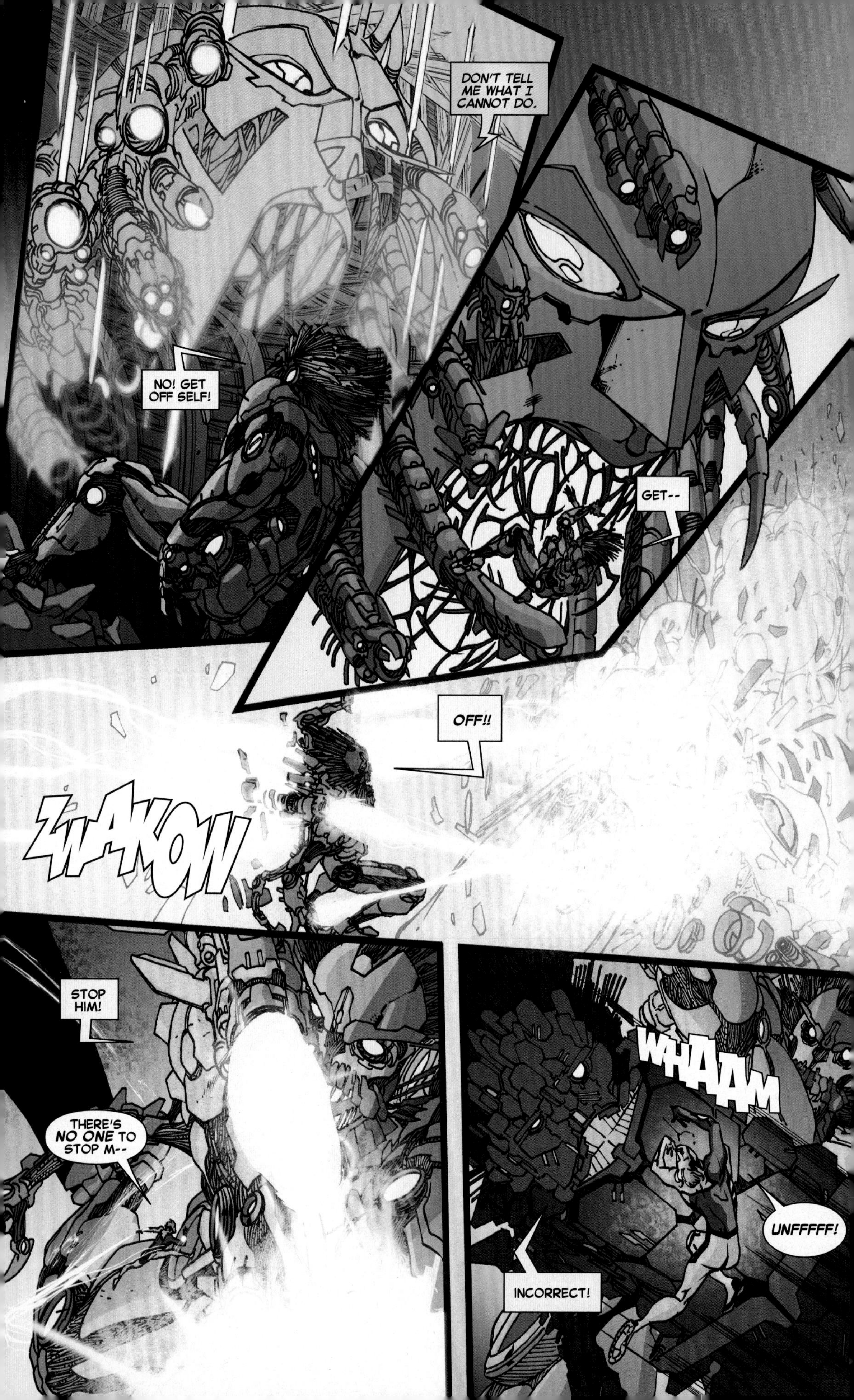
DON'T TELL ME WHAT I CANNOT DO.
NO! GET OFF SELF!
GET--
OFF!!
ZWAKOW
STOP HIM!
THERE'S NO ONE TO STOP M--
WHAAM
UNFFFFF!
INCORRECT!

WARLOCK?!

STAY DOWN, QUICKSILVER.

YOU'RE WORKING...WITH YOUR FATHER? WITH THE MAGUS? BUT... HE WANTS TO KILL YOU! I DON'T UNDERSTAN--

WHAAMM

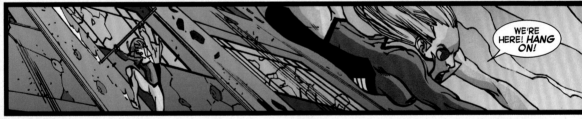

WE'RE HERE! HANG ON!

SHOULD HAVE BEEN ABLE TO DODGE THAT. I DON'T...

PIETRO? YOU ALL RIGHT?

I'M FINE. THE MAGUS... WARLOCK...

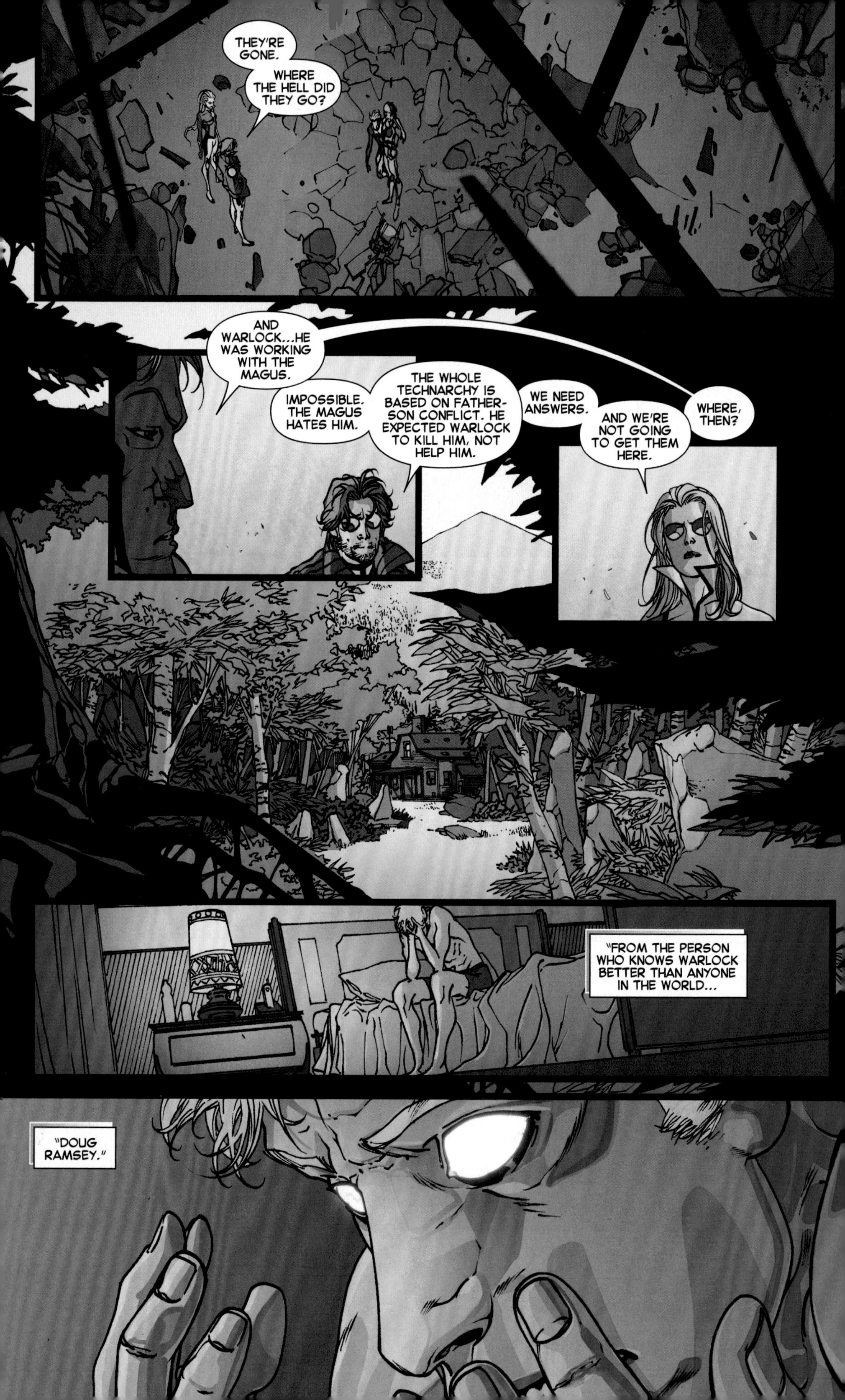
THEY'RE GONE.
WHERE THE HELL DID THEY GO?
AND WARLOCK...HE WAS WORKING WITH THE MAGUS.
IMPOSSIBLE. THE MAGUS HATES HIM.
THE WHOLE TECHNARCHY IS BASED ON FATHER-SON CONFLICT. HE EXPECTED WARLOCK TO KILL HIM, NOT HELP HIM.
WE NEED ANSWERS.
AND WE'RE NOT GOING TO GET THEM HERE.
WHERE, THEN?
"FROM THE PERSON WHO KNOWS WARLOCK BETTER THAN ANYONE IN THE WORLD...
"DOUG RAMSEY."

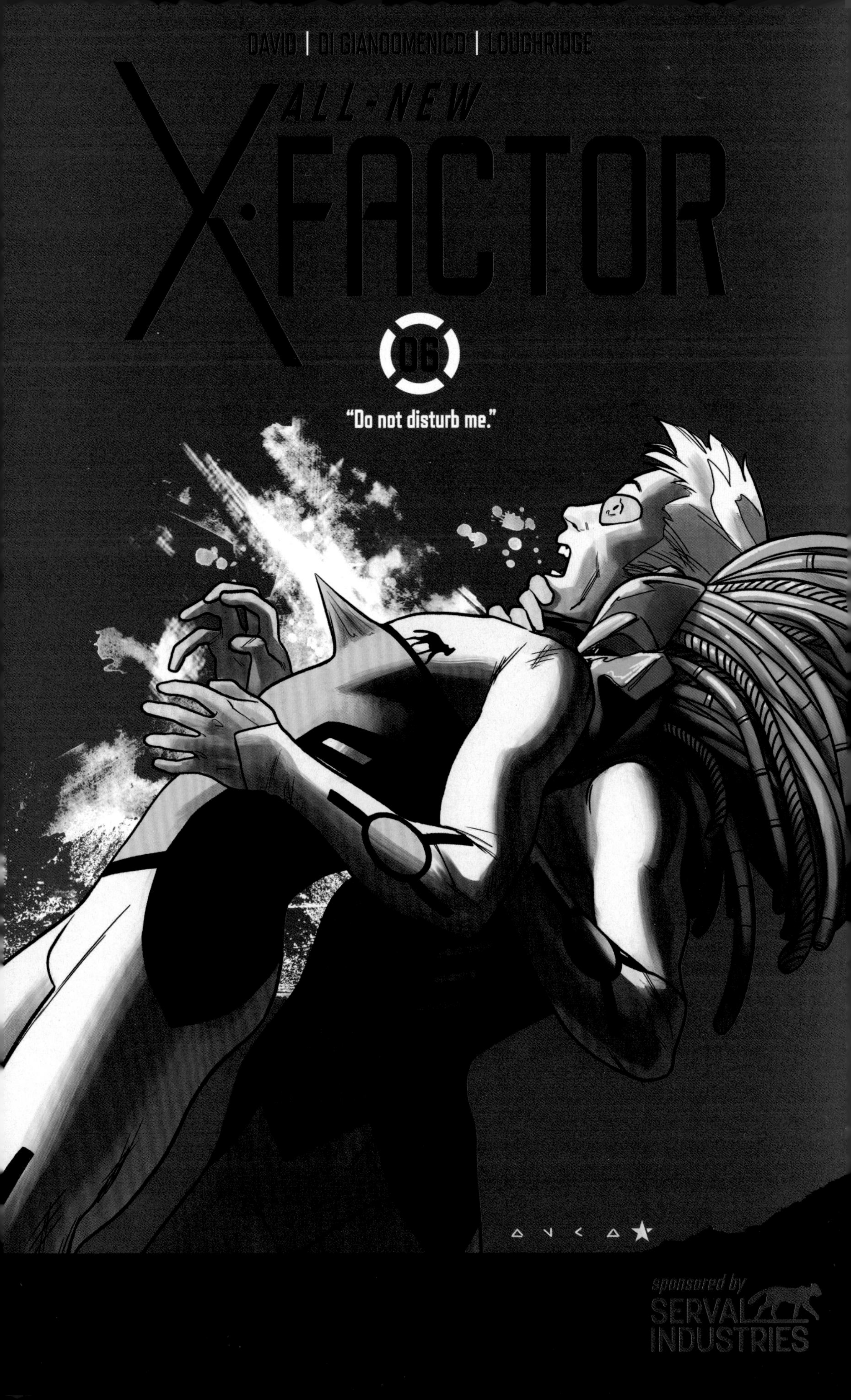
DAVID | DI GIANDOMENICO | LOUGHRIDGE
ALL-NEW
X-FACTOR
06
"Do not disturb me."
sponsored by
SERVAL
INDUSTRIES

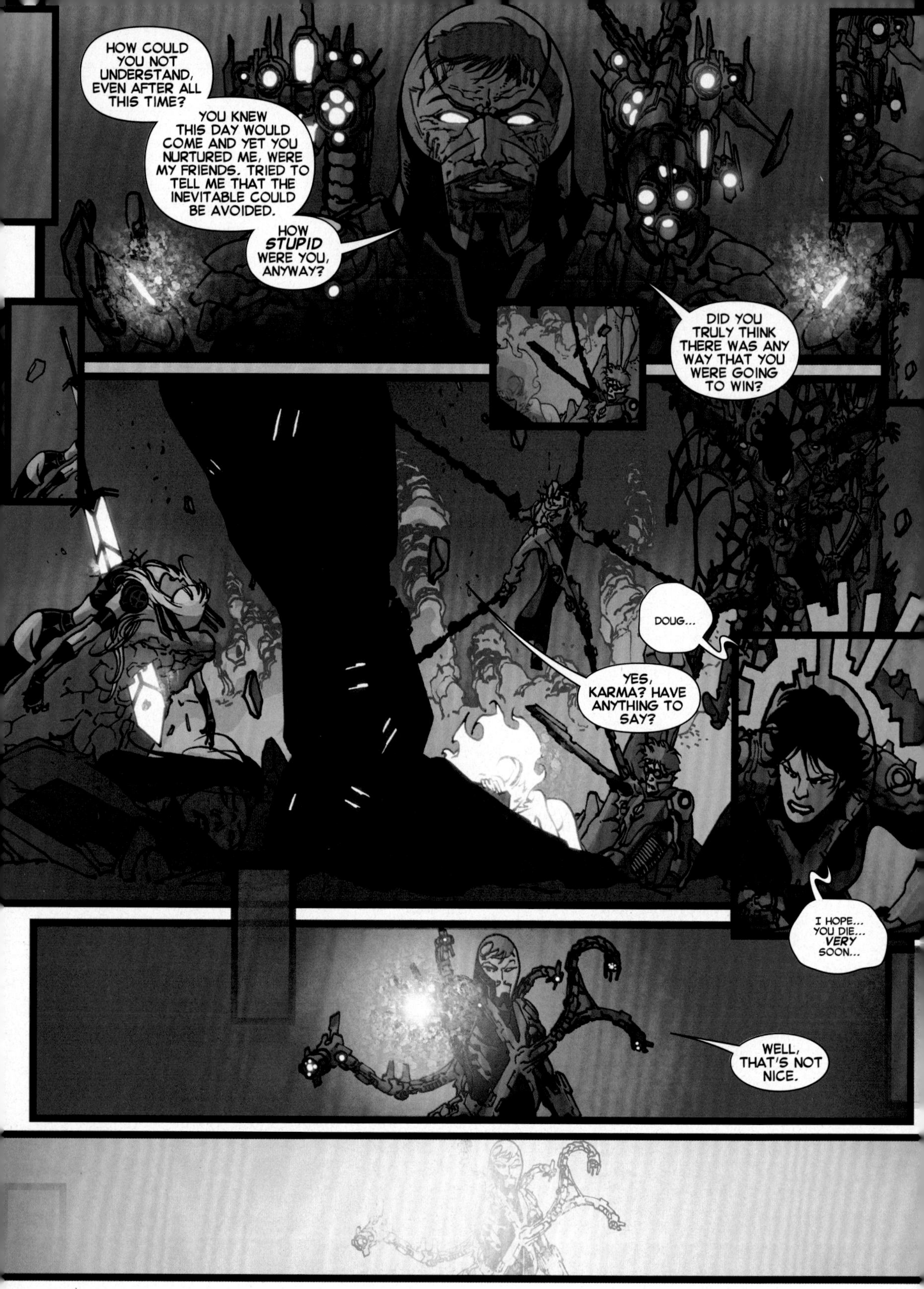
HOW COULD YOU NOT UNDERSTAND, EVEN AFTER ALL THIS TIME?
YOU KNEW THIS DAY WOULD COME AND YET YOU NURTURED ME, WERE MY FRIENDS. TRIED TO TELL ME THAT THE INEVITABLE COULD BE AVOIDED.
HOW STUPID WERE YOU, ANYWAY?
DID YOU TRULY THINK THERE WAS ANY WAY THAT YOU WERE GOING TO WIN?
DOUG...
YES, KARMA? HAVE ANYTHING TO SAY?
I HOPE... YOU DIE... VERY SOON...
WELL, THAT'S NOT NICE.

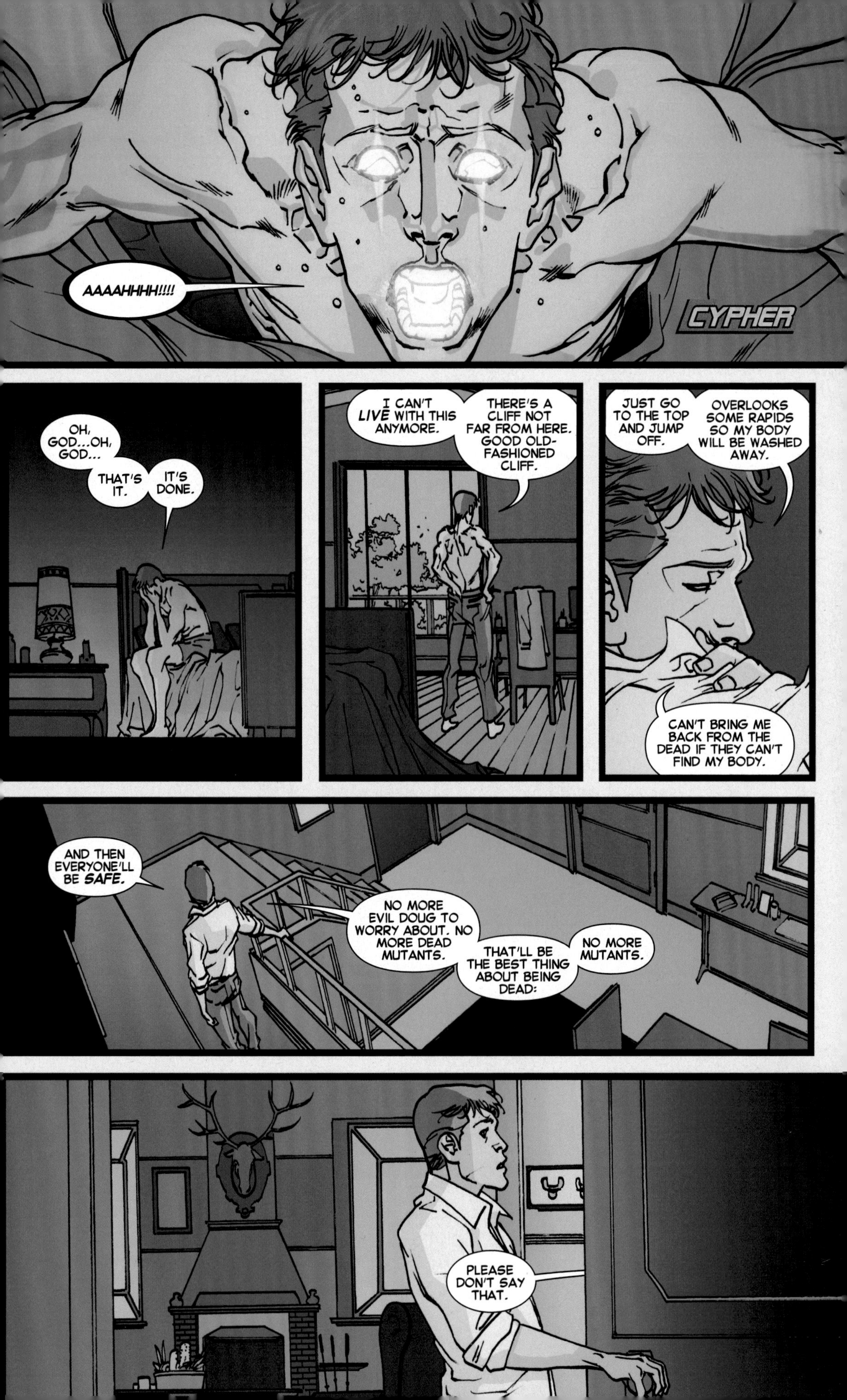
AAAAHHHH!!!!
CYPHER
OH, GOD...OH, GOD...
THAT'S IT.
IT'S DONE.
I CAN'T LIVE WITH THIS ANYMORE.
THERE'S A CLIFF NOT FAR FROM HERE. GOOD OLD-FASHIONED CLIFF.
JUST GO TO THE TOP AND JUMP OFF.
OVERLOOKS SOME RAPIDS SO MY BODY WILL BE WASHED AWAY.
CAN'T BRING ME BACK FROM THE DEAD IF THEY CAN'T FIND MY BODY.
AND THEN EVERYONE'LL BE SAFE.
NO MORE EVIL DOUG TO WORRY ABOUT. NO MORE DEAD MUTANTS.
THAT'LL BE THE BEST THING ABOUT BEING DEAD:
NO MORE MUTANTS.
PLEASE DON'T SAY THAT.

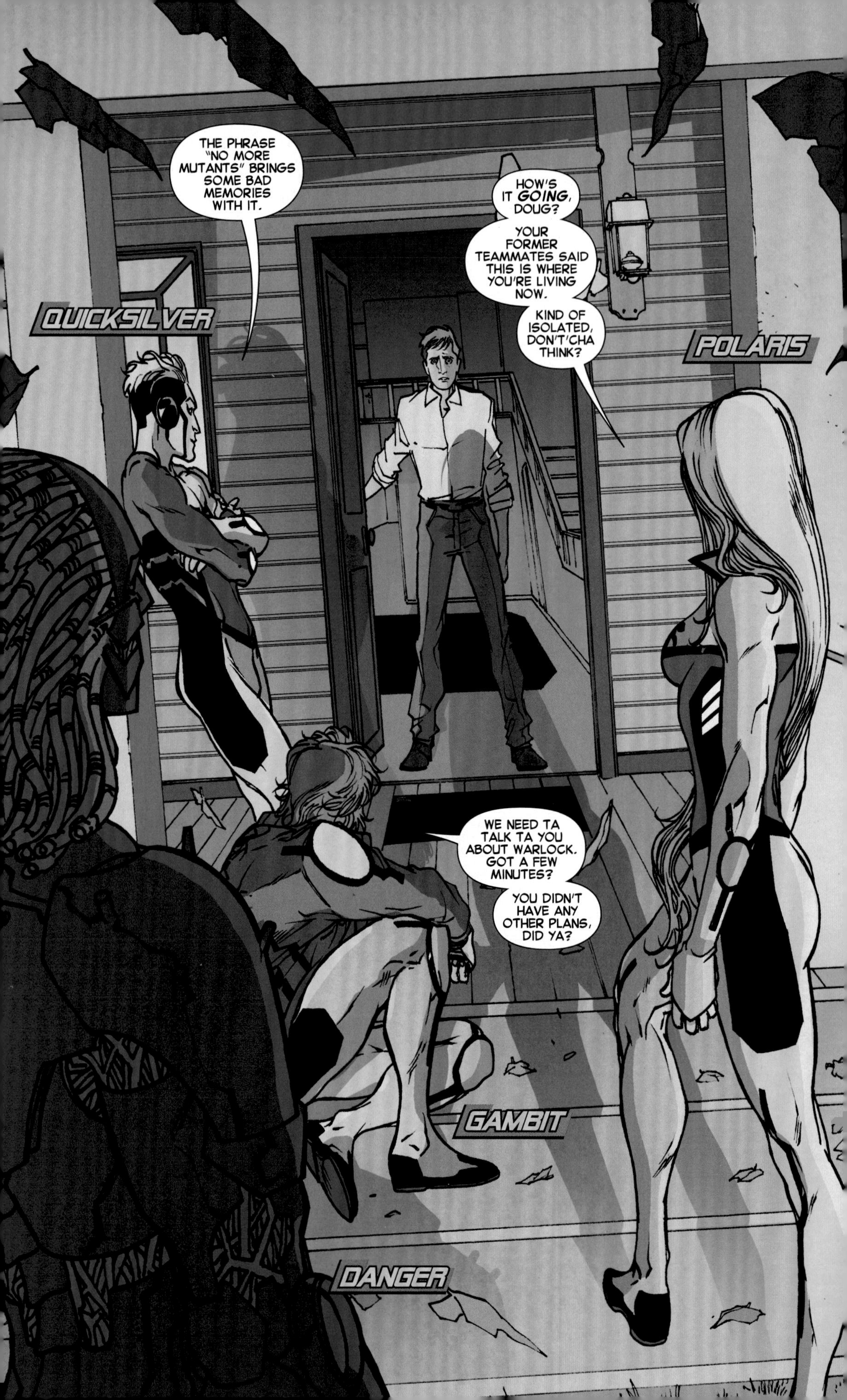
THE PHRASE "NO MORE MUTANTS" BRINGS SOME BAD MEMORIES WITH IT.
QUICKSILVER
HOW'S IT GOING, DOUG?
YOUR FORMER TEAMMATES SAID THIS IS WHERE YOU'RE LIVING NOW.
KIND OF ISOLATED, DON'T'CHA THINK?
POLARIS
WE NEED TA TALK TA YOU ABOUT WARLOCK. GOT A FEW MINUTES?
YOU DIDN'T HAVE ANY OTHER PLANS, DID YA?
GAMBIT
DANGER

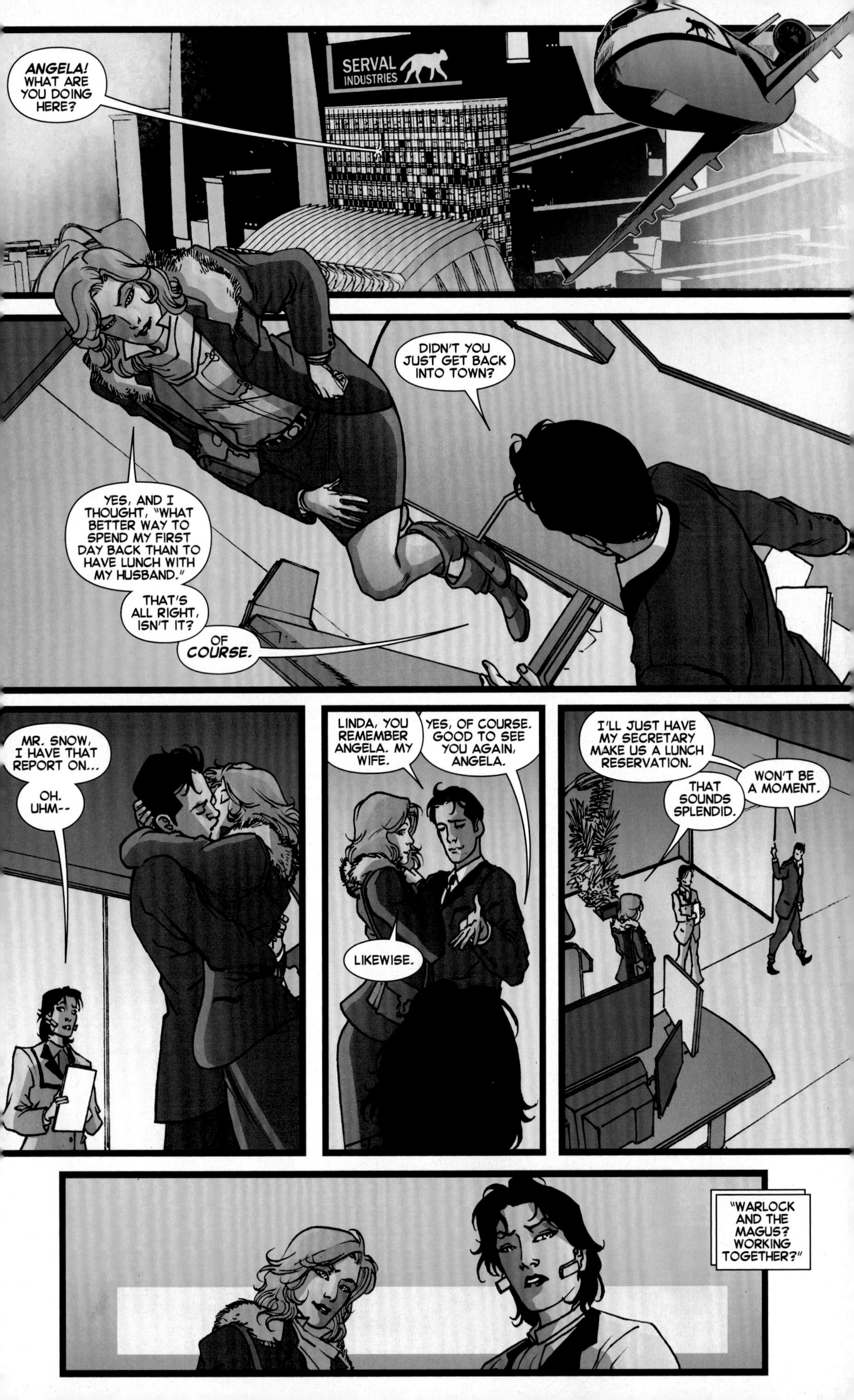

SERVAL INDUSTRIES
ANGELA! WHAT ARE YOU DOING HERE?
DIDN'T YOU JUST GET BACK INTO TOWN?
YES, AND I THOUGHT, "WHAT BETTER WAY TO SPEND MY FIRST DAY BACK THAN TO HAVE LUNCH WITH MY HUSBAND."
THAT'S ALL RIGHT, ISN'T IT?
OF COURSE.
MR. SNOW, I HAVE THAT REPORT ON...
OH. UHM--
LINDA, YOU REMEMBER ANGELA. MY WIFE.
YES, OF COURSE. GOOD TO SEE YOU AGAIN, ANGELA.
LIKEWISE.
I'LL JUST HAVE MY SECRETARY MAKE US A LUNCH RESERVATION.
WON'T BE A MOMENT.
THAT SOUNDS SPLENDID.
"WARLOCK AND THE MAGUS? WORKING TOGETHER?"

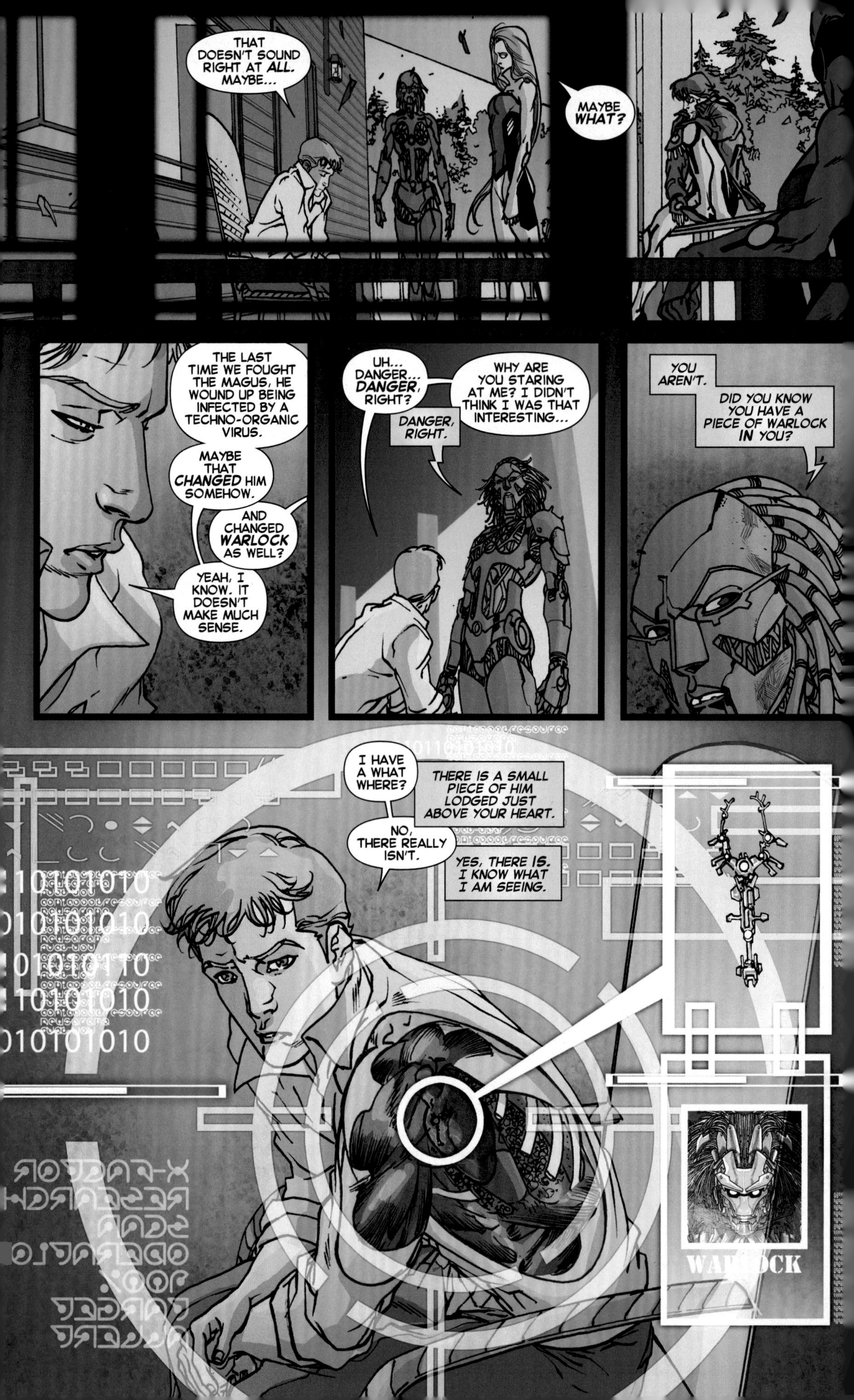
THAT DOESN'T SOUND RIGHT AT ALL. MAYBE...
MAYBE WHAT?
THE LAST TIME WE FOUGHT THE MAGUS, HE WOUND UP BEING INFECTED BY A TECHNO-ORGANIC VIRUS.
MAYBE THAT CHANGED HIM SOMEHOW.
AND CHANGED WARLOCK AS WELL?
YEAH, I KNOW. IT DOESN'T MAKE MUCH SENSE.
UH... DANGER... DANGER, RIGHT?
DANGER, RIGHT.
WHY ARE YOU STARING AT ME? I DIDN'T THINK I WAS THAT INTERESTING...
YOU AREN'T.
DID YOU KNOW YOU HAVE A PIECE OF WARLOCK IN YOU?
I HAVE A WHAT WHERE?
THERE IS A SMALL PIECE OF HIM LODGED JUST ABOVE YOUR HEART.
NO, THERE REALLY ISN'T.
YES, THERE IS. I KNOW WHAT I AM SEEING.
WARLOCK

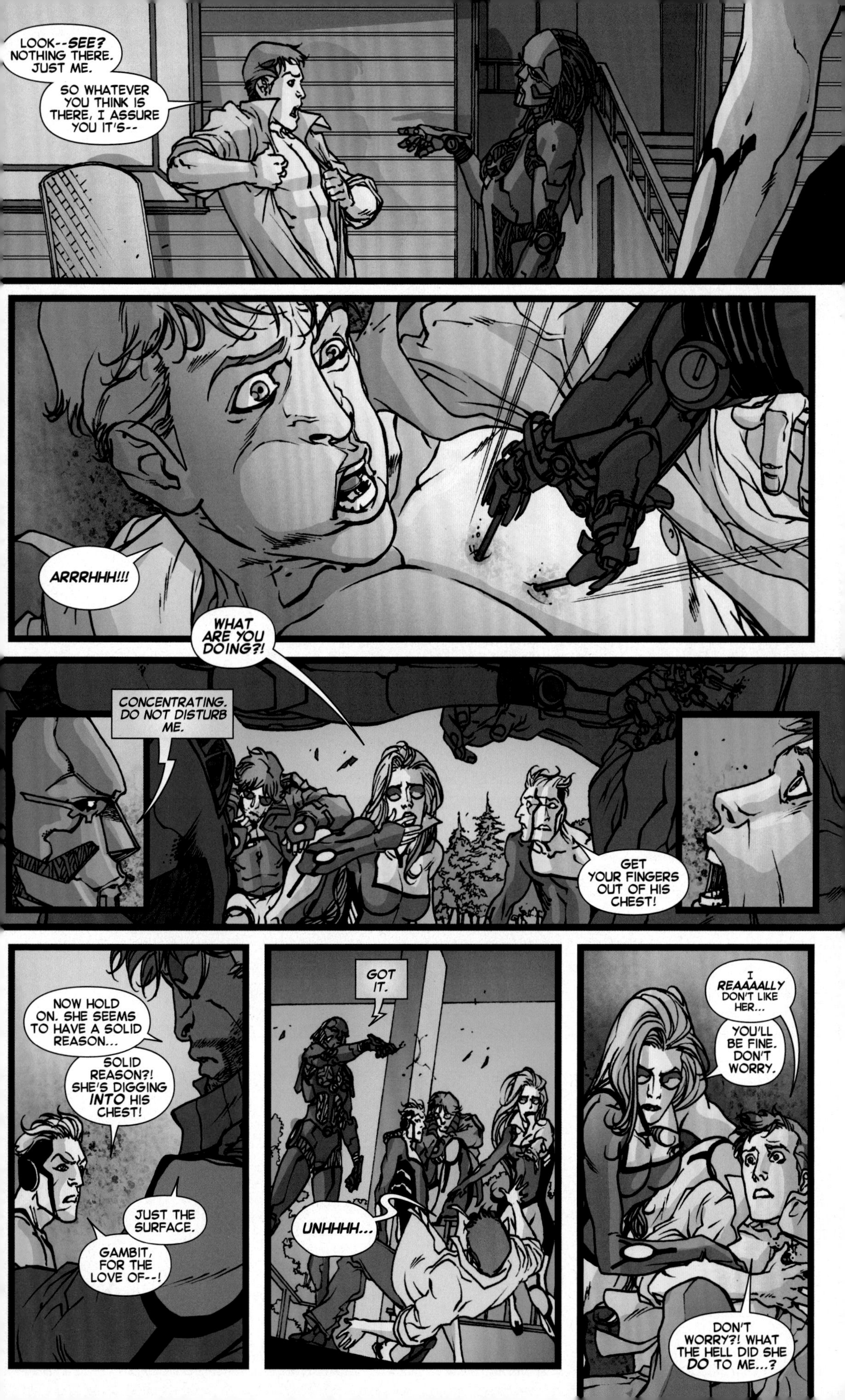
LOOK--SEE? NOTHING THERE. JUST ME.
SO WHATEVER YOU THINK IS THERE, I ASSURE YOU IT'S--
ARRRHHH!!!
WHAT ARE YOU DOING?!
CONCENTRATING. DO NOT DISTURB ME.
GET YOUR FINGERS OUT OF HIS CHEST!
NOW HOLD ON. SHE SEEMS TO HAVE A SOLID REASON...
SOLID REASON?! SHE'S DIGGING INTO HIS CHEST!
JUST THE SURFACE.
GAMBIT, FOR THE LOVE OF--!
GOT IT.
UNHHHH...
I REAAAALLY DON'T LIKE HER...
YOU'LL BE FINE. DON'T WORRY.
DON'T WORRY?! WHAT THE HELL DID SHE DO TO ME...?

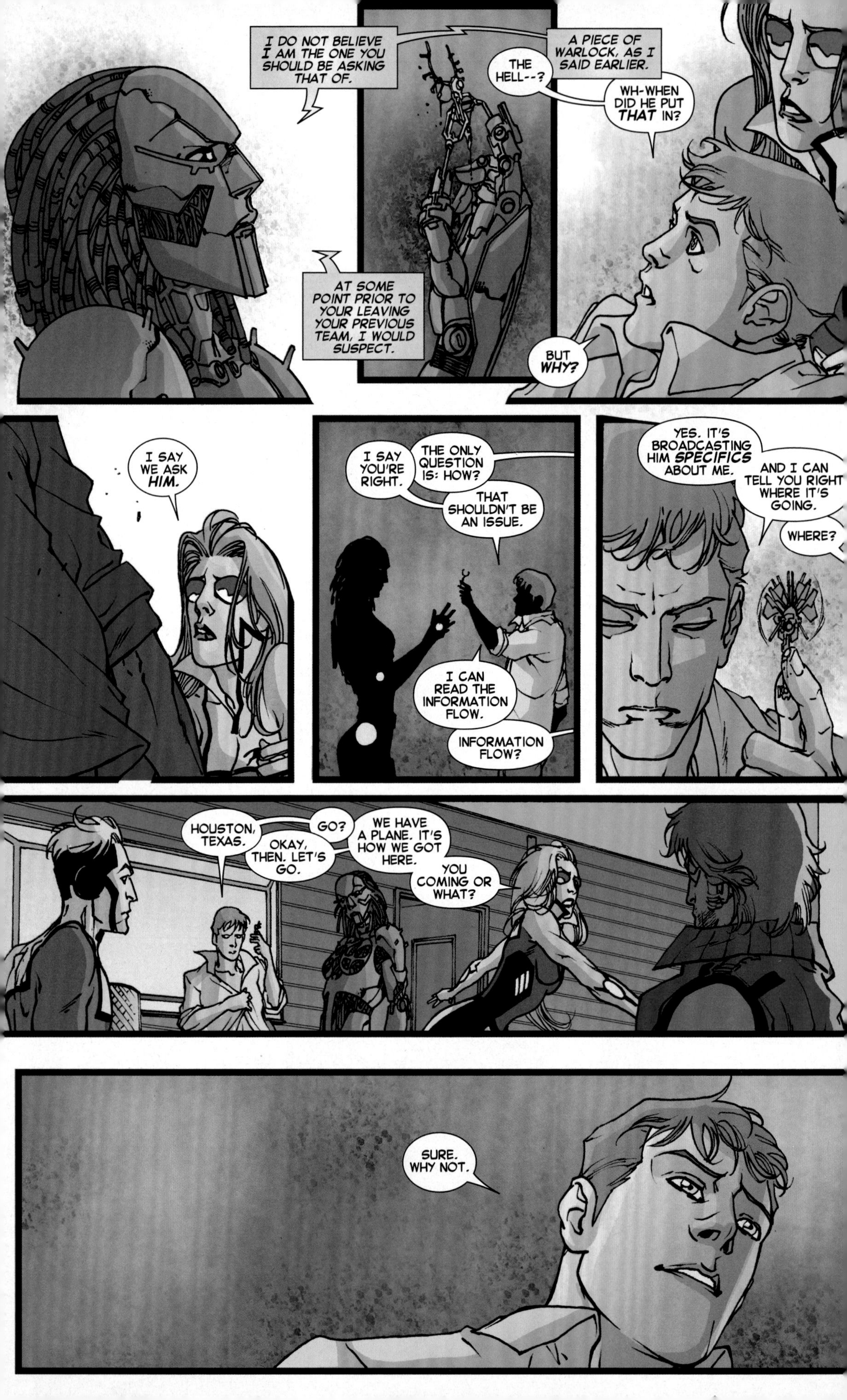
I DO NOT BELIEVE I AM THE ONE YOU SHOULD BE ASKING THAT OF.
A PIECE OF WARLOCK, AS I SAID EARLIER.
THE HELL--?
WH-WHEN DID HE PUT THAT IN?
AT SOME POINT PRIOR TO YOUR LEAVING YOUR PREVIOUS TEAM, I WOULD SUSPECT.
BUT WHY?
I SAY WE ASK HIM.
I SAY YOU'RE RIGHT.
THE ONLY QUESTION IS: HOW?
THAT SHOULDN'T BE AN ISSUE.
I CAN READ THE INFORMATION FLOW.
INFORMATION FLOW?
YES. IT'S BROADCASTING HIM SPECIFICS ABOUT ME.
AND I CAN TELL YOU RIGHT WHERE IT'S GOING.
WHERE?
HOUSTON, TEXAS.
GO?
OKAY, THEN. LET'S GO.
WE HAVE A PLANE. IT'S HOW WE GOT HERE.
YOU COMING OR WHAT?
SURE. WHY NOT.

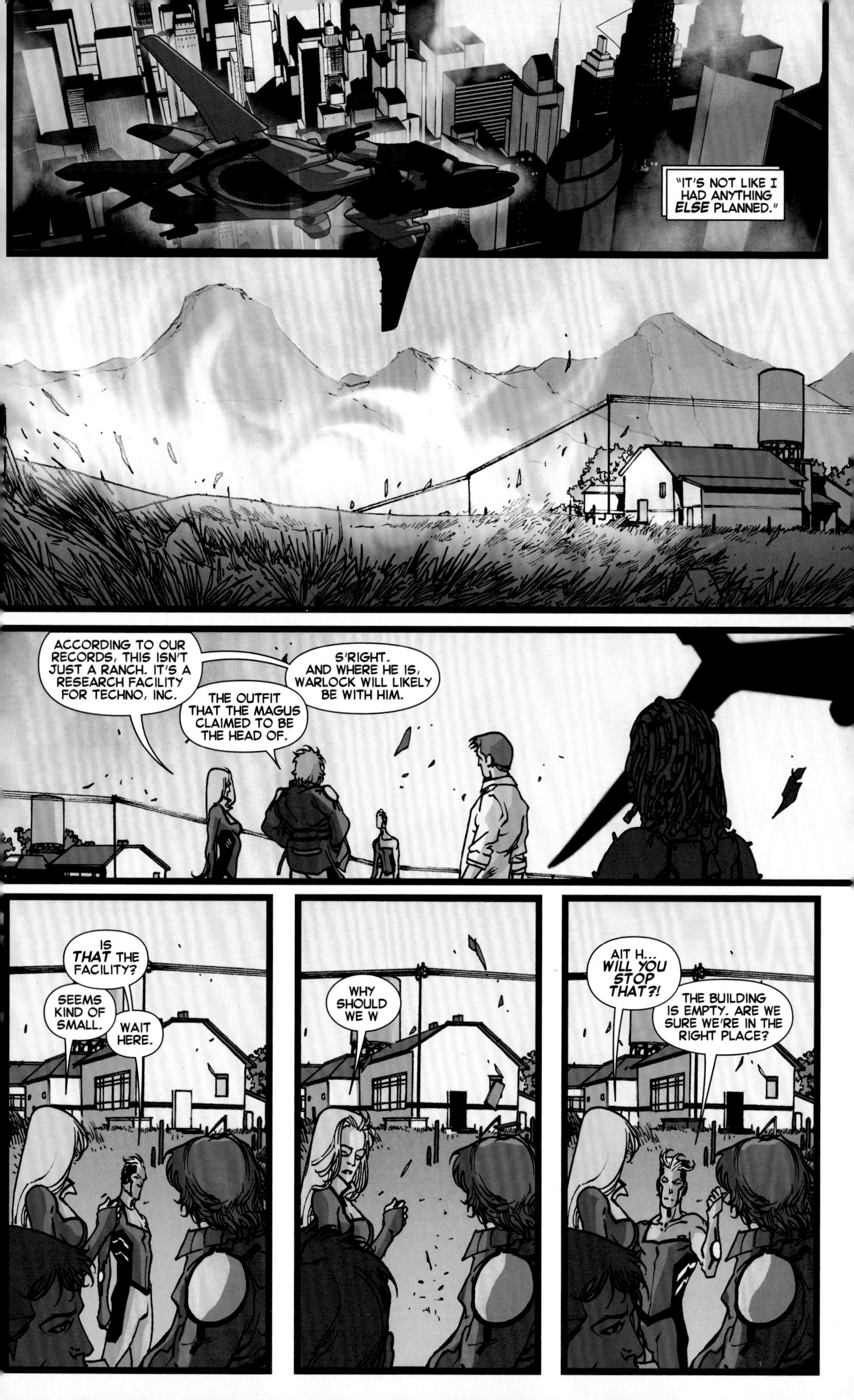

"IT'S NOT LIKE I HAD ANYTHING ELSE PLANNED."
ACCORDING TO OUR RECORDS, THIS ISN'T JUST A RANCH. IT'S A RESEARCH FACILITY FOR TECHNO, INC.
S'RIGHT. AND WHERE HE IS, WARLOCK WILL LIKELY BE WITH HIM.
THE OUTFIT THAT THE MAGUS CLAIMED TO BE THE HEAD OF.
IS THAT THE FACILITY?
SEEMS KIND OF SMALL.
WAIT HERE.
WHY SHOULD WE W
AIT H...
WILL YOU STOP THAT?!
THE BUILDING IS EMPTY. ARE WE SURE WE'RE IN THE RIGHT PLACE?

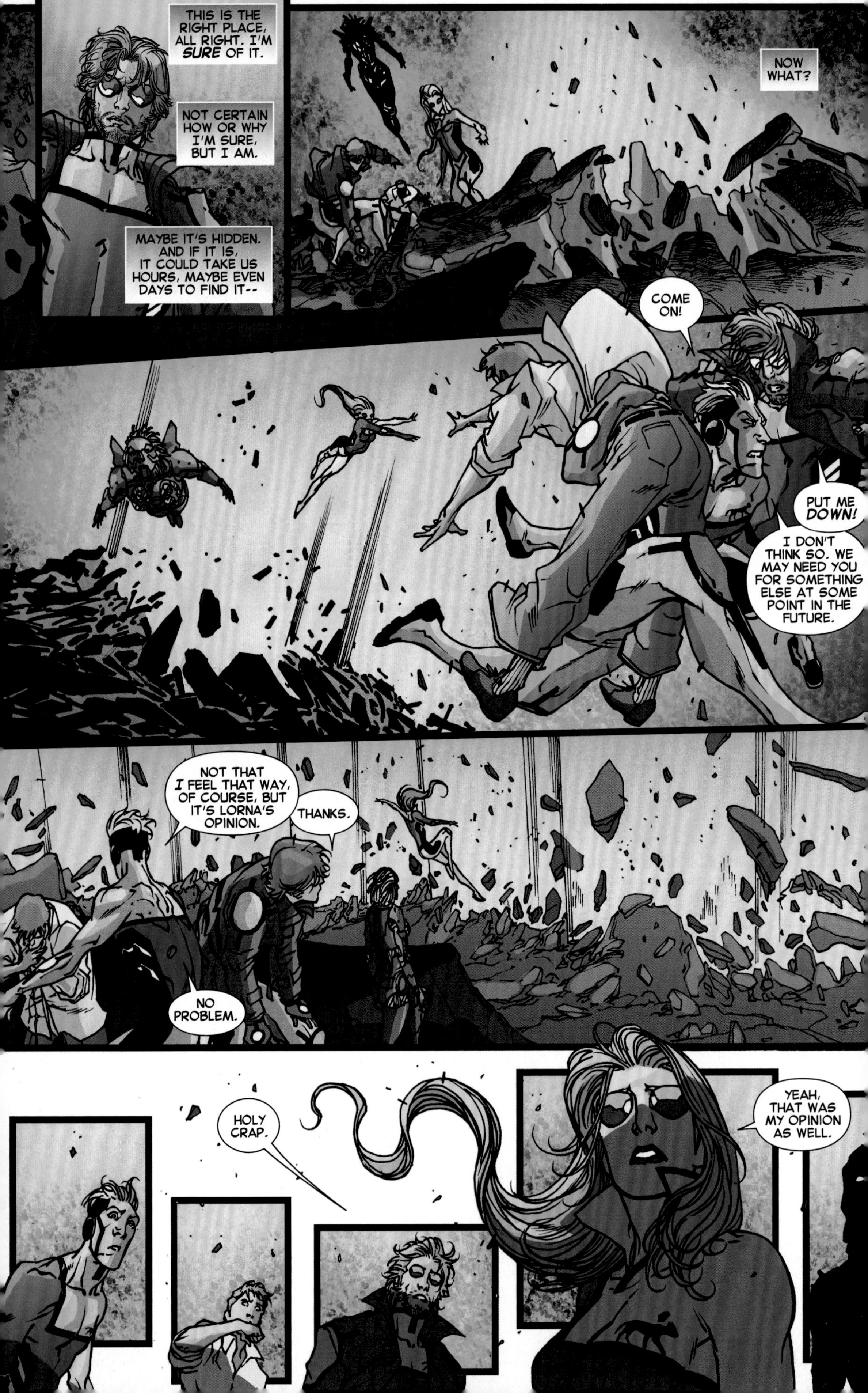
THIS IS THE RIGHT PLACE, ALL RIGHT. I'M SURE OF IT.
NOT CERTAIN HOW OR WHY I'M SURE, BUT I AM.
MAYBE IT'S HIDDEN. AND IF IT IS, IT COULD TAKE US HOURS, MAYBE EVEN DAYS TO FIND IT--
NOW WHAT?
COME ON!
PUT ME DOWN!
I DON'T THINK SO. WE MAY NEED YOU FOR SOMETHING ELSE AT SOME POINT IN THE FUTURE.
NOT THAT I FEEL THAT WAY, OF COURSE, BUT IT'S LORNA'S OPINION.
THANKS.
NO PROBLEM.
HOLY CRAP.
YEAH, THAT WAS MY OPINION AS WELL.

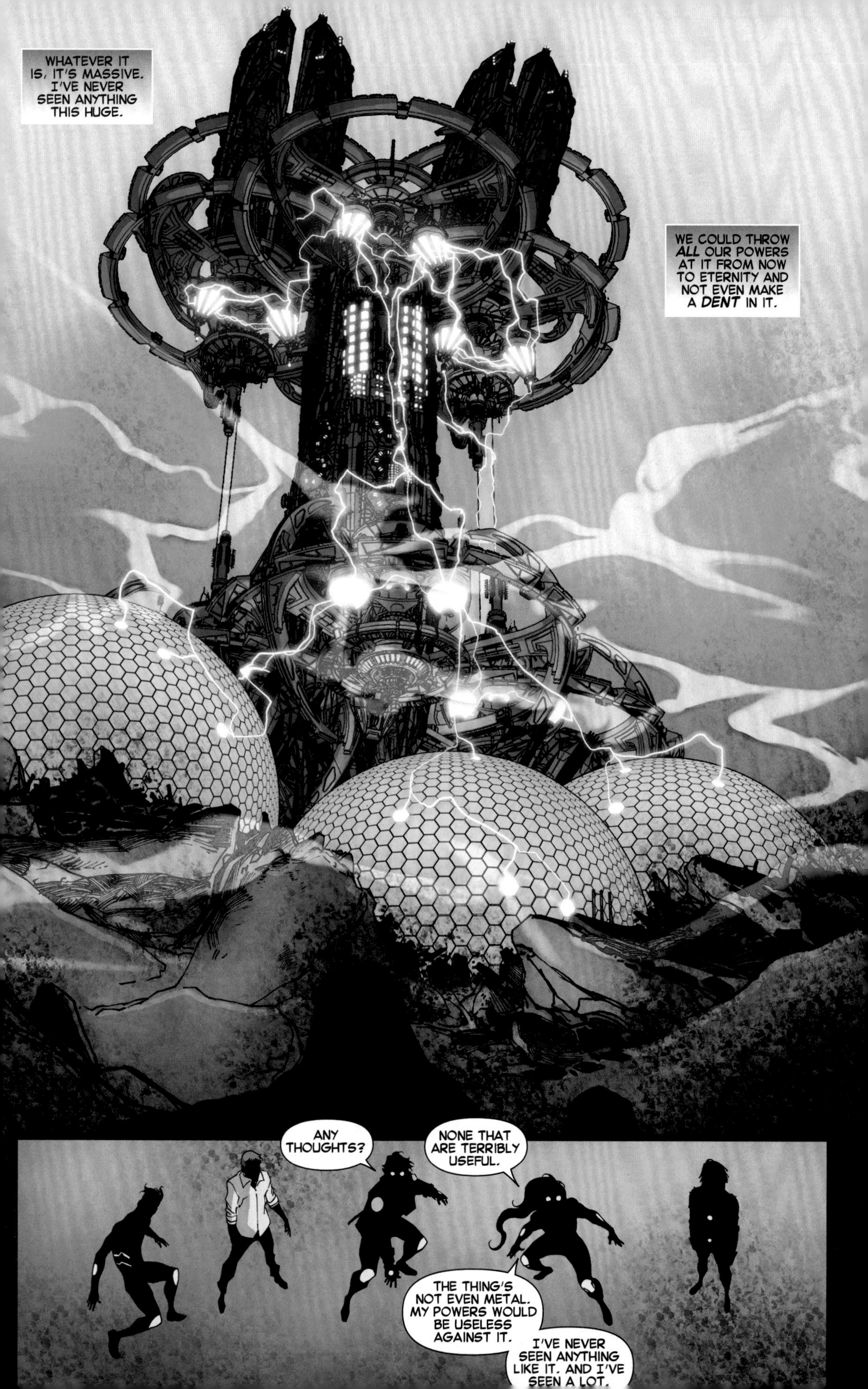
WHATEVER IT IS, IT'S MASSIVE. I'VE NEVER SEEN ANYTHING THIS HUGE.
WE COULD THROW ALL OUR POWERS AT IT FROM NOW TO ETERNITY AND NOT EVEN MAKE A DENT IN IT.
ANY THOUGHTS?
NONE THAT ARE TERRIBLY USEFUL.
THE THING'S NOT EVEN METAL. MY POWERS WOULD BE USELESS AGAINST IT.
I'VE NEVER SEEN ANYTHING LIKE IT. AND I'VE SEEN A LOT.

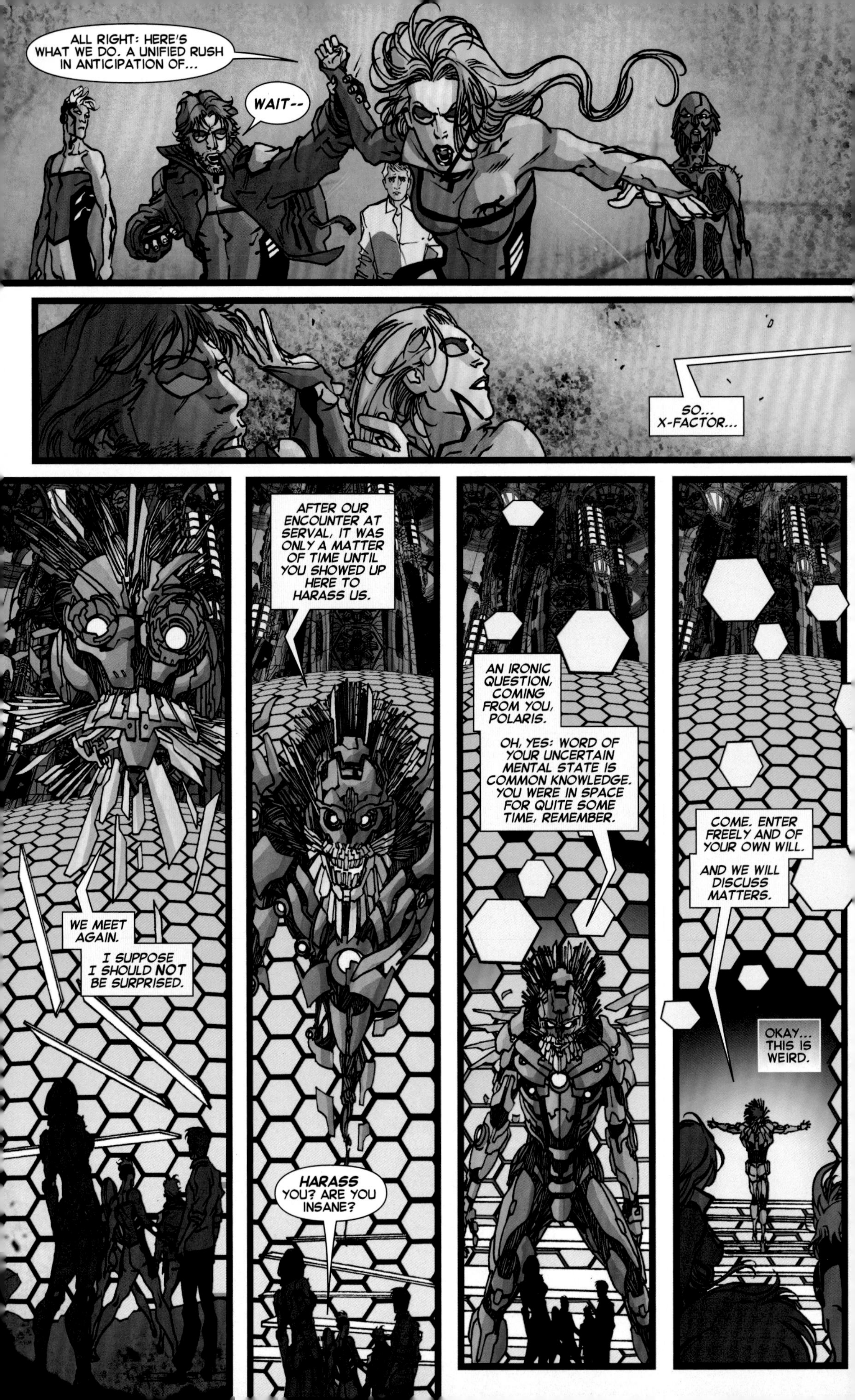
ALL RIGHT: HERE'S WHAT WE DO. A UNIFIED RUSH IN ANTICIPATION OF...
WAIT--
SO... X-FACTOR...
WE MEET AGAIN.
I SUPPOSE I SHOULD NOT BE SURPRISED.
AFTER OUR ENCOUNTER AT SERVAL, IT WAS ONLY A MATTER OF TIME UNTIL YOU SHOWED UP HERE TO HARASS US.
HARASS YOU? ARE YOU INSANE?
AN IRONIC QUESTION, COMING FROM YOU, POLARIS.
OH, YES: WORD OF YOUR UNCERTAIN MENTAL STATE IS COMMON KNOWLEDGE. YOU WERE IN SPACE FOR QUITE SOME TIME, REMEMBER.
COME. ENTER FREELY AND OF YOUR OWN WILL.
AND WE WILL DISCUSS MATTERS.
OKAY... THIS IS WEIRD.

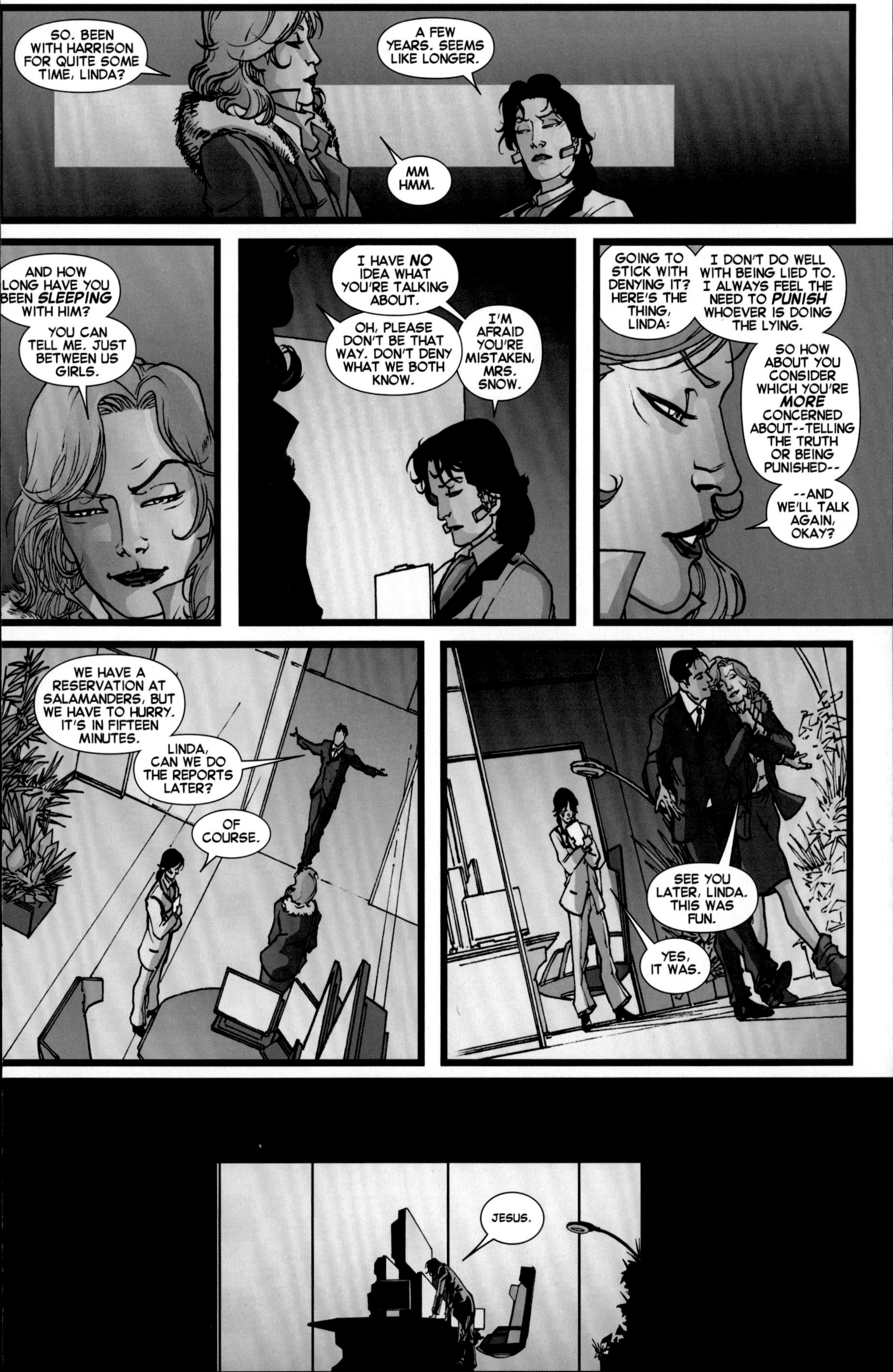
SO. BEEN WITH HARRISON FOR QUITE SOME TIME, LINDA?
A FEW YEARS. SEEMS LIKE LONGER.
MM HMM.
AND HOW LONG HAVE YOU BEEN *SLEEPING* WITH HIM?
YOU CAN TELL ME. JUST BETWEEN US GIRLS.
I HAVE *NO* IDEA WHAT YOU'RE TALKING ABOUT.
OH, PLEASE DON'T BE THAT WAY. DON'T DENY WHAT WE BOTH KNOW.
I'M AFRAID YOU'RE MISTAKEN, MRS. SNOW.
GOING TO STICK WITH DENYING IT? HERE'S THE THING, LINDA:
I DON'T DO WELL WITH BEING LIED TO. I ALWAYS FEEL THE NEED TO *PUNISH* WHOEVER IS DOING THE LYING.
SO HOW ABOUT YOU CONSIDER WHICH YOU'RE *MORE* CONCERNED ABOUT--TELLING THE TRUTH OR BEING PUNISHED--
--AND WE'LL TALK AGAIN, OKAY?
WE HAVE A RESERVATION AT SALAMANDERS, BUT WE HAVE TO HURRY. IT'S IN FIFTEEN MINUTES.
LINDA, CAN WE DO THE REPORTS LATER?
OF COURSE.
SEE YOU LATER, LINDA. THIS WAS FUN.
YES, IT WAS.
JESUS.

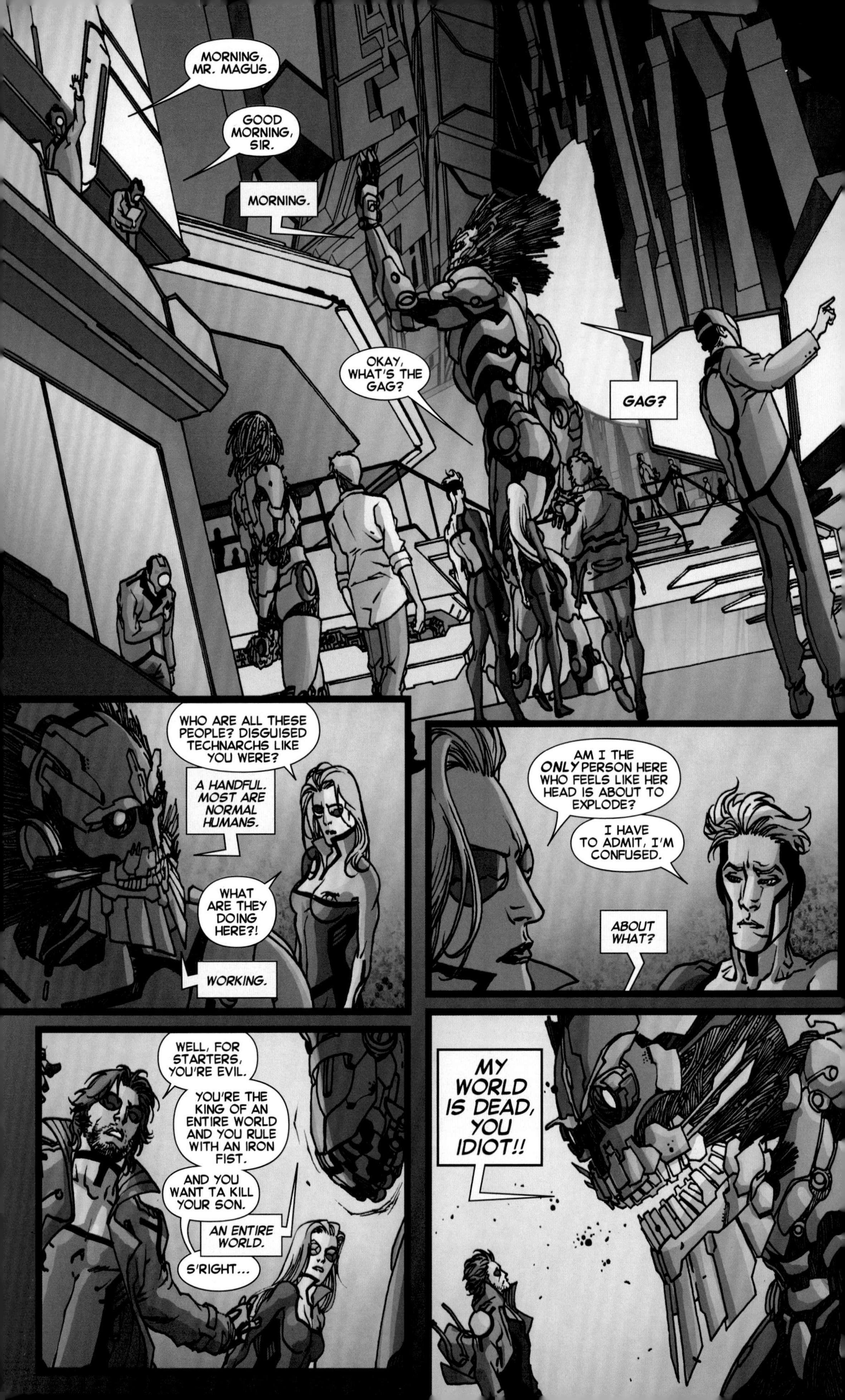
MORNING, MR. MAGUS.
GOOD MORNING, SIR.
MORNING.
OKAY, WHAT'S THE GAG?
GAG?
WHO ARE ALL THESE PEOPLE? DISGUISED TECHNARCHS LIKE YOU WERE?
A HANDFUL. MOST ARE NORMAL HUMANS.
WHAT ARE THEY DOING HERE?!
WORKING.
AM I THE ONLY PERSON HERE WHO FEELS LIKE HER HEAD IS ABOUT TO EXPLODE?
I HAVE TO ADMIT, I'M CONFUSED.
ABOUT WHAT?
WELL, FOR STARTERS, YOU'RE EVIL.
YOU'RE THE KING OF AN ENTIRE WORLD AND YOU RULE WITH AN IRON FIST.
AND YOU WANT TA KILL YOUR SON.
AN ENTIRE WORLD.
S'RIGHT...
MY WORLD IS DEAD, YOU IDIOT!!

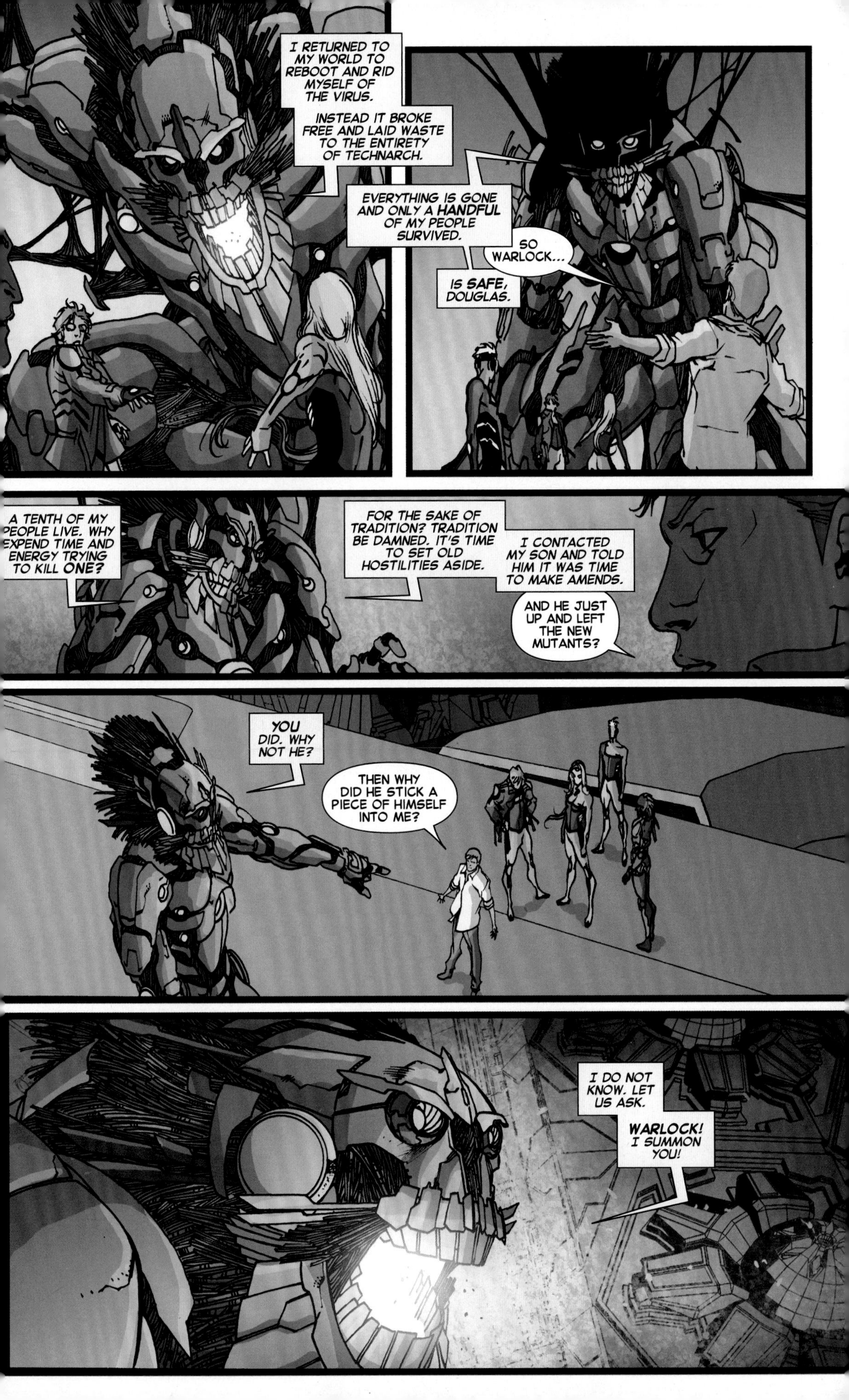
I RETURNED TO MY WORLD TO REBOOT AND RID MYSELF OF THE VIRUS.
INSTEAD IT BROKE FREE AND LAID WASTE TO THE ENTIRETY OF TECHNARCH.
EVERYTHING IS GONE AND ONLY A HANDFUL OF MY PEOPLE SURVIVED.
SO WARLOCK...
IS SAFE, DOUGLAS.
A TENTH OF MY PEOPLE LIVE. WHY EXPEND TIME AND ENERGY TRYING TO KILL ONE?
FOR THE SAKE OF TRADITION? TRADITION BE DAMNED. IT'S TIME TO SET OLD HOSTILITIES ASIDE.
I CONTACTED MY SON AND TOLD HIM IT WAS TIME TO MAKE AMENDS.
AND HE JUST UP AND LEFT THE NEW MUTANTS?
YOU DID. WHY NOT HE?
THEN WHY DID HE STICK A PIECE OF HIMSELF INTO ME?
I DO NOT KNOW. LET US ASK.
WARLOCK! I SUMMON YOU!

SELF IS HERE, FATHER. HOW MAY SELF--?

DOUGFRIEND!!

YEAH.

SELF HAD LOST SENSE OF DOUGFRIEND! DOUG REMOVED PART OF SELF THAT WAS WITHIN!

I SURE AS HELL DID!

TECHNICALLY, I DID.

RIGHT. SHE DID. YOU KNOW DANGER, RIGHT?

WE HAVE MET IN PASSING. STILL...

DANGER.

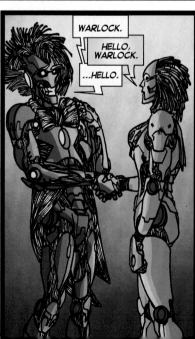

WARLOCK.

HELLO, WARLOCK.

...HELLO.

ALL RIGHT, THIS IS GETTING AWKWARD.

HMM?

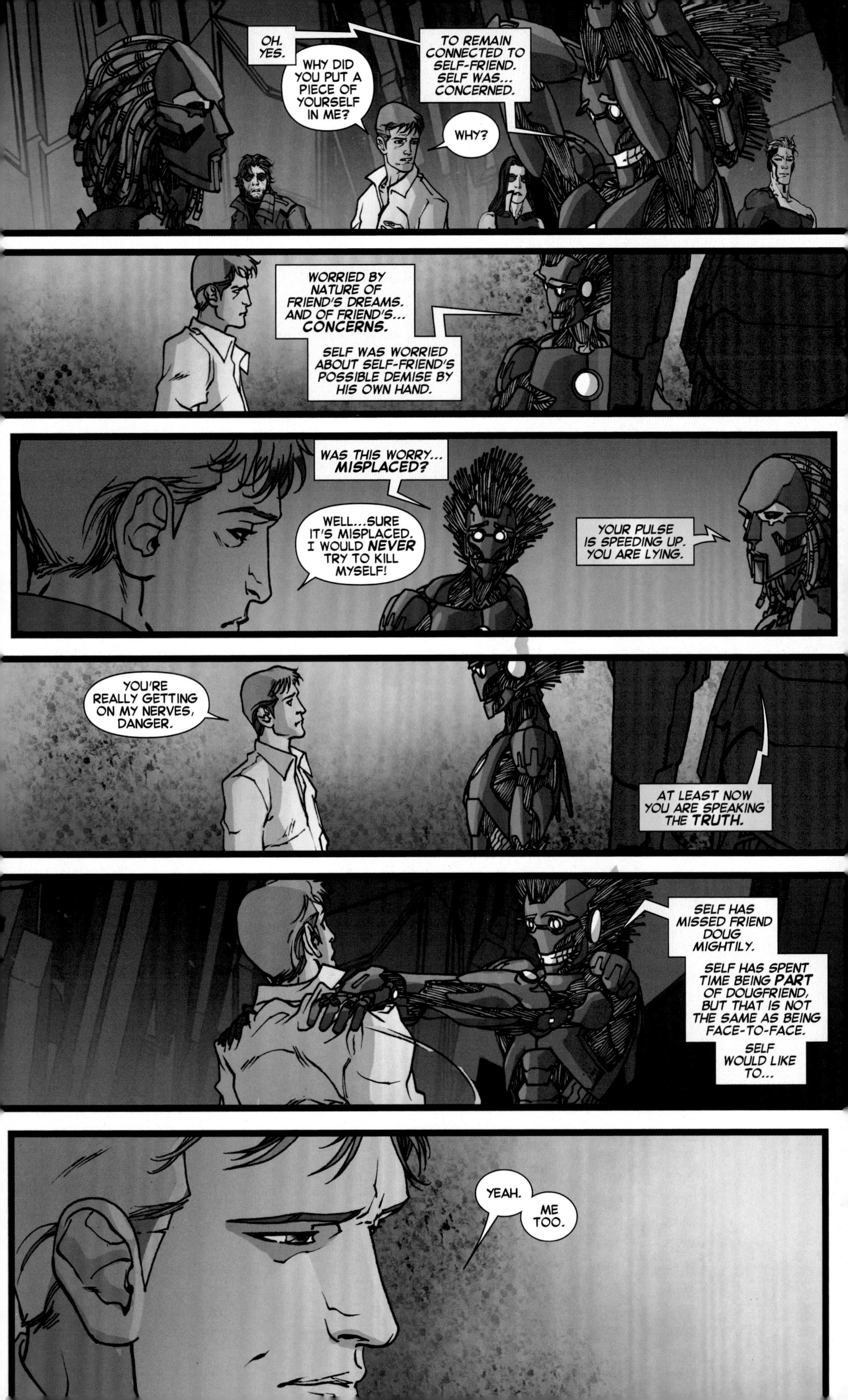
OH. YES.
WHY DID YOU PUT A PIECE OF YOURSELF IN ME?
TO REMAIN CONNECTED TO SELF-FRIEND. SELF WAS... CONCERNED.
WHY?
WORRIED BY NATURE OF FRIEND'S DREAMS. AND OF FRIEND'S... CONCERNS.
SELF WAS WORRIED ABOUT SELF-FRIEND'S POSSIBLE DEMISE BY HIS OWN HAND.
WAS THIS WORRY... MISPLACED?
WELL...SURE IT'S MISPLACED. I WOULD NEVER TRY TO KILL MYSELF!
YOUR PULSE IS SPEEDING UP. YOU ARE LYING.
YOU'RE REALLY GETTING ON MY NERVES, DANGER.
AT LEAST NOW YOU ARE SPEAKING THE TRUTH.
SELF HAS MISSED FRIEND DOUG MIGHTILY.
SELF HAS SPENT TIME BEING PART OF DOUGFRIEND, BUT THAT IS NOT THE SAME AS BEING FACE-TO-FACE.
SELF WOULD LIKE TO...
YEAH.
ME TOO.

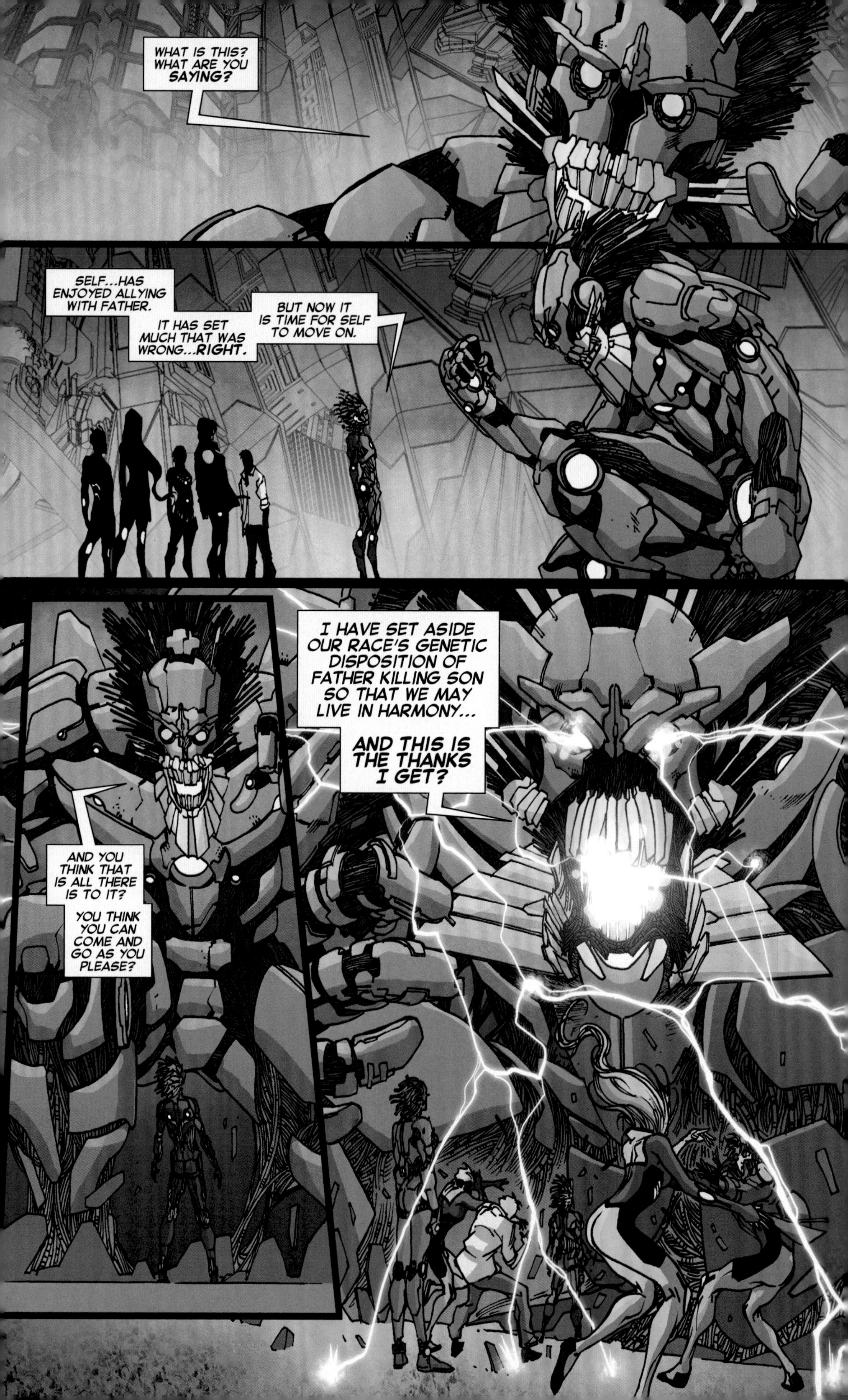
WHAT IS THIS? WHAT ARE YOU SAYING?
SELF...HAS ENJOYED ALLYING WITH FATHER.
IT HAS SET MUCH THAT WAS WRONG...RIGHT.
BUT NOW IT IS TIME FOR SELF TO MOVE ON.
AND YOU THINK THAT IS ALL THERE IS TO IT?
YOU THINK YOU CAN COME AND GO AS YOU PLEASE?
I HAVE SET ASIDE OUR RACE'S GENETIC DISPOSITION OF FATHER KILLING SON SO THAT WE MAY LIVE IN HARMONY...
AND THIS IS THE THANKS I GET?

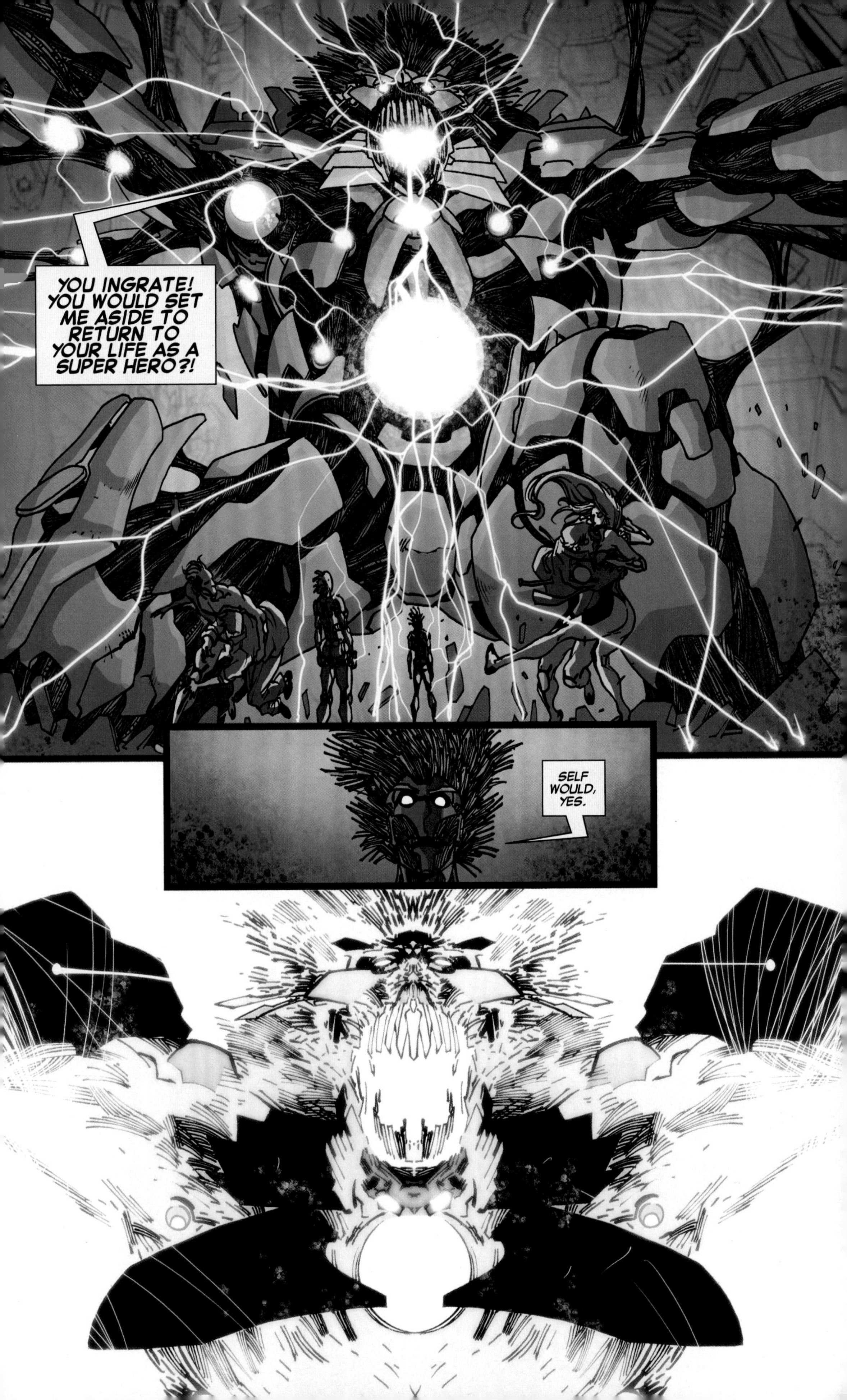
YOU INGRATE! YOU WOULD SET ME ASIDE TO RETURN TO YOUR LIFE AS A SUPER HERO?!
SELF WOULD, YES.

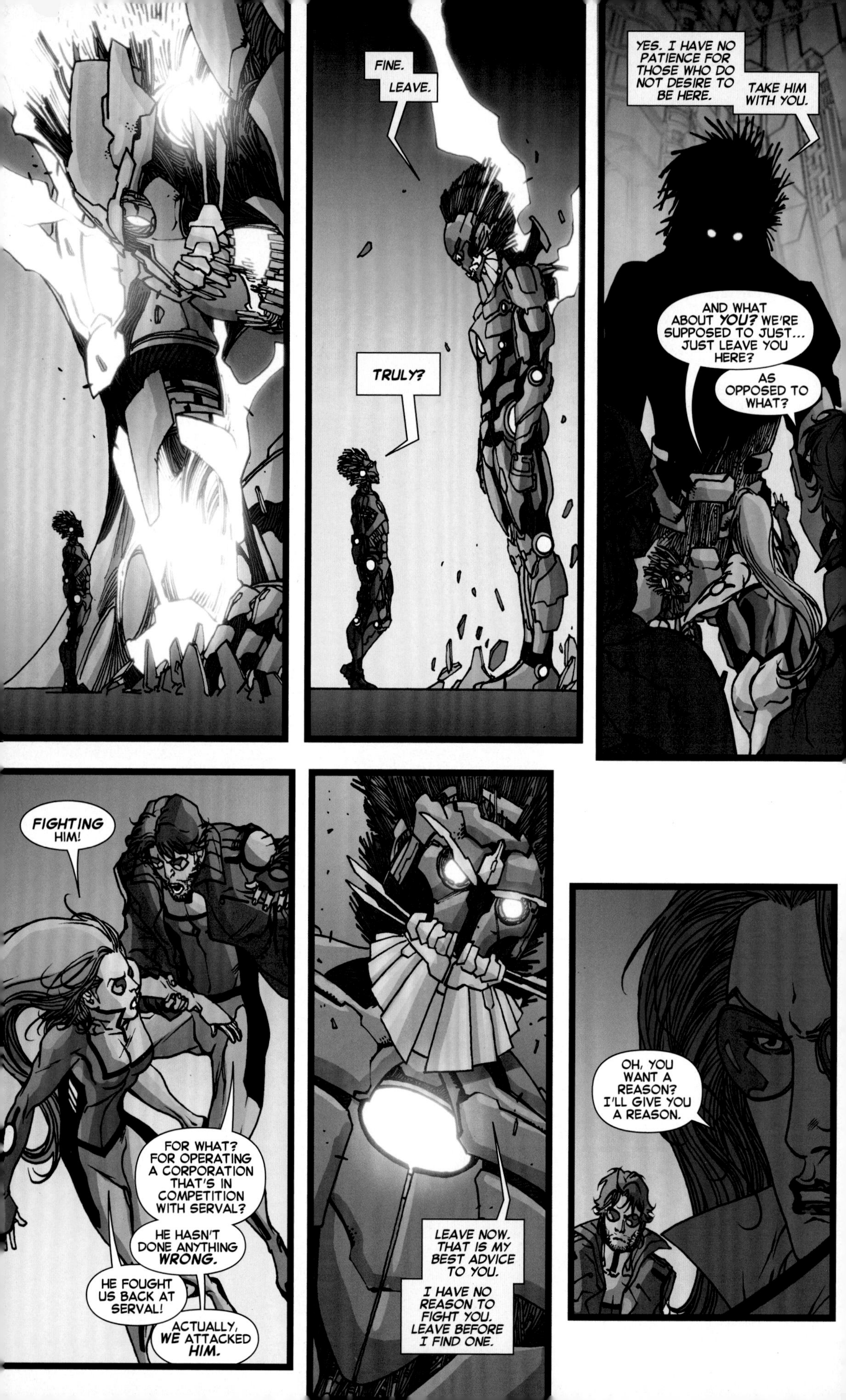
FINE.
LEAVE.
TRULY?
YES. I HAVE NO PATIENCE FOR THOSE WHO DO NOT DESIRE TO BE HERE.
TAKE HIM WITH YOU.
AND WHAT ABOUT YOU? WE'RE SUPPOSED TO JUST... JUST LEAVE YOU HERE?
AS OPPOSED TO WHAT?
FIGHTING HIM!
FOR WHAT? FOR OPERATING A CORPORATION THAT'S IN COMPETITION WITH SERVAL?
HE HASN'T DONE ANYTHING WRONG.
HE FOUGHT US BACK AT SERVAL!
ACTUALLY, WE ATTACKED HIM.
LEAVE NOW. THAT IS MY BEST ADVICE TO YOU.
I HAVE NO REASON TO FIGHT YOU. LEAVE BEFORE I FIND ONE.
OH, YOU WANT A REASON? I'LL GIVE YOU A REASON.

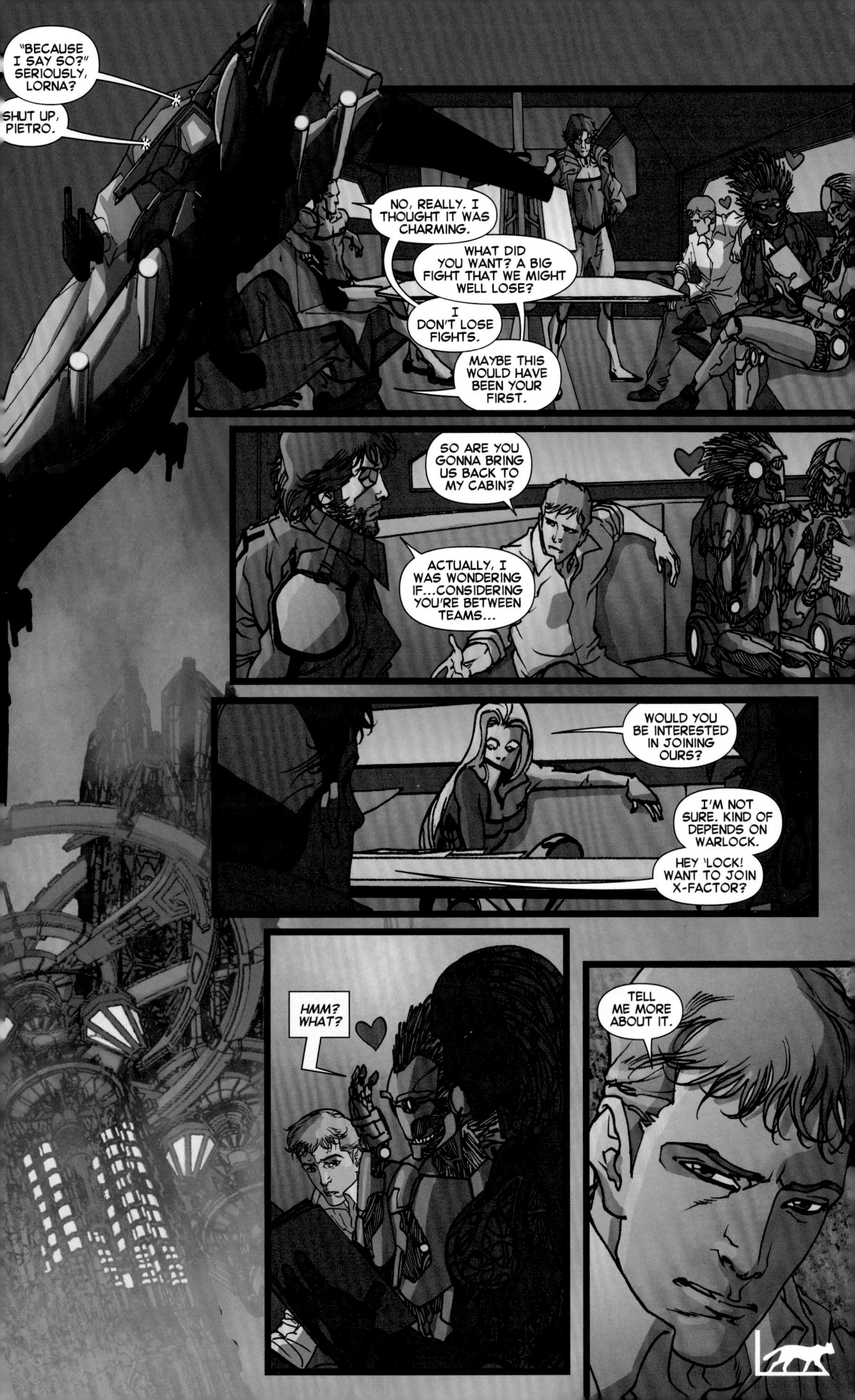
"BECAUSE I SAY SO?" SERIOUSLY, LORNA?
SHUT UP, PIETRO.
NO, REALLY. I THOUGHT IT WAS CHARMING.
WHAT DID YOU WANT? A BIG FIGHT THAT WE MIGHT WELL LOSE?
I DON'T LOSE FIGHTS.
MAYBE THIS WOULD HAVE BEEN YOUR FIRST.
SO ARE YOU GONNA BRING US BACK TO MY CABIN?
ACTUALLY, I WAS WONDERING IF...CONSIDERING YOU'RE BETWEEN TEAMS...
WOULD YOU BE INTERESTED IN JOINING OURS?
I'M NOT SURE. KIND OF DEPENDS ON WARLOCK.
HEY 'LOCK! WANT TO JOIN X-FACTOR?
HMM? WHAT?
TELL ME MORE ABOUT IT.

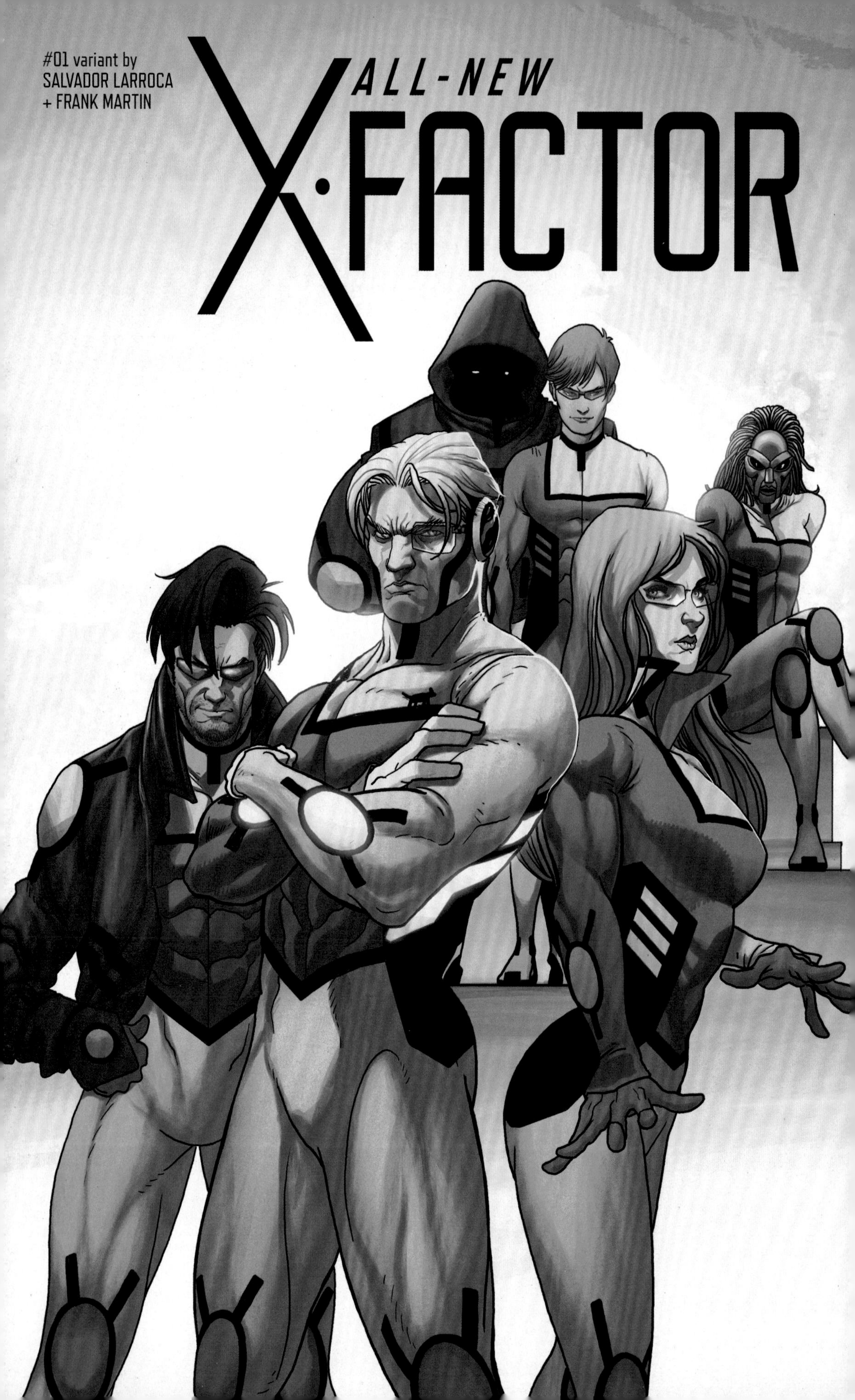
#01 variant by
SALVADOR LARROCA
+ FRANK MARTIN
ALL-NEW
X-FACTOR

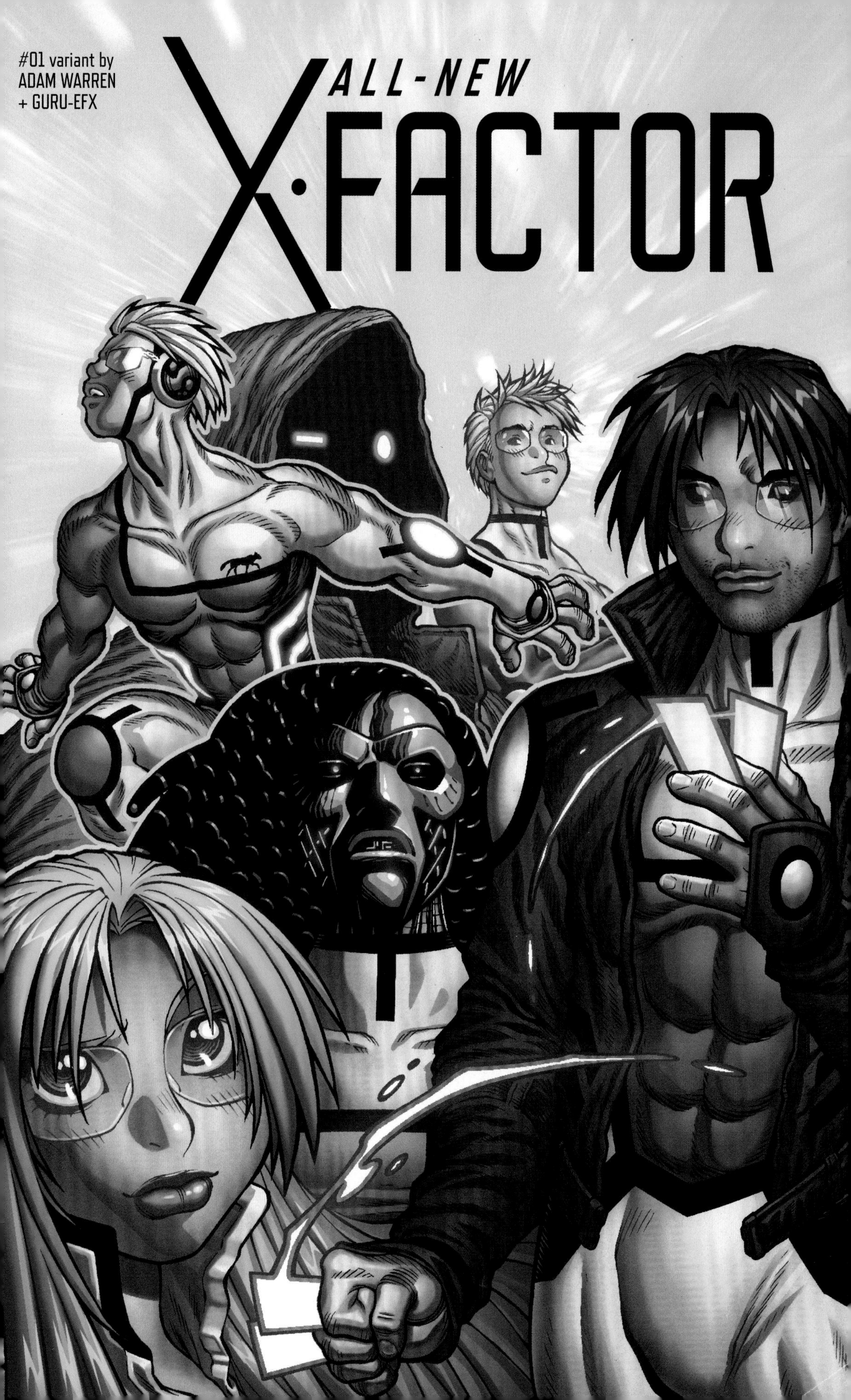
#01 variant by
ADAM WARREN
+ GURU-EFX
ALL-NEW
X-FACTOR

#01 variant by
SKOTTIE YOUNG

ALL-NEW
X-FACTOR

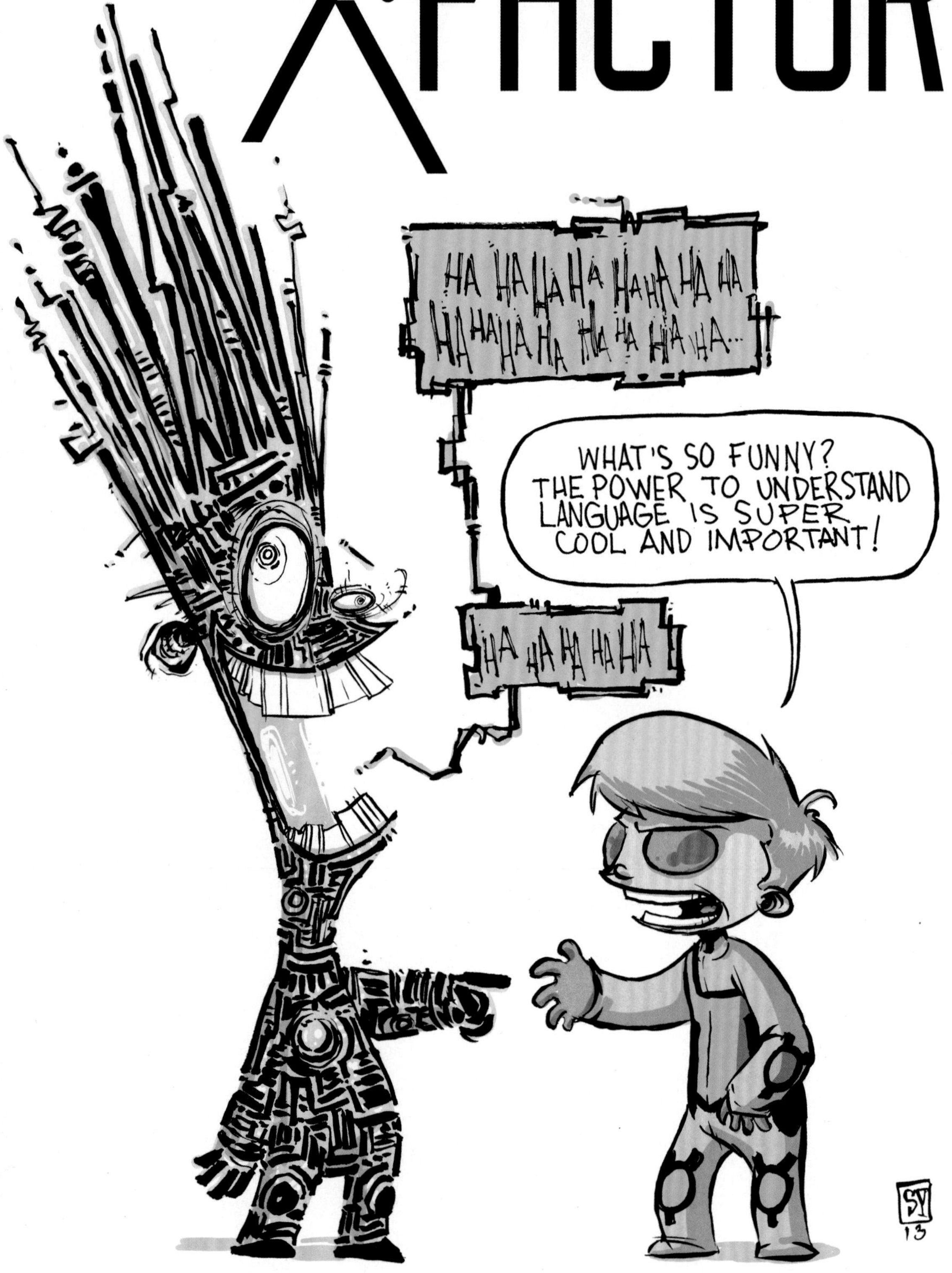
HA HA HA HA HA HA HA HA HA HA HA HA HA HA HA HA HA HA...
WHAT'S SO FUNNY? THE POWER TO UNDERSTAND LANGUAGE IS SUPER COOL AND IMPORTANT!
HA HA HA HA HA
SY 13

#02 variant by
J. SCOTT CAMPBELL
+ NEI RUFFINO

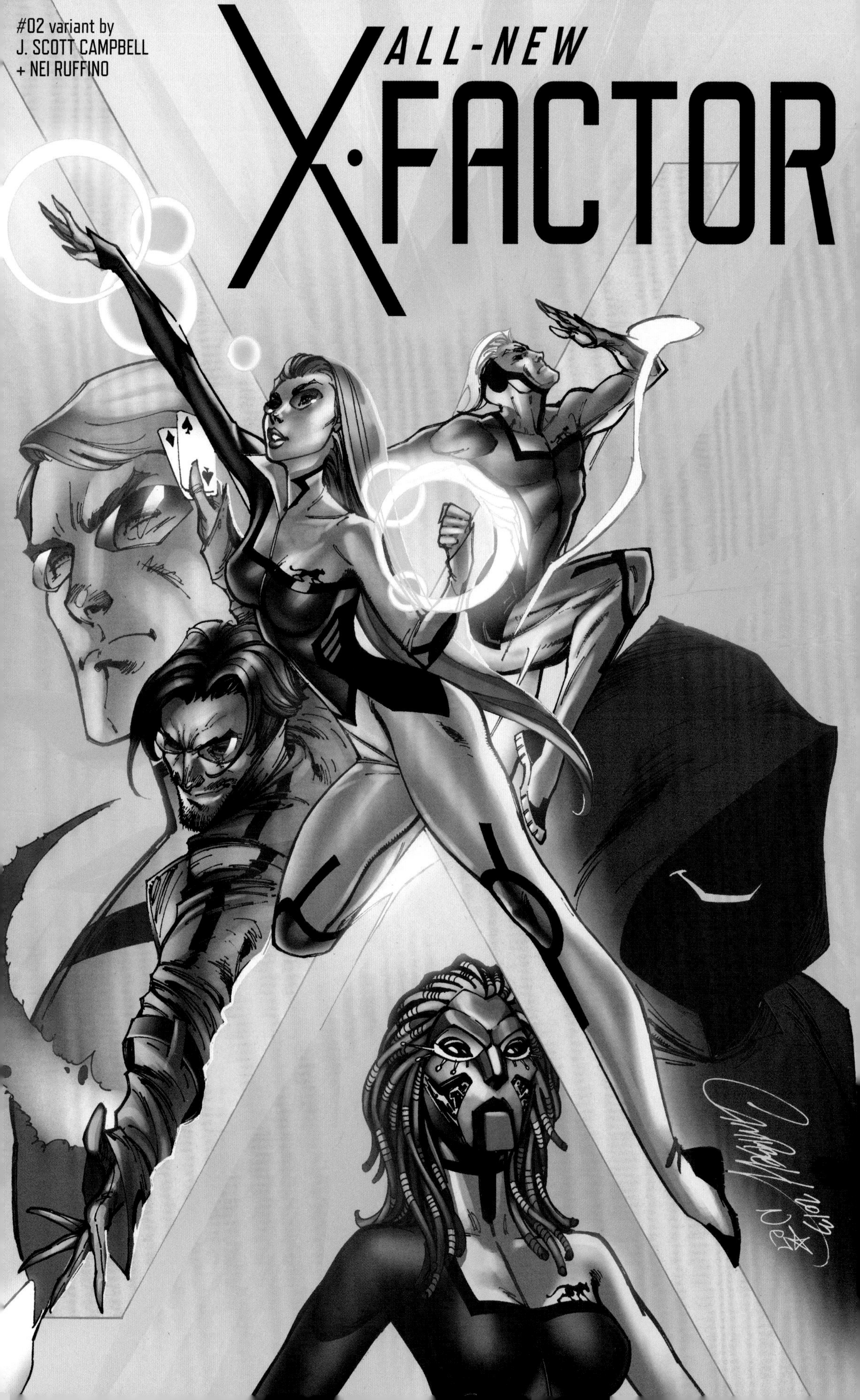
ALL-NEW
X-FACTOR

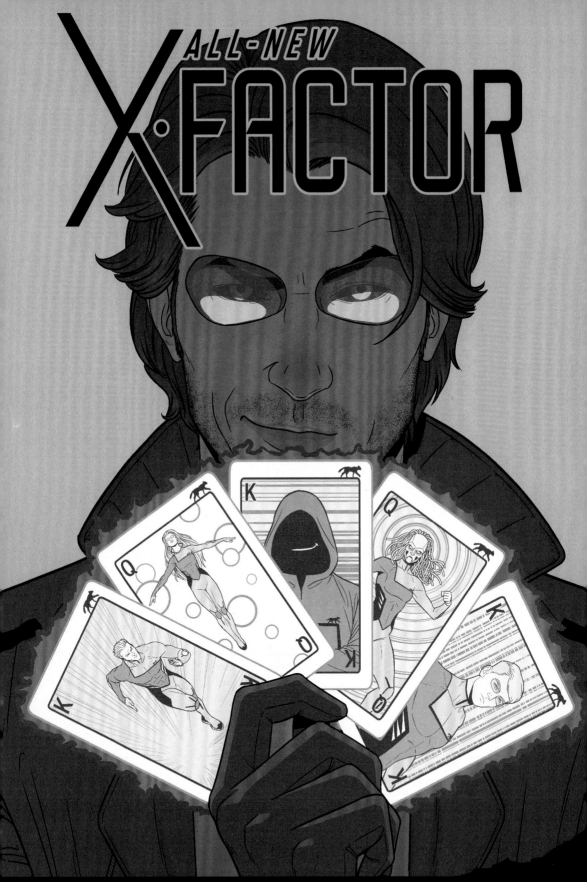

ALL-NEW X-FACTOR

#03 variant by
JAMIE MCKELVIE
& MATTHEW WILSON

sponsored by
SERVAL INDUSTRIES

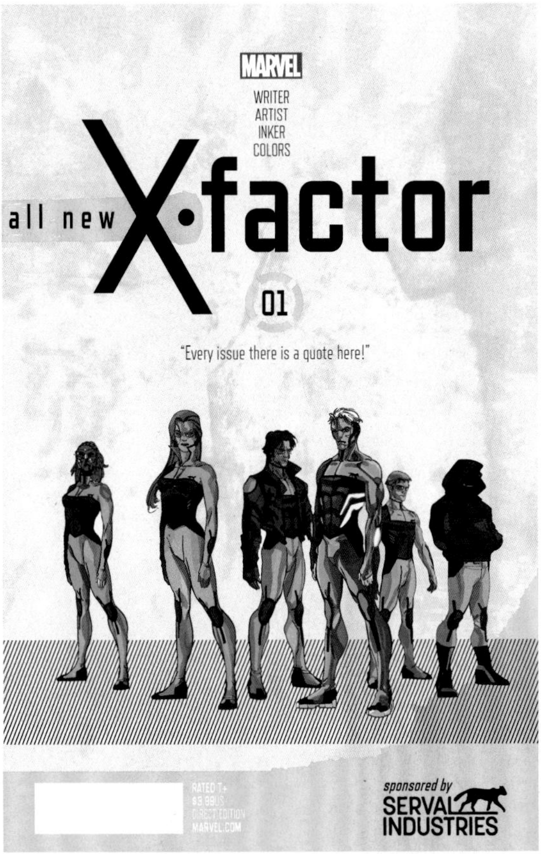
MARVEL
WRITER
ARTIST
INKER
COLORS
all new X·factor
01
"Every issue there is a quote here!"
RATED T+
$3.99US
DIRECT EDITION
MARVEL.COM
sponsored by
SERVAL INDUSTRIES

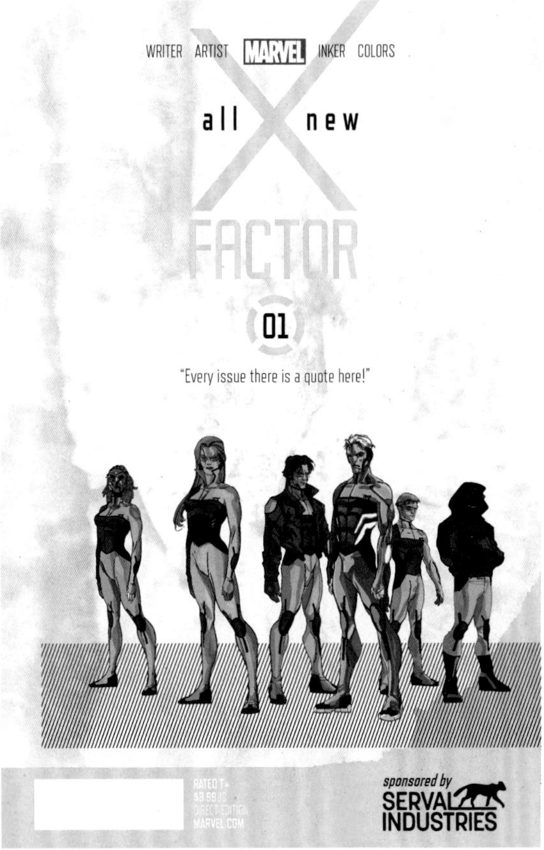
WRITER ARTIST MARVEL INKER COLORS
all new X FACTOR
01
"Every issue there is a quote here!"
RATED T+
$3.99US
DIRECT EDITION
MARVEL.COM
sponsored by
SERVAL INDUSTRIES

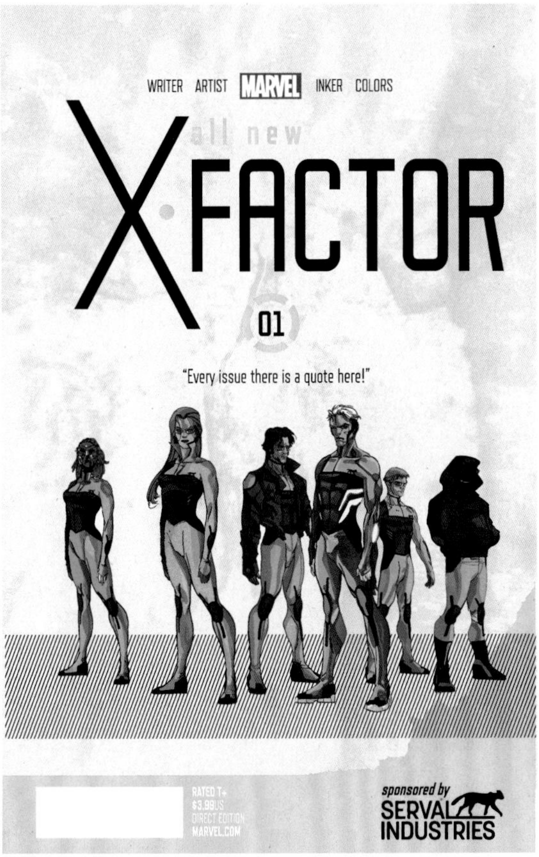
WRITER ARTIST MARVEL INKER COLORS
all new X·FACTOR
01
"Every issue there is a quote here!"
RATED T+
$3.99US
DIRECT EDITION
MARVEL.COM
sponsored by
SERVAL INDUSTRIES

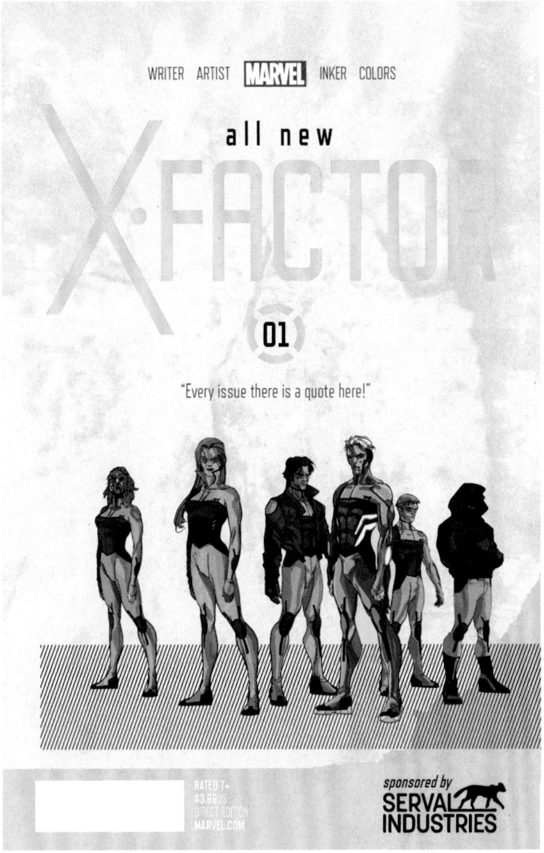
WRITER ARTIST MARVEL INKER COLORS
all new X·FACTOR
01
"Every issue there is a quote here!"
RATED T+
$3.99US
DIRECT EDITION
MARVEL.COM
sponsored by
SERVAL INDUSTRIES

JARED K. FLETCHER'S early cover layout and logo designs

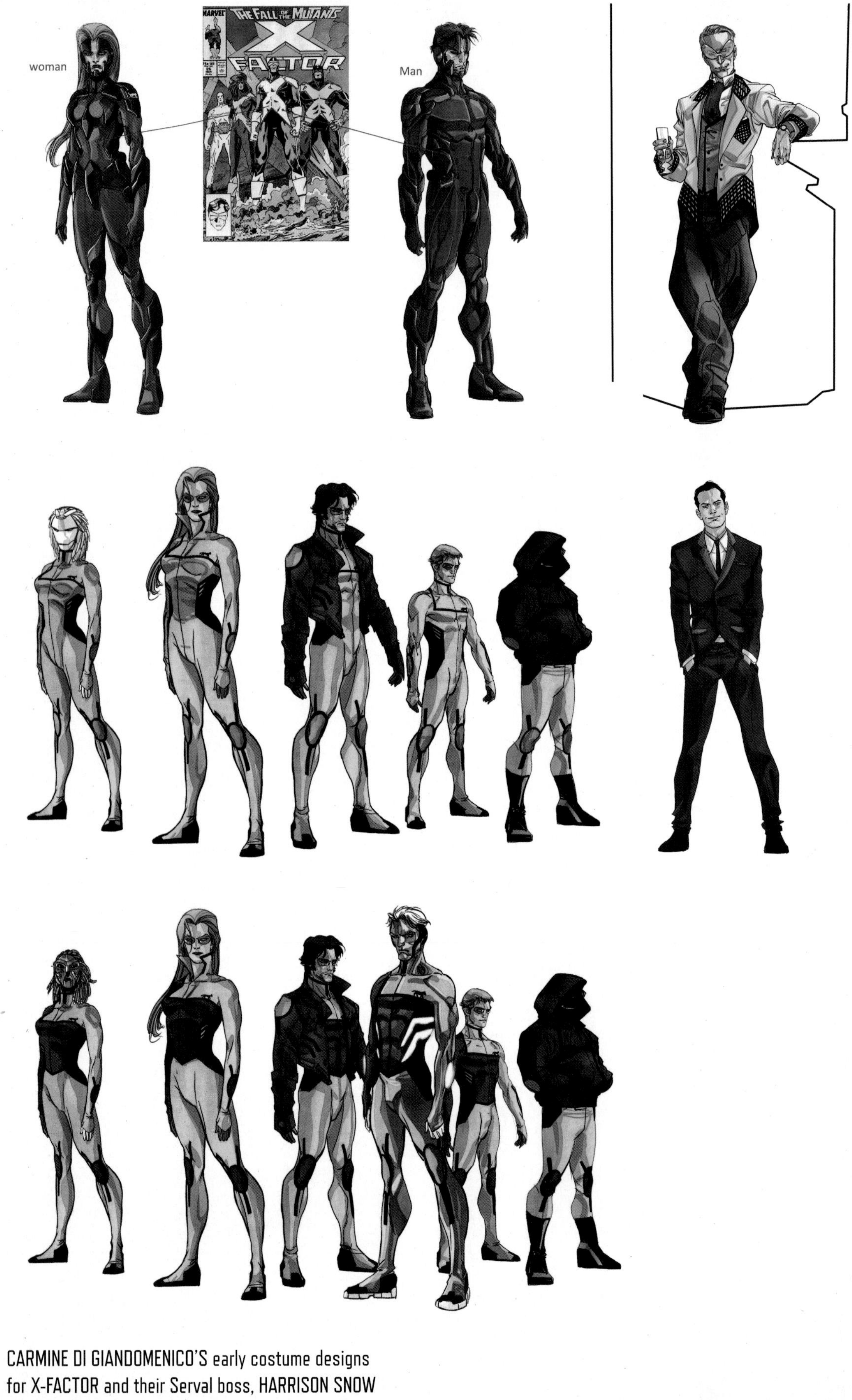
woman
MARVEL
THE FALL OF THE MUTANTS
X-FACTOR
Man

CARMINE DI GIANDOMENICO'S early costume designs
for X-FACTOR and their Serval boss, HARRISON SNOW